COMMUNAL LOVE AT ONEIDA

A PERFECTIONIST VISION OF
AUTHORITY, PROPERTY, AND SEXUAL ORDER

by
Richard DeMaria

THE EDWIN MELLEN PRESS
New York and Toronto

Richard DeMaria

COMMUNAL LOVE AT ONEIDA

(Texts and Studies in Religion, Volume 2)

Library of Congress Cataloging Number 78-60958

ISBN 0-88946-986-5

Printed in the United States of America

TO

Fred A. DeMaria

MY FATHER

CONTENTS

INTRODUCTION

Communal life is a siren which has mesmerized the idealistic of every age. The vision of men and women sharing all—property, talents, time and love—has been particularly influential in America where the number of communal undertakings in the 19th century alone must be placed conservatively in the hundreds. Unfortunately, most of these attempts in community living disbanded long before they saw a tenth anniversary, despite, in many cases, considerable idealism and careful planning. Only a few succeeded, at least if we judge success in terms of longevity. Among those successes was a community established in the mid-nineteenth century at Oneida, New York—a community important not only because it survived thirty years, but also because of its impressive financial and cultural attainments. The source of Oneida's unity and strength was the religion of Christian Perfectionism as taught by John H. Noyes and practiced by the members. Of special interest in the story of Oneida is their practice of communal marriage. The members of Oneida held theological and spiritual ideals which, they believed, dictated the abandonment of traditional marriage in favor of a system of nonexclusive, sexual loving, whereby each person considered himself married to and responsible for every other member. They called this social arrangement Complex Marriage.

It is the topic of Complex Marraige which has attracted the greatest interest among those who have written and read about Oneida, but, for the most part, studies of Complex Marriage have not attempted to understand the

theology and spirituality which gave rise to and supported this unorthodox form of communal relationship.
Such neglect is not entirely inculpable, for John Humphrey Noyes repeatedly reminded his readers that only
those familiar with the theology upon which his social
system was based could appreciate it. The Community's
Handbook insisted that the communism of Oneida could not
for a moment be dissevered from its theology; the two had
to be considered together, for together they either stood
or fell. Yet according to Noyes, Oneida's social theory
was repeatedly seized upon by outsiders, separated entirely from its religious principles, and then dragged in
its denuded state into the open court.[1]

The present writer intended at first to study the
practice of communal marriage as lived at Oneida Community. But as research progressed, it was the underlying
theology of love which attracted and demanded attention
and interest. It bcame apparent that the Oneida system
of social relations reflected a philosophy of Christian
love which was not only different from, but essentially

---

[1]*Circular,* 15 February 1852, p. 59. Three studies
which do attempt to consider the system of Complex Marriage in the context of theology are: Allen Estlake, a
former member of the Community, wrote *Oneida Community,
A Record of the Attempt to Carry Out the Principles of
Christian Unselfishness and Scientific Race Improvement*
(London, 1900), a work which is valuable though largely
apologetic and by no means comprehensive. Robert Parker
in his history of Oneida (*A Yankee Saint: John Humphrey
Noyes and the Oneida Community* [New York, 1935]) treats
Complex Marriage in a theological context, but briefly.
Benjamin Breckinridge Warfield (in his "John Humphrey
Noyes and his 'Bible Communists,'" *Bibliotheca Sacra,*
Vol. 78, pp. 27-72, 172-200, 319-367 and in the chapter
by the same title in his *Perfectionism,* Vol. II [New York,
1931], pp. 219-333) also approaches the topic in the context of theology, but the treatment appears to be unsympathetic from the outstart, and again lacks the scope
with which the topic needs to be explored.

opposed to, love as it was understood in the world. The
elucidation of that philosophy became the main goal of
the research, and interest in the actual social system of
Oneida became important only to the extent that they reflected and incarnated this unusual concept of love.
John Noyes and his community were greatly impressed by
the fundamental Christian doctrine that one loves God in
loving his neighbor. But they were also convinced of
another truth: that not all which is called "love" rightly
deserves the title. In fact, they maintained that much of
what is popularly regarded as love is a form of idolatry
which thwarts rather than aids man's quest for God. The
members of the Oneida Community, having rejected as
idolatrous and debilitating the romantic love of their
contemporaries, advocated a love which was non-possessive,
non-exclusive and sacramental.

The specific intention of the present study is,
then, to analyze the concept of love which was operative
in the Oneida Community and which was implemented by them
in the different social institutions of the Community.
There is no one source where the student can find a complete treatment of the principles of love which were operative at Oneida. Available, however, is a considerable
volume of primary literature. Noyes was enamored of the
power of the printed word. From the time of his conversion to Perfectionism, he looked to the press as the
instrument through which the world would be converted to
his religion. From 1834 until 1880, he and his followers
published newspapers on a regular, usually weekly basis.
(His goal was a daily newspaper, and for several years he
did succeed in publishing three times a week.) The Community assigned the paper a priority importance, and, even
during the years when the Oneida experiment was threatened
by economic pressures, when food was scarce and living

others or to another time.

One final point with regard to method: actual
source texts are only rarely cited in the body of this
work, though many are given in the footnote section.
However, as the reader may soon realize, whenever possible,
the words of Noyes have been integrated into the text.
There is some history behind this procedure: the present
writer at first intended to "translate" Noyes' concepts--
especially those which he felt would be offensive to contemporary readers--into language and models which would be
perhaps more palatable, more attuned to current thought
forms. Efforts at translating a philosophy usually dis-
tort the original understanding; this is a price one is
often prepared to pay in order to revivify its basic message for another generation. But because this study represents, to the author's knowledge, the first efforts at
a full presentation of Noyes' theology of love, it was
thought best to preserve the particular theological termi-
nology in which Noyes expressed himself. Till later must
be left the interesting project of contemporizing this
man who in his ideas, if not in their mode of expression,
was a man out of his time.

The writer's interests in Oneida were initially
historical. But as research continued, he found himself
wondering whether there is not to be found in the Oneida
chronicle more than an eccentric, perhaps historically
interesting, philosophy. Admittedly, its concept of love
opposes everything which is considered obvious about love
and its ways. But Oneida's critique of current concepts
of love, and its case for a non-possessive, non-exclusive
way of love calls forth serious interest and reflection.
At least the writer found it so. Perhaps it is man's efforts to possess, to control and to isolate the loved one
which in the end destroys love--and himself. Noyes'

expenses were whittling away the initial capital resources, the Community continued to print its newspapers
and to sustain the drain which it invariably made upon
funds. These papers (the titles and format of which
changed many times over the fifty year period) are
fortunately extant, a relatively complete collection being available at Cornell University. Substantial partial
collections can be found in the libraries of the State
Historical Society of Wisconsin, Harvard University,
Dartmouth College, the Library of Congress, Syracuse University, and the Boston and New York Public Libraries,
among others. These newspapers deal with subjects of
every sort, ranging from methods of fruit preserving to
analyses of contemporary events. But scattered throughout
the 1800 issues of these newspapers, as well as in the
twenty-five books and pamphlets published by the Community
on theological or polity issues--in an article, a personal
reflection, a poem, a confession, a sermon, a report on
some event at Oneida--often between the lines, one finds
references to their concept of love. The student must
then search these pages for the clues which, when placed
together, do reveal in rather clear detail the concept of
love which inspired Oneida. To assemble these pieces together in an ordered way, and to reconstruct from these
the theology of love which inspired the Oneida Community,
is the intention of this book. The author hopes that this
construct, as well as the gathered references and cita-
tions, will prove of value to others who do not have the
opportunity or time to search fifty years of publications.

This study, then, is largely the result of a thorough
familiarity with the published literature of the Community.
It should be mentioned in passing that this literature
would be of relatively little value if one were attempting
a study of the Oneida experiment itself, or were attempting

a critique of the success of its fellowship system. But
the goal of this study is to explicate the *theory* of
love behind the Oneida experiment. Its interest in the
institutions which the Community proposed will be only
to increase understanding of this theory by asking how
Noyes would apply his principles to a real life situation.
The study is primarily concerned with ideals, and only in
passing with the actual success or failure of the Community to fulfill the goals set. And for that purpose the
published sources are most appropriate.

        Chapter one of this study consists in a general
overview of the history and theological thought of Oneida,
with special emphasis on those points which are important
for an understanding of its social theory. Chapter two
will consider the concept of love at Oneida under its
many aspects, after introducing certain philosophical notions which underlie this concept. Chapter three centers
upon a description of the polity with regard to social relations at Oneida, insofar as we can deduce how the Community intended to incarnate its vision of Christian love.
In the final pages, some tentative suggestions and con-
clusions concerning the success, the demise and the contribution of the Oneida experiment will be offered.

        There is much that this study leaves undone: it
does not attempt to answer the important question (with
the exception of a few passing observations) about the
success of the Community in fulfilling its own ideals; it
does not attempt a critique of Oneida's theory of love,
but sets as its goal simply to assemble a sympathetic,
ordered, and documented presentation of that theory; it
does not attempt to trace the stages in which the theory
of love evolved, but is content to elucidate the basic,
perduring dynamics and directions of that theory. These
projects which have not been attempted must be left to

insistence that love is true only when it leads one beyond the individual, that one love never excludes others,
that because all loves are the same there is no need to
cling to a particular love--all these suggestions deserve
respect.

Recently, America has witnessed a resurgence of the
communal movement; a new generation of utopianists has
come upon the scene. Understandably, they are looking to
the past for theoretical and practical wisdom in the art
of making community. Those would-be-communitarians who
envision a life style which extends the ideal of sharing
into the sphere of affection and sexuality understandably
are looking to the precedent of the Oneida Community to
support and shape their hopes. Research into the actual
meaning of Complex Marriage as understood by Oneida is
prerequisite to determining the value of this historical
precedent as a model and guide for today's reformers.
Those who learn of the asceticism and spirituality which
in fact informed the experiment at Oneida might be tempted
to caution present utopianists against citing the Oneida
Community too quickly as an ally. In any case, it is
hoped that the present study may help to clarify the nature of this important precedent in the area of communal
marriage. While Noyes' ideas will be of particular interest to those trying to live one form or another of communal life or communal marriage, their application (as he
always insisted) need not be restricted to these. His
suggestions may well prove important to all who are attempting to follow the moral demand of loving all men as
brothers.

Richard DeMaria
Iona College

CHAPTER ONE

HISTORICAL ORIENTATIONS

MEETING ONEIDA

The Oneida Community was the offspring of John
Humphrey Noyes. Born in 1811, in Brattleboro, Vermont,
John Noyes grew up in Putney, Vermont, attended Dartmouth and, until his religious conversion at the age of
19, prepared himself for a career in law. Thereafter,
he studied theology at Andover, and Yale Theological
Seminary in New Haven. During these years he associated
himself with the Free Church movement in New Haven.
Though not separated from the parent Churches (Presby-
terian and Congregational), the Free Church groups met
in separate places for worship, and could be distinguished from their forebears by their attachment to
evangelism and protracted meetings, by their zeal for
revivals, and by a spirit of general radicalism.[1] Noyes
was increasingly attracted by a theology called "Perfectionism", which maintained that Christianity, properly
understood, was the call to a *sinless* life of union with
Christ. Perfectionism maintained that to the extent to
which the orthodox Churches tolerated sinfulness in the
Christian life, they failed to preach Christianity.[2] So
convinced was Noyes of these new doctrines and of the

---

[1] *Perfectionist*, 22 March 1845, p. 2.

[2] See below, pp. 16ff, for a more complete account
of John Noyes' Perfectionist Theology.

failure of the established Churches to spread the Christian gospel, that he retracted an earlier promise to work in the foreign missions and dedicated himself to the task of Christianizing the American people (who needed conversion quite as much as the heathens).[3]

· When word of his new ideas reached the faculty of the Yale Theological Seminary, Noyes' licence to preach was withdrawn, and he found himself without means of support. The next years were years of wandering, of spiritual anxiety, of financial difficulties. His sister, who lived in New Haven, wrote the following letter to her sister living at home:

> I know not what to think of John... I cannot reconcile his practice and feelings with my ideas of perfection, and if he is not deranged, there is no consolation for me. If he is deranged, he is more an object of pity than any one I ever heard of. He is a homeless wanderer, and is entirely dependent upon charity.[4]

Such was not, however, the analysis which John Noyes made of his situation. He saw these years as a period during which God was leading him to a deeper and expanded understanding of Perfectionism, a period from which he would emerge a man prepared for a mission. He returned to his Putney, Vermont home in 1838, married, and gathered about him followers willing to help publish a paper dedicated to the spread of Perfectionism. This group of disciples, meeting for spiritual instruction and co-laborating in the printing room, gradually metamorphosed into a single community, sharing goods and

---

[3]*Handbook of the Oneida Community, with a Sketch of its Founder and an Outline of its Constitution and Doctrines* (Wallingford, Conn., 1867), pp. 7f. Hereafter cited as *Handbook, 1867.*

[4]George Wallingford Noyes, ed., *Religious Experience of John Humphrey Noyes, Founder of the Oneida Community* (New York, 1923), p. 229.

talents, dwelling together as one family.

Noyes and his small community believed that communal sharing should extend into the area of the affections and the physical expression of love. Their practices in this regard eventually became common knowledge
and incensed the people of Putney who forced the disbanding of the fledgling community in 1847.[5] Another
group of Perfectionists who were attempting an experiment in communal living in central New York heard of the
problems at Putney, and invited Noyes to join them at
Oneida Creek as leader of the incipient community.[6]
Noyes accepted the offer and in time his presence attracted to Oneida former members of the Putney group, as
well as others who had been readers of the Putney publications. By 1849, there were eighty-seven members in
the Oneida Community, living in a large "Mansion House"
which the industrious founders had erected. One year
later, there was a population of 172 inhabiting an expanded Mansion House, and by 1851 the Community reported a membership of 205 souls.[7] During the following
years, several associated communities were founded: in
Brooklyn (dedicated to publishing newspapers), in New
York City (a business agency for the products of the
Community), in Wallingford, Connecticut, in Vermont, and
in New Haven (for students attending Yale). With the
exception of the Wallingford Community, these associated
foundations were eventually dissolved, and their members

---

[5]The events leading to this practice of communal
love and affection will be considered in greater detail
in a later section of this chapter.

[6]Walter D. Edmonds, *The First Hundred Years: 1848-
1948* (Oneida, New York, 1948), p. 16.

[7]*Circular,* 12 February 1866, pp. 386ff.

reassigned either to Oneida or Wallingford.[8] For the major part of the Community's history, membership in the combined communities was kept at approximately 275, the majority of whom lived in Oneida.[9]

If membership remained relatively stable after the first years, it was by design and not for lack of interested applicants. The *Circular* of 5 November 1866 reported that should the Community have accepted all who had made application during that year alone, it would have become an overgrown encampment.[10] Regularly, the Community advised readers of its publications that it was not in a position to increase membership.[11] The reasons given for this no-admittance policy were many: lack of accommodations; the difficulty of forming new members in the ways of communal life;[12] existing debts; the problem of how to control financial demands made by seceding members; the pressures of persecution from

---

[8]In later years, some of the Perfectionists lived on a property some distance from the Mansion House, and to an extent this group formed a third community, Willow Place. See *American Socialist,* 1 November 1877, p. 347.

[9]*Circular,* 7 August 1865, p. 168.

[10]p. 289.

[11]See *Free Church Circular,* 6 May 1850, p. 104f; *Circular,* 30 December 1867, p. 332; *Circular,* 9 January 1871, p. 13.

[12]The difficulty of living communal life is reflected in this stand. The Community estimated that only one out of every hundred persons who presented himself for membership was actually suited for communal life. Moreover, it found that new members, no matter how good their intentions, adjusted to communal life only after considerable education, a process which the Community said it had come to dread "much as women dread bearing children." (*Oneida Circular,* 11 December 1871, p. 397.) See also *Circular,* 17 October 1870, p. 244.

without and disharmony within. Noyes insisted to his
readers that the propensity of a community to propogate
itself beyond its financial and spiritual means was the
vice which most often vitiated the efforts of beginning
communities. For all these reasons, the Oneida Community resisted the temptation to expand membership throughout its history.[13]

There are two other, less pragmatic, reasons behind
the refusal of the Oneida Community to expand its membership, and an appreciation of these sheds light on the
particular genius of Oneida. First, Noyes understood the
Oneida Community to be an experiment whose existence was
justified in terms of the service it could provide to
society as a whole. He saw community as a setting in which
he and his followers could explore the full meaning of the
Perfectionist Theology, could develop through experiment
and evaluation a morality proper to Christian Perfectionism, and could publish, then, a report of their experience
for the edification of the public. Noyes did not, at least
originally, intend to precipitate any movement toward community living. Rather he looked to the day when the virtues
and values developed through communal experiment and preached
through communical publications could be spread to the world.[14]
The Perfectionists of the Community at Oneida cast themselves
in the role of soldiers in combat, scouting new territories.
They reported that participation in this war was painful

---

[13]*Circular*, 5 November 1866, p. 265; *Circular*, 30
December 1867, p. 332.

[14]*Oneida Circular*, 10 July 1871, p. 220; *Oneida
Circular*, 3 November 1873, p. 357; *Oneida Circular*, 5 January 1874, p. 12.

and demanding; they were spurred on by the hope that the
world was profiting vicariously from their sacrifices.[15]
Noyes saw no point in a proliferation of similar experiments, especially since he knew well the cost of participation and the meager chances of success. He dissuaded
others from leaving home to form new communities, and
encouraged them to remain in their present situations,
and to apply there the morality demonstrated by Oneida.[16]

In adopting this position, Noyes placed himself in
the true tradition of utopian experiments. The man who
leaves society in order to create a new community, is
not--in his own mind--"dropping out" of society, or
evading responsibility; rather, he leaves in order to
develop in isolation a style of life which he hopes society at large will be persuaded to adopt when it observes in practice the feasibility and results of a more
idealistic way. The Oneida Community was intended to
serve as a demonstration that the anti-selfish principle
could be trusted in all the relations of life, and that
all the human passions could be made to work harmonious-
ly and safely without restraints of law. The publications of the Community were intended to enable readers
throughout the country to observe the experiment in communal living and to profit from that experience.   It
would seem that in later years Noyes did move toward an
increasing emphasis upon the values of communal life itself, especially toward the late 70s when he ceased the
publication of the *Oneida Circular* and replaced it with
the *American Socialist,* a journal dedicated to spreading

---

[15]*Circular,* 16 December 1867, p. 317; *Circular,* 30
March 1868, p. 9.

[16]*Free Church Circular,* 6 May 1850, pp. 104f.

information concerned with communal life in its different forms. Yet even in that journal, we find statements
advising readers against the immediate establishment of
new communities. This is understandable when we consider the second key factor behind Noyes' reluctance to increase membership at Oneida.

Noyes believed that only men who had achieved a
high degree of holiness could meet the demands which
communal life makes upon its participants. He argued
that unless members were filled with the virtue of selflessness, it was foolish to expect any success in a communistic venture.[17] Noyes repeatedly asserted that the
Oneida Community's success could not be understood by
those unaware of the importance of religion within that
commune.[18] Noyes was firmly convinced that the success
or failure of any communal undertaking would depend upon
the presence or absence of religious maturity in its
members. In this he could point to the history of

---

[17]*Oneida Circular,* 6 February 1871, p. 44.

[18]The original impetus for forming the Oneida Community had come, Noyes would remind readers, not from
the writings of social reformers such as Fourier, but as
an immediate corollary to the religious tenets of Perfectionism. "Historically, the communal relation of the
Oneida system grew out of the spiritual relation which
its original members conceived they had come into toward
Christ. Understanding from the New Testament and from
personal experience that in accepting Christ as a Savior
they come individually into a heart-marriage to him,
they found that the correlated New Testament fact followed, that all who are thus married to Christ come into
the relation toward one another of mutual brotherhood."
(*American Socialist,* 20 February 1879, p. 63.) See also
[Oneida Association], *Bible Communism: A Compilation
From the Annual Reports and Other Publications of the
Oneida Association and its Branches; Presenting, In Connection with Their History, a Summary View of Their Religious and Social Theories* (Brooklyn, 1853), p. 7.

American socialism to corroborate his position: of the
hundreds of attempts at community living in the 18th and
19th centuries, the handful which had succeeded were all
ones in which religion had played the key role. Thus,
even if in later years Noyes did envision community life
as a goal for many rather than as just a temporary experiment for the few, he continued to advise the post-
ponement of this widespread movement until men had been
converted, purified and informed by the living Spirit of
Jesus, and the morality of selflessness.[19]

Government in the Oneida Community did not depend
upon the force of law, but upon the willing subordination of the members to their elders. There were no written constitutions which were to be obeyed in minute detail; but each man and woman was expected to seek perfection, and to submit himself to the advice and criticism of his elders.[20] Noyes' school of Perfectionism
differed from other branches of Perfectionism here: the
latter insisted on the absolute independence of the individual and scorned any form of organization. The followers of John Noyes, while rejecting a law-based religion, insisted that unity and harmony could be attained
through the willing subordination of men to one another.[21]
One way in which this advice could be sought was through
the process called Mutual Criticism, in which a man or
woman, especially when troubled by depression or moral
weakness, asked that his or her character be criticized

---

[19]*Oneida Circular*, 6 February 1871, p. 44; *Oneida
Circular,* 7 October 1872, p. 324; *American Socialist,* 30
January 1879, p. 34.

[20]*Bible Communism*, p. 9; *Oneida Circular,* 29 July
1872, p. 244.

[21]*Handbook, 1867*, p. 22.

in open session before the Community. During these ses-
sions any member present was encouraged to speak publicly concerning the faults and strengths of the "patient",
suggesting ways toward improvement. During these criticisms, the person under scrutiny was required to maintain
absolute silence and control over the desire to defend
himself against the accusations. Usually criticism was
voluntary, but in extreme cases of disobedience or recal-
citrance it was administered without being solicited.[22]
That this process was painful and never easy, the Community did not deny. But they insisted that its effects
were nearly miraculous and that its value was never
doubted within the membership. Rather, we are told, its
popularity grew with the years.[23] Surprisingly, the Community often administered criticism to those who were
ill as a means of restoring them to health. Noyes was
convinced that all sickness is the result of sin, and
that the first step toward overcoming poor health is to

---

[22] [Oneida Association], *Mutual Criticism* (Oneida,
New York, 1876), p. 18

[23] Many departures from the Community were attributed
to the inability of the weaker members to undergo the pain
of Mutual Criticism. Even after years of experience, we
are assured, most found the ordeal a difficult one to
bear. The *Circular*, 15 August 1864, p. 172, reported that
once, when a visitor was exclaiming rapturously on the
beauty of the communal life-style, a member observed: "I
wonder if she would think it was a paradise after she
had...gone through three or four criticisms." See also
Harriet M. Worden, *Old Mansion House Memories by One
Brought up in it* (Kenwood, New York, 1950), p. 92; George
Wallingford Noyes, ed., *John Humphrey Noyes: The Putney
Community* (Oneida, New York, 1931), p. 123; *Oneida Circular*, 2 February 1874, p. 45. In spite of this pain,
the Community maintained that no thought could be given
to dropping the practice, so beneficial was it. See
Mutual Criticism, p. 15; *Circular*, 4 April 1864, p. 18.

attack the source of the malady: a sickly spirit.   The
Community reported on several occasions how children,
as well as adults, suffering from lingering illnesses
were restored to health immediately after undergoing
the ordeal of criticism.[24]   Over the years the Community
members developed real skill in the art of criticism,
exhibiting both sharpness and delicacy, blending whenever possible commendation with criticism.[25]   Over the
years, experiments with variations of the Criticism were
tried.   At one time, Criticism was administered by small
committees of inquiry rather than by the whole community.
Another variation was the development of what they
called "historical criticism" in which emphasis was
placed upon searching out faults and failings from the
past which, though long forgotten, continued to poison
present experience.[26]   Noyes often attributed the success of the Oneida venture to the restorative effects of
Mutual Criticism.   He recommended its practice to all
his readers as a means of improvement, especially to
families, schools and clubs threatened by chords of dis-
unity.

It is difficult to give a *horarium* of life in the
Oneida Community, for variety, change of schedule, and
flexibility were introduced on principle into the daily
schedule there.   Noyes constantly exhorted his brethren
against the tendency to settle into permanent schedules,
for he believed that, should life there become habitual,

---

[24]*Mutual Criticism*, pp. 71f.

[25]*Mutual Criticism*, pp. 26-35; *Circular*, 12 December 1870, p. 309; Oneida Circular, 1 January 1872, p. 4;
Oneida Circular, 5 August 1872, p. 253.

[26]*Mutual Criticism*, pp. 70f.

it would lose its inspiration and become a source of
evil. He wrote concerning habit:

> The great mistake...is in distinguishing between
> different kinds of habits, calling some good and
> others bad, and considering it a merit to have
> what are termed good habits; whereas in truth,
> and in the sight of God, all habits are bad, and
> in some senses, "good habits" are the worst of all.[27]

New experiments, new schedules, new policies were regularly introduced at Oneida, if for no other reason than
for the sake of change. Noyes regarded any attachments
to fixed ways as "a hankering after the flesh pots of
Egypt." He encouraged his community to entertain all
sorts of odd notions and experiments, for any change, he
thought, is a source of growth among people who are
searching for newness of life.

> ...the particular luxuries and good things...of
> yesterday are not to be repeated today; something
> different and better is in waiting for us, and we
> must watch for it...the warfare of life is to
> know how to take hold of things and then let go
> of them.[28]

One who wished to progress must eschew habit and tolerate only the minimum of repetition. The *Circular* was
even prepared to define genius as freedom from habit.[29]
This wariness of habitual action was a factor which influenced John Noyes' thinking greatly and is an important key for understanding his positions on fellowship.

The goal Noyes set for his brethren was to combine

---

[27]*Circular*, 21 September 1853, p. 355. See also:
Free Church Circular, 20 December 1850, p. 329; *Circular*,
18 May 1868, p. 65; *Circular*, 28 November 1870, p. 289;
Circular, 12 December 1870, p. 305.

[28]*Circular*, 18 June 1864, p. 141. See also *Circular*, 18, July 1852, p. 141; *Circular*, 21 September 1853,
p. 355; *Circular*, 18 May 1868, pp. 65f.

[29]*Circular*, 19 October 1864, p. 235.

the monk's fondness of contemplation with the Capital-
ist's spirit of enterprise.[30] Surprisingly enough,
there were no Church services, prayers or other forms
of ritual worship at Oneida; but the Community members
did set aside several hours daily for Bible study and
private spiritual pursuits. Great emphasis was placed
upon attendance each evening at a community conference
which blended spiritual and business concerns. At these
evening meetings, the whole community gathered for dis-
cussions of house matters and business proposals; for
the reading of suitable novels and newspapers; for public criticisms and religious testimonies; for a "home
talk" by Noyes or one of the other elders.

All possessions were held in common, different committees being appointed to oversee the allotment of
money and materials for personal needs.[31] The first
years of the Community's existence were times of grave
poverty; food was scarce and accommodations poor. The
Community initially looked to agriculture as their means
of support, but this proved to be a losing venture. They
had lost some $40,000 of their initial resources before
they turned their efforts to manufacturing. Here re-

---

[30]Alfred Barron and George Noyes Miller, eds.,
Home Talks by John Humphrey Noyes, Vol. I (Oneida, New
York, 1875), p. 39.

[31]At one time the Community experimented with the
idea of allowing members to cultivate side industries
to cover special personal expenditures, but they abandoned this program when it was seen to result in individualism and possessiveness. (*Circular,* 13 January
1859, p. 203.) Another experimental venture, instituted
for the purpose of teaching the younger members the meaning of economy, was a budget system, in which each individual was allotted a certain amount for clothing, to be
spent at his own discretion. (*Oneida Circular,* 23 February 1874, p. 68.)

sults were more encouraging, and the Oneida Perfectionists soon found themselves managing several flourishing
industries, developing profitable trades in fruit preserving, steel traps, steel chains, silk and silver-
ware.[32] Efforts were made to move men and women from
one industry to another in order to diminish the factor
of boredom, and to provide all with a well-rounded education in business. So successful was the Community in
its endeavors that in later years Noyes asked whether
affluence and concern for expansion were not undermining
the future of the Community. He urged the Community to
practice a voluntary poverty and asceticism lest they
be destroyed by wealth.[33] He advised his followers to
continue to put in a day's work, even though resources
might make it possible to depend mainly on hired help.[34]

The Community encouraged its members to seek learning and to cultivate a taste for things cultural: musi-
cal concerts and theatre presentations were held regularly in the Oneida Mansion; classes in mathematics,
philosophy and other subjects were attended by the old
as well as the young; a library and museum were established and prized by the members; speakers passing
through the area were invited to address the Community;
capable young men were sent to Yale for further education.

John Humphrey Noyes was insistent in distinguishing

---

[32]See [Oneida Community, Ltd.], *Oneida Community,
1848-1901* [n.p., n.d.], pp. 6-17 for an account of the
different industries through which the Oneida Community
prospered.

[33]*Circular*, 8 June 1868, p. 94; *Oneida Circular*,
13 December 1875, p. 393.

[34]*Circular*, 25 July 1870, p. 146; *Oneida Circular*,
23 March 1874, p. 98.

the Oneida Community from the experiments based on
writings of Fourier, Owen, Brisbane and other Associa-
tionists. The latter all shared the belief that by establishing new social structures they could overcome
the evil dimensions of man's character, since they
viewed the latter as entirely the result of poor environment. They believed that, should a man be placed into a
wholesome atmosphere, such as that of shared community
life, he would respond positively, dropping the selfish
propensities which had been learned as protection against
a cruel world. In contrast to this theory, Noyes maintained that change of conditions could never eradicate
the evil side of man. The evil which man does is the
result, he maintained, of an inherent selfishness within
man, and until that selfishness is eradicated, attempts
at communal life are neither possible nor therapeutic.
Noyes wrote:

> ...We have not the slightest faith in Brisbane's
> doctrine...that a man is selfish, cruel and de-
> graded simply because of the dwarfish, distort-
> ing and depressing conditions by which society,
> surrounds him.[35]

In Noyes' thinking, the true process is quite different:
community life is possible only when composed of men and
women who are engaged in the process of ridding *themselves* of selfishness and sin. Noyes looked for a radical, inner change in man as a prerequisite for his participation in association. A member of the Community
wrote: "[Fourier and others] trusted to Association for
individual conversion, when only by individual conver-

---

[35]*American Socialist,* 19 April 1888, p. 121. See
also *American Socialist,* 6 November 1879, p. 356.

[36]*Circular,* 13 September 1855, p. 134.

sion was Association...possible."[37] It is not community life which perfects men, but perfected men who make community life possible.

Above, brief mention was made of Noyes' conviction that only communities which assigned priority to religious idealism could expect success. It was Noyes' conviction that religion is the only means by which the radical change of man can be effected, because the gospel of Christ and the grace of God are the only powers which produce men fitted to live together in communal life.[38] He advised those who felt a religious foundation unnecessary to the project of communal life to consult the testimony of history: of some hundred attempts in America to form community on a non-religious basis, all had resulted in distress and failure. While the few successful experiments in American Community life had been made by men who accorded to religion a key role in their lives.[39]

---

[37]*American Socialist,* 25 October 1877, p. 340. See also *Circular,* 26 December 1864, p. 322; *Circular,* 30 November 1868, p. 289.

[38] "Our experience in Association convinces us that the gospel of Christ only can supply [community]--that the grace of God which saves men from sin, is the only power which will ever produce good and reliable men, fitted to meet either the present emergencies of associate life, or the temptations accruing to future prosperity." *(Free Church Circular,* 27 February 1851, p. 25.) See also *Handbook, 1867,* p. 9; *Circular,* 22 November 1869, p. 284; *American Socialist,* 19 April 1877, p. 121; *American Socialist,* 19 December 1878, p. 401.

[39] "But those who are sanguine that a religious platform is unnecessary, and that association can be successfully achieved with the principles and motives which belong to ordinary selfishness would do well before setting out on the experiment to consult the history of about a hundred attempts that have been made in this country in the non-religious theory, which resulted in distress and failure." *(Circular,* 5 March 1866, p. 401.) "The one feature which distinguishes these [successful] Communities from the transitory

However, Noyes felt that Orthodox Protestant theology did little to precipitate this radical religious rebirth of individuals which was the crucial prerequisite to a successful communal undertaking. Rather than drawing men to greatness, Orthodox theology allowed them to wallow in feelings of degradation, and discouraged any innate aspirations to holiness and sanctification. By contrast, the theology which Noyes preached brought to man's attention the greatness and holiness of which he is capable. Noyes called this theology Perfectionism. Because it is impossible to appreciate the Oneida Community in general, and their social theory in particular, without an understanding of the main thrusts of this theology, the next section of this chapter will consist in an overview of the theology of Perfectionism as formulated by John H. Noyes.

THE PERFECTIONIST THEOLOGY OF JOHN HUMPHREY NOYES

The phrase "formulated by John H. Noyes" accurately describes the way Noyes viewed his theology. He considered it to be unique and original. The term "Perfec-

---

sort, is their religion; which in every case is of the earnest kind which comes by recognized afflatus, and controls all external arrangements. It seems then to be a fair induction from the facts before us that earnest religion does in some way modify human depravity so as to make continuous association possible, and insure to it great material success." (John Humphrey Noyes, *History of American Socialisms* [New York, 1966], p. 655.) See also *Free Church Circular,* 18 February 1850, p. 42; *Circular,* 23 November 1868, p. 285. Most students of the communal movement agree, if reluctantly, with Noyes' analysis here. It is difficult to deny the coincidence of successful communities with religious motivation. Of value would be a study which could isolate those aspects of personality which religion develops among its adherents enabling them to sustain community life.

tionism" can be attributed to a whole movement within
theology during the 19th century, and Noyes was a parti-
cipant in that movement, undoubtedly influenced by the
many Perfectionist theologies popular at the time. But
within a few years of his conversion to Perfectionism,
Noyes had made major strides toward formulating his own
particular theology, and thereafter he rarely acknowledged the influence of other theologians on his thinking. He attributed his ideas solely to his patient and
constant searching of the Scriptures. If some of his
tenets seemed to be the same as those of other theologians, Noyes assured his reader that the similarity was
only superficial: his theology differed on essential
points from the thinking of any other divine. In fact,
Noyes argued, he was the first Christian since the days
of the Primitive Church to have discovered the true message of Christianity, present but unnoticed in the pages
of Scripture.[40]

---

[40]A theologian who believes himself the first in
1900 years to have recovered the Christian gospel cannot be expected to acknowledge the influence of previous
writers on his thought. In his writings, Noyes evi-
dences familiarity with many other theologians, but
this is usually in a context of showing how they have
erred in their thought. (See John H. Noyes, *The Berean:
A Manual for the Help of Those who Seek the Faith of the
Primitive Church* [Putney, 1847), pp. 301-304, 310-316,
351-366.) While studying at Yale, Noyes was most impressed by the teachings of Dr. Nathaniel W. Taylor, who
opposed the "miserable sinner" concept of orthodox theology in favor of a position which ascribed moral
strength to the redeemed Christian. At the same time,
Noyes was reading and considering the writings of John
Wesley, which nurtured his growing conviction that not
only is perfection attainable in this life--the call to
this state is the essence of Christianity. Noyes was
also familiar with the thought of Swedenborg, and with
the thought of other American Perfectionist preachers,
notably Charles Finney. Though undoubtedly influenced
by all these, Noyes rarely acknowledged any such debt.

The essential message of Christianity, according
to Noyes, is that men can be radically transformed by
the inner presence of Christ. Orthodox theology considered man as essentially unchanged by conversion; it
taught that he remained a sinful, sick and weak creature, incapable of performing good.[41] But true doctrine
teaches, Noyes maintained, that in conversion a change
occurs so radical that it can only be described as a
"new birth" or as the making of a "new creature".[42]
Jesus came--not merely to *forgive sins,* for that was accomplished in the Old Testament--but to give purification, that is, *freedom from sin.* The message of Christianity is that man can be freed from sin completely:

> Whoever abideth in him, sinneth not. Whosoever
> sinneth hath not seen him, neither known him
> (1 John 3:6). By one offering he hath forever
> *perfected them* that are sanctified (Heb., 10, 14).

According to Noyes, those who taught a doctrine of salvation which still allowed for the continuance of sins
arising from a sinful nature, did not know Christianity.
They were still working out of the Old Testament notion

He mentions these authors in order to contrast his own
theology with that of men who had not, he felt, yet discovered the central doctrines of Christian holiness.
(See *Berean,* pp. 236-242; 270-276.) See Benjamin Breckinridge Warfield, "John Humphrey Noyes and his 'Bible Communists'", *Perfectionism,* Vol. II [New York, 1931], p. 311
who argues that many of Noyes' key doctrines were borrowed
directly from Shakerism.

[41]*Berean,* p. 200.

[42]*Circular,* 2 May 1864, p. 50. See also *Salvation
from Sin: The End of Christian Faith* (Oneida, New York,
1876), pp. 3f.

of imputed holiness: forgiveness without healing.

Noyes' doctrine of sinlessness was met with ridi-
cule from many quarters. How, he was asked, could he
sanely propose that men might live without sinning?
Noyes responded that this is possible only because
Christ dwells within the converted man, possesses him
and directs his actions. Noyes understood the scriptural dictum "Christ dwells within me" literally. He believed that Christ takes control of a person through a
dynamic similar to that by which the mesmerist directs
the actions, thoughts and will of the patient.[43] The
individual is made holy, sinless, perfect because Christ
has taken possession of him.[44] It is, therefore, the
righteousness of God and not of good works which is at
issue in Noyes' theology:

> If he lives in us, we are justified because he is
> justified--we are holy because he is holy--we are
> in the resurrection, because he is in the resur-
> rection. Self is extinguished....[45]

---

[43]*Berean*, pp. 47-51, 54-55; Allan Estlake, *The
Oneida Community: A Record of an Attempt to Carry out
the Principles of Christian Unselfishness and Scientific
Race Improvement* (London, 1900), pp. 126f. The popularity of mesmerism in this country during the 19th century provided both a model and milieu which made Noyes'
doctrine of possession by Christ understandable and
credible. This important concept will be discussed and
applied in Chapter II.

[44]*Spiritual Magazine*, 18 September 1849, p. 242;
Oneida Circular, 7 April 1873, p. 118. Noyes provided
for two conversions: the first, to discipleship in which
the person believes on Christ but has not yet been re-
created; and the second conversion, whereby Christ takes
possession of the believer. See *Handbook, 1867*, pp.
23-25.

[45]*Spiritual Magazine*, 18 September 1849, p. 241.

> The enlightened, practical believer in Christ must
> see that by virtue of his identity with Christ he
> is saved from sin and selfishness as truly as
> Christ himself. The spirit of Christ lives in
> him, and he naturally by the working of spiritual
> laws disseminates a good spirit.[46]

Noyes maintained that when Paul said "I can do all
things through Christ who strengthens me", he claimed
for all believers the consequences of union with a perfect, immortal and almighty being.[47]

Noyes' antagonists would ask him to show them a
man who never did wrong, who never fell into transgres-
sions of Christian morality. But this objection came
from men who failed to recognize that, for Noyes, sin
was primarily a matter of motivation. According to
Noyes, Jesus introduced a radical conception of holiness
and sin by affirming that, though right action is important, right intent is of prior necessity.[48] In judging
actions, the intent is the true measure of the character
of an act. Sin does not consist in the transgression of
specific rules of external conduct, but in selfishness
of intention or will; and righteousness does not consist
in undeviating conformity to external rules, but in
obedience of the will to the spirit of perfect love of
God.[49]

---

[46]*Circular*, 25 April 1865, p. 52. See also: George
W. Noyes, *Religious Experience*, pp. 136, 142; John H.
Noyes, *The Doctrine of Salvation from Sin, Explained
and Defended* (Putney, Vermont, 1843), p. 25; *Spiritual
Magazine*, 1 September 1847, p. 118. As Warfield, *Per-
fec.ionism*, p. 262, comments: "The affinites of his
[Noyes'] doctrine...were less Pelagian than mystical."

[47]*Circular*, 24 October 1864, p. 249.

[48]George W. Noyes, *Religious Experience*, p. 90.

[49]"God tells me that he does not care so much what I do as
how I do it, and by this word I walk in all things. I never

Elsewhere, Noyes takes a position which would lo-
cate the morality of actions more remotely still. He
indicates that the goodness of actions depends, not on
their objective nature, not even on intention, but on
the inner reality of the one performing them. In other
words, an action is either good or bad, not in terms of
the action performed, not even in terms of the reasons
why it was performed, but in terms of the healthiness
of the life which gives birth to the action. Actions
are evil because the man who performs them is evil; actions are good because the man who performs them is good.
Noyes wrote: "What we are is more important than what we
do; because being is the countain of doing...."[50] Because, according to Noyes, the saving grace of Jesus
transforms the inner life of the Christian, the actions
of the converted man are informed with healthiness and
goodness, and are therefore sinless. Noyes did not deny
that external faults might still occur in the life of
the holy man. Freedom from sin did not mean, he would
insist, that one no longer fell into external faults,
or that there was no need for further purification and
growth.[51] He was, in fact, insistent on the need for

---

inquire whether it is right to do this, or wrong to do that, but
whether God leads me to do it or not." (*Oneida Circular*, 28
June 1875, p. 202.) "But we agree...that the substance of the
second birth itself, is a change effected only by the Spirit of
God--a change, not of purpose or acts, but of spiritual conditions--
a divorce of the human spirit from the power of Satan, and a junction with the Spirit of God." (*Berean*, p. vii.)

[50]*Circular*, 25 October 1869, p. 250. In fact, according to Noyes, the chief value of good actions is
simply that they improve the quality of one's being.
See *Free Church Circular*, 28 January 1850, p. 6.

[51]*The Doctrine of Salvation from Sin*, p. 23.

discipline, for regular self-examination, and for efforts toward improvement. In fact, the sign of true
conversion was an unquenchable desire for pressing forward and improvement.[52] Noyes wrote in this regard:

> The distinction between being free from sin on
> the one hand and being past all improvement on
> the other, however obscure it may be to some,
> was plain to me as soon as I knew by experience
> what freedom from sin really was. To those who
> endeavored to confound that distinction and
> crowd me into a profession of unimprovable per-
> fection I said: 'I do not pretend to perfec-
> tion in externals. I only claim purity of
> heart and the answer of good conscience toward
> God. A book may be true and perfect in senti-
> ment and yet be deficient in graces of style
> and typographical accuracy.'[53]

Perfect holiness meant a purity of heart which gives
good conscience, and this purity could exist prior to
all external improvement or good works.[54]

As was indicated above, Noyes was not alone in
teaching the possibility of perfection in the Christian
life. Wesley's doctrine of Christian Perfection predated

---

[52]*Berean,* pp. 242-245.

[53]George W. Noyes, *Religious Experience,* pp. 119f.
See also: *Circular,* 20 December 1853, p. 27; *Spiritual
Magazine,* 15 May 1846, p. 33; *The Doctrine of Salvation
from Sin,* p. 23.

[54]Noyes pointed out that his antagonists who insisted that this doctrine of Perfectionism was blasphe-
mous and unreasonable believed similar things about the
state of men in heaven. The main difference, then, between Perfectionism and Orthodoxy, Noyes pointed out,
was that, for the former, participation in the life of
Christ begins while still living in this world. See
John H. Noyes, *Paul's Prize* (n.p., n.d.), p. 16; John
H. Noyes, *The Way of Holiness* (Putney, Vermont, 1838),
pp. 11f; Robert A. Parker, *A Yankee Saint: John Humphrey Noyes and the Oneida Community* (New York, 1935), p.
23; Gilbert V. Seldes, *The Stammering Century* (New York,
1928), p. 17.

Noyes; and other Perfectionist groups, notably that inspired by Charles Finney, were forming throughout the
Northeast. But Noyes insisted on distinguishing his
theology from these other Perfectionist groups. He rejected the thinking of Taylor[55] because the latter failed
to see that the call to perfection is the essence of
Christianity and not an extra to which some few are
called. Noyes distinguished his positions from those of
Swedenborg who, he said, relied more on a system of
spiritual philosophy than on the Christian gospel. Noyes
claimed that Swedenborg made the divine indwelling to be
part of the nature of man, and thereby denied the doctrine of security. Wesley had concluded after much consideration that even the trace of entire sanctification
could be lost, that holiness was maintained on a moment
to moment basis. Here, according to Noyes, he failed,
neglecting to "clear away fully the rubbish" which
blocked the entrance to holiness.[57] Noyes argued that,
although according to Scripture the salvation of the *sinful disciple* is uncertain, this statement does not apply
to the *perfect disciple* whose salvation is assured.[58]
Noyes also opposed himself to the teachings of Finney
and the Perfectionists at Oberlin on two counts: first,
like the Methodists, they denied security in perfection;
and secondly, they made perfection but a secondary ap-
pendage to the message of Christianity, instead of seeing

---

[55]See above, footnote 40.

[56]Berean, p. 272.

[57]Berean, p. 241.

[58]*Berean*, pp. 236ff, 270ff; George W. Noyes, *Religious Experience*, p. 91; *Circular*, 25 April 1864, pp.
52f. *Perfectionist*, 22 March 1845, p. 2; *Perfectionist*,
4 May 1844, p. 13.

that it is the central concept which was revealed by
Christ.[59]

Noyes insisted that belief in the doctrine of perfection had critical and *pragmatic* consequences. The
man who believes that Christ dwells within him and works
through him will find himself capable of a moral life
unthinkable to the man who believes himself to be in a
sinful condition.[60] In Noyes' opinion, the man who is

---

[59]Noyes argued that the Oberlin group failed to insist that the Christian is capable of perfection. They
simply urged converts to aim at holiness. He saw this
to be only the smallest step toward shifting emphasis
away from the ideas of human inability and imperfect
sanctification. On the relation of Noyes to other Perfectionist teachers, see Benjamin B. Warfield, "John
Humphrey Noyes and his 'Bible Communists'", *Bibliotheca
Sacra,* Vol. 78, pp. 188f.

[60]Noyes wrote, *Berean,* p. 176: "The *effect* of simple
belief on the conduct and condition of men, may be illustrated by
many familiar examples....suppose a poor outcast is made heir by
the will of a friend to a large estate. He is informed of his good
fortune. Now if he refuses to believe that the will exists, and
that he is actually the owner of the estate, he remains a beggar in
feelings and condition, though he is a rich man, by lawful title.
On the other hand, if by any means he is persuaded to believe the
truth in the case, his feelings and actions immediately come into
correspondence with that truth: he becomes in his own consciousness
as well as in fact a rich man." Earlier, Noyes had observed,
Berean, p. 51: "As the manifest indwelling of God is the essence of Bible religion, so it is the corner stone of Bible morality,
education, social order, and physical well-being. All schemes of
reform and improvement for soul and body, which have not this for
their starting point and their end, however popular and promising
they may be, are as certainly impostures as the Bible is a book of
truth, and man was made to be the temple of his Maker. Who but a
madman can expect to check the spiritual and physical disorders of
social life and restore mankind to harmony and happiness, while the
first great wheel of the whole machinery by which the result is to
be attained, is wanting? Trees without roots will as soon bud and
blossom and bring forth fruit, as man will attain holiness of heart,
virtue of action, wisdom of thought and health of body, without
the indwelling of God." See also: George W. Noyes, *Religious Experience,* p. 239.

told, and believes, that he is incapable of radical
goodness will remain in mediocrity. But the man who is
convinced that he is an angelic creature, able to overcome selfishness and sin because he has access to hidden
sources of power, can achieve a moral perfection quite
beyond expectations. Men live up to their self image!
Noyes contended that they are mistaken who believe that
a sense of sin and wretchedness can motivate men to live
good lives. The doctrine of sinful holiness leads only
to spiritual impotence.[61] Noyes regularly reiterated
his advice to the reformers of his day (anti-slavery
groups, temperance groups): their efforts were doomed to
failure because addressed to a public formed by a theology which considered sinfulness inevitable.[62] Noyes
believed that the great obstructing wall confronting
all efforts toward improvement is man's lack of faith in
himself. The doctrine that men are embodiments of the
spirit of Christ, Noyes insisted, would generate a people willing and able to live fruitful lives. Noyes told
his followers to engage themselves in a war against self-
condemnation and the torments of an evil conscience by
being mindful of Christ's dwelling within them.[63]

The Oneida Community had succeeded, he insisted,
because it was composed of men and women who refused to
think of themselves as miserable sinners, subject to an
irresistable gravitation towards wickedness, but who believed that, through the generosity of God, they had
been lifted out of the slough of sin and condemnation

---

[61]*Berean*, pp. 199f.

[62]*Berean*, pp. 451ff.

[63]*Circular*, 15 June 1868, pp. 103f; *Circular*, 15
March 1869, p. 410; *American Socialist*, 16 August 1877,
p. 260.

and were thus fitted to participate in the life of
sharing and generosity so necessary to successful community.[64]

Noyes was not counseling men to *imagine* they were
holy, but to become *aware* of their holiness, of the
sources of energy within them consequent upon Christ's
real presence to human nature. According to Noyes,
Christ, by his death and resurrection, has entered into
a permanent relation with human nature, with all flesh
and thus with all men.[65] But the effectiveness of this
relation depends upon the *recognition* of it by the individual. Noyes understood the passage: "The light shineth
in the darkness and the darkness comprehendeth it not" to
apply to the presence of Jesus within every man, and the
contraceptive effects of ignorance or unbelief.[66] Men do

---

[64]Henry J. Seymour, *The Oneida Community, A Dialogue* [n.p., n.d.], pp. 2f.

[65]According to Noyes, *Salvation from Sin,* p. 41,
Jesus' spirit is present within every man, believer and
unbeliever alike: "The life then of the Son of God is
actually and unconditionally given to every man *before
believing....*" Later, p. 43, he writes: "Christ has
come *in the flesh*--not in a single man, merely, but in
the whole of human nature." Thus all men are in touch
with two natures: the one prone to sin, the other
"adapted to the fulfillment of righteousness", says
Noyes, p. 42. But man's ignorance of this presence has
"crucified the Son of God in you and...he only waits for
the permission of your faith, to burst the tomb of your
heart and manifest his presence" (p. 40). See also:
Seymour, *The Oneida Community, a Dialogue,* p. 20. The
model Noyes used most often to explain the nature of this
presence was that of mesmerism. Just as the spirit of the
mesmerist can transcend the limitations of body to inspire
another, enabling the former to control the thoughts and
actions of his patient, so Christ's spirit is present to all
men, awaiting release. Further consideration of this concept of presence will be given in Chapter II.

[66]*Salvation from Sin,* p. 40.

not attain what they do not expect. Noyes stated that
unless men are made aware of their salvation from sin,
they will not expect it; and if they don't expect it,
they will never seek or attain it. Noyes argued that,
while no one can earn holiness by good actions, it is
man's belief in the presence of Christ within him that
occasions his salvation from sin.[67]

Noyes taught that the man who has recognized Christ's
power within him is introduced into a state which exempts
him from the laws applying to ordinary men. The world
does not treat all men alike: criminals do not expect
to be given the rights of the good citizen; the insane
are governed by different laws than the sane; and the
sick do not presume to live the life-style of the well.
In a similar way, Noyes insisted, it is to be expected
that the laws and restrictions which apply to the ordinary, unregenerated man may not be necessary in the case
of the Christian who has entered into the state of holiness.[68] The law was made for sinful and depraved men,
and was never intended to apply to those already converted to the Lord. The law, while necessary for the
non-spiritual, produces only a forced conformity, which
can never lead to full Christian maturity.[69] Noyes'

---

[67]See Henry J. Seymour, "Oneida Community: Confession of Christ", a reprint of a letter dated 3 November
1897 [n.p., n.d.]; Spiritual Magazine, 15 July 1847, p.
67.

[68]Oneida Circular, 2 January 1871, pp. 1f; Oneida
Circular, 25 December 1871, p. 409. Noyes taught that
the Christian who is crucified with Christ enters into
a posthumous state, wherein he is beyond the laws of
ordinary men. Even marriage, which lasts until death
parts the couple, is dissolved for the man who has died
in Christ. (Bible Communism, pp. 86-87; Handbook, 1867,
pp. 58f.) See also below, footnote 184 in Chapter II.

[69]Free Church Circular, 23 September 1850, p. 242.

teaching here should not be too hastily labeled antino-
mian, for he sought to avoid the pitfalls of irresponsible antinomianism as well as the impotence of legalism.
Noyes insisted that the Christian, though freed from the
imperative of law, was called to improve his life, to do
good works, and to fulfill the code of the law. Absolute personal liberty, he said, is essential to holiness--
that is Paul's doctrine. But, he would add, in Paul's
doctrine there are a thousand safeguards against antinomianism, which the "liberty maniacs" know nothing about.[70]

Noyes maintained that the law had failed to bring
man to holiness. Jesus had come, and by giving men his
spirit, he had made it possible for them to achieve the
holiness they had sought in vain. The essential point,
Noyes contended, is that the *obliging* nature of law had
proven to be ineffectual. Threats, commands and exhortations were unable to bring about holiness. Only the
grace which changes man was able to accomplish this.
Thus when Noyes said that the law had been done away
with, he meant that the attempt to achieve holiness
through enforced, threatened goodness had been abandoned.
He did not mean that the moral code which the law taught
was made unnecessary. Noyes maintained that the content
of the law, the law considered merely as a standard of
righteousness, remains a perfect expression of the will
of God for man.[71] He wrote:

> Whatever is contrary to the command of the law is
> also contrary to the doctrine of the gospel. The

---

[70]George W. Noyes, *Religious Experience*, pp. 369,
382.

[71]*Berean*, p. 215; George W. Noyes, *Religious Experience*, p. 196; George W. Noyes, *The Putney Community*, pp.
77f; [John H. Noyes], *The Twofold Nature of the Second
Birth* (Putney, Vermont, 1841), pp. 15f.

> difference between the law and gospel is not in
> respect to their standards of right and wrong,
> but in respect to their mode of indulgence in
> securing or seeking conformity to those stand-
> ards. The law is imperative, the gospel is per-
> suasive. The law addresses fear, the gospel
> addresses love. The gospel carries its per-
> suasions to the heart by spiritual power. And
> yet they have a standard of right and wrong in
> common.[72]

And again:

> Christ has a 'yoke' for his followers, and it
> binds them to subordination and cooperation,
> not less stringently than the yoke of the law.
> It is 'easy', not because it is weak and uncon-
> trolling, but because it carries a good dis-
> position with it.[73]

In this regard, Noyes pointed to the example of Paul
who, while insisting that Christians were free from law,
filled his letters with precepts and exhortations. They
were not laws, they were not given nor received in the
imperative. Paul, Noyes taught, had re-enacted the in-
dicative portion of the law as fast as he had abolished
the imperative.[74]

A much longer treatment of Noyes' attempt to steer
a course between antinomianism and legality would be
necessary in order to properly understand it. Suffice
it to say that, while Noyes insisted on the freedom of
the Christian from law and saw obedience to the law as
mere imitation of holiness and inherently incapable of
bringing salvation, he nevertheless insisted that the
doctrine of the law was to be respected, and that the
Christian, though unaffected by the force of the law,
was called to fulfill its teachings.

---

[72]*Berean*, p. 215.

[73]*Berean*, p. 463.

[74]*Berean*, pp. 215ff.

An argument which was often directed against the doctrine of Perfectionism pointed to the obvious sinfulness of men throughout history. The Old Testament saints, the apostles, and men throughout the Christian era have confessed both by word and deed to their sinfulness. In the face of this testimony, how, John Noyes was asked, could he advocate the doctrine of sinless perfection? The solution to this argument, the Perfectionists responded, was a correct understanding of salvation history. Stated briefly, history should be divided into two parallel salvific dispensations: the Jewish and the Gentile. In each dispensation, God intended that a period of "discipleship", during which his chosen would live under the law in a state of sinful regeneration, should be followed by a period of perfect holiness, which in turn would give way to Resurrection. Noyes traced this pattern in the history of the Jewish people: after a period of sinful regeneration which extended from the time of Adam into the early years of the Primitive Church, a chosen group of men (the apostles and their true disciples) entered into a state of Christian perfection which they lived for some years until the Parousia, when they were taken into heaven. With their departure, the Jewish dispensation came to an end, and mankind entered the second dispensation. Those followers of Christ who had failed to perceive the true doctrine of Jesus (perfect holiness) were left behind to form the nucleus of a new dispensation, once again characterized by sinfulness and dependence on outward ordinances. But Noyes believed that this group, too, was destined to give birth to a true Church able to grasp the central message of Christian perfection.[75] John Noyes and his followers viewed

---

[75]Noyes wrote, *Berean*, p. 277: "As God divided mankind into two great families--the Jews and the Gentiles--so he has

themselves as the first to perceive the advent of this
new phase. They believed that they were the nucleus of
a new, perfect Church which would in turn usher in the
second and final resurrection and judgment.[76]

This account of history enabled Noyes to insist
that the possibility of perfection had not existed for
the Old Testament saints, nor for Christians in the *earliest* years of the Primitive Church, nor for the Christians of the centuries since the destruction of Jerusalem (the date of the Parousia), and thus none of these
groups could be studied in order to ascertain the truth
of the doctrine of perfect holiness.[77] But Noyes did

---

appointed a separate judgment for each. The harvest of Jews came
first, because they were ripened first. God separated them from
the rest of the nations, and for two thousand years poured upon
them the sunshine and the rain of religious discipline. When Christ
came he said the fields were white. By the preaching of Christ and
his apostles, the process, necessary to make way for the judgment,
was complete. At the destruction of Jerusalem, the Jews as a nation
were judged. Then the kingdom of heaven passed from the Jews to the
Gentiles. Matt.21:43. God commenced a process of preparation for a
second judgment. The Gentiles came under the sunshine and rain,
which had before been sent upon the Jews. For nearly two thousand
years the Gentile crop has been maturing, and we may reasonably look
to the Gentile harvest as near." This statement is a concise
summary of Noyes' treatment of history, which is a key
to understanding his theology.

[76]*Berean*, pp. 414ff; *Handbook, 1867*, p. 16.

[77]The Old Testament saints were, Noyes noted, servants of God, but not yet heirs. At death they were still
living in hope of the perfect salvation promised. Therefore, Noyes argued, no one should even expect to find
among them witnesses to perfection. (*Doctrine of Salvation from Sin*, pp. 5f.) Although Jesus' atonement effected the union of the divine and human natures, and
thus made true holiness possible for his disciples, a
period of assimilation was necessary before the new
Christians became aware of it, and therefore benefited
from the indwelling of Christ within them. Therefore,
in looking to the Primitive Church for examples of perfection, Noyes insisted that it was necessary to dif-

assemble an impressive series of texts from the New
Testament which he interpreted to prove the sinlessness
of the Primitive Church *in its more mature years.* According to Noyes, by the time John wrote his epistles,
perfection had become the *norm* Christians understood:
"Whoever is born of God doth not commit sin."[78] And,

---

ferentiate reports of the earliest years from those describing the more mature Apostolic Church. (*Doctrine of
Salvation from Sin,* p. 2.) See also *Berean,* pp. 154-169;
188-199, where Noyes discussed those scriptural texts
which seem to suggest that the Primitive Church continued to sin.) Finally, the dispensation which followed
the Parousia was not, in Noyes' scheme of history, a
continuation of the period of holiness brought to fulfillment by Christ, but the first stage of a new dispensation. Therefore, Noyes contended, it would be foolish
to look to the men and women of the post-Parousia Church
for models of perfection. (George W. Noyes, *Religious
Experience,* pp. 73, 289.) Noyes summarizes these positions in the following paragraph from the *Berean,* pp.
161f: "Thus we have shown, first, that salvation from sin, present
and future, was the great object of the mission and sacrifice of
Christ; secondly, that the sins of the Old Testament saints cannot
be adduced as evidence against this doctrine, because they were committed before Christ came into the world; thirdly, that the sins of
the disciples during Christ's personal ministry, cannot be so adduced, because they were committed before the death and resurrection
of Christ, and the effusion of the Holy Spirit; fourthly, that the
sins of many in the primitive church after the day of Pentecost cannot be so adduced, because they were committed before the truth concerning Christ's death and resurrection was fully developed and applied; and fifthly, that according to the testimony of Paul and
John, Christianity in its maturity, did actually make believers perfectly holy in this world." For a development of this theory,
see also *Salvation from Sin,* pp. 6f, 13.

[78]Noyes wrote, *Berean,* p. 161: "However carnal then the
Primitive Church may have been as a mass, and in its early days, it
is manifest that in Paul's time there was a class within it who were
properly denominated PERFECT. It is also manifest from what we have
before said, that this class became more and more numerous and distinct, as the harvest time of the apostolic age approached, till at
last, when John wrote his epistles, Perfectionism was fully developed, and had become the acknowledged standard of Christian experience." See also George W. Noyes, *Religious Experience,* p.
97; *Salvation from Sin,* pp. 16ff.

Noyes argued, what had been attained by the Primitive
Church in the years before its entrance into heaven was
being realized again by those who were accepting the
doctrine of Perfectionism.

In a long series of articles, Noyes labored to support his contention that the Parousia had occurred in
the year 70 A.D.[79] There were several reasons why he
considered this doctrine crucial to his theology. First,
he believed that to deny its occurrence would be to un-
dermine the whole of the Scriptures, for quite plainly
both Jesus and the early Church looked to an immanent
Parousia. Secondly, this doctrine enabled Noyes to explain why the concept of Perfection, which he considered
central to Christianity, had been ignored or forgotten
since the Patristic period. Thirdly, this doctrine enabled him to justify his withdrawal from the Orthodox
Churches without denying that Jesus did intend that all
Christians should be members of the Church he founded.
Noyes defined the Church as the community of saints taken
to heaven by Jesus at the time of the Parousia, who continue to inspire those Christians who turn to them for

---

[79]There are three strands in Noyes' argument concerning the occurrence of the Parousia: first, the
Scriptures (which are without error) clearly predict a
Second Coming of Jesus within the lifetime of the first
generation of Christians. Second, Noyes maintained, all
the signs which were to precede the Second Coming did in
fact occur before 70 A.D. Third, Noyes argued that by
saying he would come as a thief in the night, Jesus had
indicated that only the true believers who were to be
taken into heaven should see him. Thus, Noyes concluded,
we cannot expect to find any documentation or chronicles
of the event other than the hiatus in the historical records. And Noyes found just such a break: he claimed
that there are no records of the Church during the seventy years following the date he assigns to the Parousia,
and that when the Church does reappear in chronicles,
its character is totally changed. See *Berean*, pp. 310-
316; *Circular*, 20 July 1868, p. 137; George W. Noyes,
Religious Experience, pp. 78-82.

advice and strength.[80] Just as Jesus "inspires" or
"possesses" Christians through spiritual indwelling, so,
Noyes taught, the saints in heaven can influence the actions and thoughts of people who remain open to them.
Noyes encouraged the Perfectionists to seek the company
and guidance of the saints in heaven, who were able to
share the wisdom they had accumulated over 2000 years of
experimenting. Noyes believed that it is a mistake for
the Christian to model his life on the social institutions which the Primitive Church practiced while still
on earth, when he could learn directly from the saints
in heaven the experience of so many years.[81]

This, then, concludes our sketch of the theology of
John Noyes. Our treatment has been necessarily brief,
and there are many aspects of Noyes' theology which have
been left unmentioned. Some distortion of his thought
may have been introduced by our method of selection: it
is the more unorthodox and unexpected aspects of his
theology which have been mentioned, since it is necessary that the reader be informed about these. Such a

---

[80]*Berean,* pp. 275-300; *Circular,* 20 July 1868, p.
138; George W. Noyes, *Religious Experience,* pp. 83f.

[81]Despite his belief that the Christian should be
open to the guidance and direction of the saints, Noyes
rejected the Spiritualist movement of his day--not because he doubted the validity of their intercourse with
spirits, but because the Spiritualists failed to distinguish the influences of good and evil spirits, and Noyes
had no doubt that the latter were equally capable and
desirous of influencing the lives of men on earth. See
Circular, 23 January 1865, p. 353; *Circular,* 5 February
1866, p. 369; *Free Church Circular,* 28 January 1850, p.
12. A slight shift in position can be noticed in the
Oneida Circular of 5 October 1874, pp. 324f. By the
time of the dissolution of the Community, many members
were deeply interested in Spiritualism, according to
Estlake, p. 125.

selection process may leave the reader with the impression that the whole of John Noyes' theology is characterized by such maverick tendencies, and this would be unfair to a theologian whose writing is usually balanced, insightful, always logical, and generally impressive. Before concluding this section, a few brief observations with regard to Noyes' methods may be helpful.

The main compendium of Noyes' Perfectionist theology is entitled *The Berean,* a significant choice since it indicates the method which John Noyes claimed to utilize in forming his thought. The Bereans were a group of early Christians, mentioned in the *Acts of the Apostles,* who "searched the Scriptures daily" in pursuit of truth. And this, Noyes maintained, was the sole source of his theology: he would read the Scriptures repeatedly, often ten times or more, with a particular question in mind until he discovered there the gospel of Jesus. Noyes believed that the true doctrines of Christianity lay within the Scriptures, but that they had been buried under years of misinterpretation by a people who had eyes to see, but saw not.

Noyes believed the Scriptures to be without error, and he was apparently willing to propose rather eccentric theses in order to defend the inerrancy. Noyes seems to have moved in a milieu which rarely brought the criterion of "common sense" or "likelihood" to bear upon a subject. As long as a particular position--no matter how unlikely--was faithful to the canons of Scripture and logic, then Noyes (and his followers) were apparently able to accept it. Noyes' reading of Scripture would generally seem to be fundamentalist and unhistorical. Yet this stance did not reflect ignorance of more critical analyses of the Testaments. For example, Noyes'

position with regard to Jesus' Second Coming was taken
despite his cognizance of more "sophisticated" inter-
pretations.[82] Noyes himself demonstrated a certain
facility for "translating" Scripture in ways which departed from traditional readings. For example, he in-
terprets "crucifying the flesh" in Paul to refer, not to
physical fasting, but to efforts at curbing selfishness
and exclusivity. "Recognizing the Lord's body" was
translated by Noyes as a mystical doctrine of reverence
for the world rather than a reference to the reality of
the sacramental presence. One last observation with regard to Noyes' use of Scripture: in certain instances
the impression is given that eisegesis rather than exegesis better describes Noyes' method. One asks whether
his procedure was not in fact to study Scripture in order to find corroboration for ideas which he *already* held.
How significant is the complete text of Acts 17, 11 with
reference to the Bereans: "The Bereans received the
word of the Apostles with all readiness of mind, and
searched the Scriptures daily to *see whether these things*

---

[82] "We confess we cannot but be astonished at the pertinacity
with which the churches and their great men keep themselves away
from the marrow of the truth in relation to the second coming of
Christ. The simple idea that he actually came according to his
promise, and commenced the judgment in the world of souls, immediately after the destruction of Jerusalem, seems to be avoided as
though it were forbidden fruit. The commentators of Germany and
this country go around and around it, and seem to be ever drawing
near to it.... The old ways of managing the 24th of Matthew are
all abandoned. The double-sense scheme is scouted at Andover.
Twisting the word 'generation' is given up. Still the learned
come to no conclusion that is satisfactory to themselves or to one
another. In Germany, where skepticism is licensed, one wise man
thinks the evangelists misreported Christ. Another thinks Christ
mistook the purport of his own visions, and misreported the Holy
Ghost. In this country, Robinson finds a dubious history of Jewish wars subsequent to the destruction of Jerusalem, and forthwith
applies to them the splendid prophecy of the second coming. And
Bush thinks that 'the grand nodus of this remarkable prophecy remains yet unsolved.'" *(Berean,* pp. 315f.)

were so." The corollaries with which he concludes his
theological articles may often have been the starting
points, rather than the deductions, of his biblical med-
itations.

Noyes characterized his theology as an attempt to
stand squarely between polar positions. For example,
his attempt to steer a middle course between antinomianism and legality reflects his general effort to bridge
the polar positions found with reference to any major
theological question.[83] Another example: although armed
with, and prepared to use, the iconoclastic principle
that Christianity after the Parousia was a return to
pre-Christian morality, Noyes cautioned his disciples
against waging indiscriminate war on antiquity, tradi-
tions and existing institutions. He was fearful that
the needed attacks on Orthodoxy by his contemporaries
would include the jettison of much valuable wisdom.

The aspect of the Oneida experiment which has attracted the greatest interest among observers and which
will be the main concern of this book centers around
the social relation they called "communal marriage" or
"Complex Marriage". Before turning to a detailed study
of the theology which produced this system, it may be
valuable to sketch quickly the events which led to and
surrounded this practice.

THE HISTORY OF THE COMMUNAL MARRIAGE EXPERIMENT AT ONEIDA

Apparently soon after his conversion to Perfectionism, John Noyes began to consider the question of marriage in the life of the perfected Christian. He became
acquainted with the doctrine of spiritual affinities,

---

[83]*Circular,* 1 August 1852, p. 152.

popular among the Spiritualists of his day, which refused to recognize the bonds of marriage whey they pro-
hibited the union of two souls destined by God for one
another.[84] Though attracted to this teaching, John
Noyes made no public avowal of these ways, but chose to
ponder the question further. After several years, he
arrived at a doctrine of universal marriage.[85]

Apparently important in the crystallization of his
thought was the marriage of Miss Abigail Merwin, a young
woman whom Noyes had loved deeply since his first days
in New Haven. She had been his faithful disciple and
collaborator in those days, and, although she had refused to see him for two years previous to her marriage,
Noyes was evidently shaken by the turn of events. Soon
after, in a letter to a friend, Noyes expressed his
ideas concerning love and marriage for the Christian.
This letter was passed among other acquaintances, one of
whom presumed to send it on to a magazine, *The Battle
Axe*, which published it without naming the author in
January of 1837. In this letter, which came to be known
as the "Battle Axe letter", Noyes wrote:

> When the will of God is done on Earth as it is
> in heaven, there will be no marriage....every
> dish is free to every guest. Exclusiveness,
> jealousy, quarreling have no place there.
>
> I call a certain woman my wife.... She is yours,
> she is Christ's and in Him she is the bride of
> all the saints. She is dear in the hand of a
> stranger and, according to my promise of her, I
> rejoice.[86]

---

[84]This doctrine will be considered in greater detail in Chapter II.

[85]*Oneida Circular,* 24 August 1874, p. 276.

[86]*Oneida Circular,* 24 August 1874, p. 276. It is
difficult to ascertain with any assurance the degree to

Noyes' letter caused consternation and disgust among many readers of the *Battle Axe*, and soon angry speculations regarding the author's identity were about. Although aware that he might jeopardize the future of the fledgling Perfectionist movement by admitting his authorship, Noyes felt obliged to inform society of the facts and to accept the repercussions. In a public acknowledgement, he insisted that, although he was the author of the ideas contained in the letter, he was not their publisher. He assured his readers that he would never have obtruded these ideas onto the public conscience, lest his liberty become a stumbling block for others.[87] However, he also argued that he saw the hand of God in this unexpected publication of his ideas, directing him to champion the concept of non-exclusive love. Henceforth, he declared, he would accept and follow this call of God, even should it mean the loss of popular support for his work. In defending his position, Noyes pointed out his strong insistence in the "Battle Axe letter" that communism of love was a suggestion for the *future*. It was a social system which was to be adopted only when men and women had reached a state of selflessness and holiness. Until that time, Noyes in-

---

which the marriage of Miss Merwin was responsible for Noyes' rejection of marriage and espousal of free love policies. That the event seriously upset Noyes and that it precipitated his writing some ideas on the matter does seem to be the case. But Noyes claimed that he had begun to think along these lines at a much earlier date, and that the rejection by Abigail of his attentions was hardly as critical as his critics would make it, if for no other reason than that at that time he had intended to remain celibate for life. (*Oneida Circular*, 24 August 1874, p. 276.)

[87]*Oneida Circular*, 24 August 1874, p. 277.

sisted, marriage must be retained as a means of regulating concupiscence. This was the position he had
clearly maintained in the "Battle Axe letter" when he
had written: "Woe to him who abolishes the law of apos-
tasy (marriage) before he stands in the holiness of the
resurrection."[88]

Soon after, John Noyes proposed marriage to Harriet
Holton, a disciple and supporter, making it clear in his
letter of proposal how the relationship he had in mind
would be based on his principles of Christian love, and
how it would differ from marriage as commonly understood
in the world. While they would not presume to enter into the heavenly state of free love,[89] while they would
be faithful to the responsibilities of marriage and
scrupulously careful to avoid anything of a licentious
nature in their relations with others, there would be
nothing of an idolatrous or sentimental nature in their
love for one another.[90] Noyes wrote to Harriet:

> I desire and expect my yokefellow will love all
> who love God whether they are male or female,
> with a warmth and strength of affection unknown
> to earthly lovers, and as freely as if she stood
> in no particular connection with me.[91]

---

[88]Cited in the *Oneida Circular*, 2 February 1874, p. 41.

[89]In the early years, Noyes referred to the ideal
social relation between the sexes as "free love", to indicate its non-possessive, non-exclusive character. But
later, when a free love movement sprang up in this country,
Noyes discontinued the use of this term to describe his
vision, for fear that his ideas would be associated with
a movement which he considered to be mean, irresponsible,
and the antithesis of Christian love.

[90]*Circular*, 3 September 1866, p. 195; *Circular*, 8
January 1866, p. 337.

[91]Cited in Hubbard Eastman, *Noyesism Unveiled: A
History of the Sect Self-Styled Perfectionists; with a
Summary View of Their Leading Doctrines* (Brattleboro,
Vermont, 1849), p. 134.

John and Harriet were married in June of 1838.[92]   The
love of John and Harriet for one another, based strictly
on the principles of non-exclusive love, free from the
heat and excitement of romantic love, perdured throughout their lives, grew in warmth and depth, and served as
a model of true love for the Community.

Noyes' main concern in the years following his marriage was the advancement of Perfectionism.   A few disciples came to join Harriet and himself in Putney, Vermont in order to study with them the Scriptures and the
doctrines of holiness, and to help with the publication
of a newspaper.   This loose confederation of people con-
solidated with time, gradually adopting different practices of communal sharing.   Step by step, they bound themselves into a community: in 1843, 1844, and 1845 they
adopted increasingly binding contracts of partnership.
But, true to the policies outlined in the "Battle Axe
letter", they refrained from any form of communal marriage.   This they saw as a temporary policy.

In the "Battle Axe letter", Noyes had insisted that
no one enter into the practice of free love who did not
stand in the holiness of the Resurrection.   In 1845 he
assured his followers that no one stood in that condition:

> Believe no one who professes to have attained the
> resurrection of the body.... Profession and imagi-
> nations of this kind have constantly been connected
> with licentious tendencies among Perfectionists....
> We may be sure that any one who cannot prove his

---

[92]By his marriage, Noyes said that he hoped to free
himself from the slander which was occasioned by his
bachelorhood, and to testify by example that he, with
Paul, held marriage as an honorable state during the in-
terim period.   The marriage also gave him access to monies which enabled him to advance the cause of Perfectionism.   John H. Noyes, *Dixon and His Copyists; A Criticism,*
2nd ed. (Wallingford, Connecticut, 1874), p. 9

> attainment of the glorified state by a glorified
> body has not passed beyond a state of discipline;
> and if he thinks he has, we may set him down as a
> candidate for folly and chastisement.[93]

Exactly what Noyes meant by the "holiness of the resurrection" or "resurrection body" in these statements is
difficult to ascertain. Determining his meaning is made
even more difficult because it appears that he later
changed his position with regard to the necessity of the
resurrection state as a prerequisite for abandoning traditional sexual morality. The following, tentative, explanation of the data seems to be a viable hypothesis.

Noyes originally thought of the "resurrection state"
as something over and above the state of perfection, but
a state which could be attained by the members of the
Second Church, while still on earth, even though the members of the Primitive Church did not attain it until the
Second Coming. Exactly what the characteristics of the
man in the "resurrection state" would be are not carefully outlined, but it would probably involve an elimina-
tion of sickness, concupiscence, death. Until this state
was attained, no man was to abandon the traditional sexual morality. Later, Noyes changed his position in this
regard. He saw the new morality to be an option for
those who were in the state of perfection as a *means* of
bringing about the "resurrection state". There is evidence to support this interpretation in Noyes' use of a
curious analogy: the shell ought not to be broken until
the chick inside is strong enough to bear the world; but
the shall bursts *before* the chick comes forth. Just so,
Noyes reasoned, the breaking up of the fashion of this
world [marriage], though it must not commence until the

---

[93]*Perfectionist,* 12 July 1845, p. 34.

power of Christ is established in the heart, must *pre-cede* the attainment of the "resurrection state".[94] Accordingly, Noyes later saw universal love as an option for those who had entered the state of perfection but who had not yet attained the "resurrection state".[95]

If these suggestions are correct, it was certainty as to their participation in the state of perfection which caused the Putney group to hesitate about entering communal marriage. Just as a period of assimilation had been necessary between the day of Pentecost and the day when the members of the Primitive Church had entered

---

[94]George W. Noyes, in *Putney Community,* p. 119, cites the following statement written by Noyes in an unnamed pamphlet published in 1849:   "It is true that, since life works legitimately from within outward, the social revolution ought not to be commenced until the resurrection power is established in the heart. The shell ought not to be broken until the chick itself is strong enough to make the breach. Yet in the order of nature, the shall bursts before chick comes forth. Just so the breaking up of the fashion of the world must precede the resurrection of the body." Later in his text, p. 194, George Noyes states: "But nothing that could be accepted as a resurrection of the body had been attained. Reconnoitring the whole position from his new standpoint, Noyes perceived for the first time that there was an interaction between life and environment: that increased life tended to improve environment, and improved environment to increased life. He therefore announced his belief that Complex Marriage was one of the means by which the resurrection power would be let into the world."

[95]This hypothesis explains a contradiction in Noyes' writings with regard to the Primitive Church. In one place, Noyes suggests that the Primitive Church did not enter the "resurrection state" until the time of the Second Coming, which would suggest that the practice of universal love was never an option for them. Yet, as will be shown, Noyes maintained in other places that the only reason the Primitive Church did not enter into new forms of social relations was the shortness of time and their concern with other, more pressing, matters. *Perfectionist,* 12 July 1845, p. 33; *Perfectionist,* 27 September 1845, p. 54; George W. Noyes, *Putney Community,* pp. 119, 194

fully into the state of perfection, so Noyes expected
that a similar period of assimilation would be necessary
for his small community before they would be completely
transformed by the power of Christ. Until that transformation took place, Noyes insisted that no one in the
Community venture outside the bonds of traditional morality. The first years at Putney, then, were years of
preparation and waiting. The Perfectionists at Putney
watched for some sign that the time of preparation was
completed, that mankind had, in their persons, entered
again into the period of Perfection. And only when that
day dawned would they consider abandoning marriage in
favor of free love. Just how they would recognize that
this time had arrived, Noyes was not sure.

In 1846, the Community cautiously embarked upon a
program of communal marriage. This action on the part
of the Perfectionists of Putney had been called into
question by many critics of the movement: first, because
no special sign was given upon which to base their decision; and, secondly, because the decision was precipitated by an incident in which John Noyes and Mary Cragin,
a close disciple, came very close to sexual relations.[96]
The following seems to account for the actions of the
Community. After many years of waiting, no sign had been
given to indicate the coming of the Kingdom, and thus the
passing of the law of marriage for the members of the
young Community. This unexpected delay caused Noyes to
ponder the matter and to rethink his position. As was
pointed out above, relying on the image of the little
chick breaking the shell in order to come into the world,
Noyes suggested that the adoption of a new morality with

---

[96]*Oneida Circular,* 28 September, 1874, pp. 316f.

regard to sexuality could be a *means* of bringing about
the Kingdom.[97] Thus, some members of the Putney group
entered formally into the system of communal marriage,
affirming that henceforth there would be no intrinsic
difference between community of persons and community
of things.

On June 1, 1847, Noyes called a Community conference and asked the members whether or not the time had
come for them to publicly confess their conviction that
the Kingdom of God had dawned among them. He asked them
to review the record of life within the family. Was the
spirit of charity, of unity, of growth in holiness such
that it indicated the presence of Christ within the members? Noyes asked his brethren to consider the analogy
of the seasons. Just as it is impossible to pinpoint
the actual moment of the arrival of Spring, so one cannot label a particular moment as the actual hour of the
Kingdom's advent. The coming in both cases is gradual
and without any exceptional sign. It is the congruence
of many indications which signifies advent. In the case
of proclaiming the Kingdom, one had to watch for indications of the presence of a new power within the world.

> All expressed themselves deliberately and freely.
> The indivisible unity and unfeigned brotherly
> love, the growing momentum of improvement, the
> increasing intimacy of communication with God's
> invisible kingdom

were cited as proofs of God's presence. After such de-
liberations, those present unanimously agreed to confess

---

[97]See above, footnote 94. See also George W. Noyes,
Putney Community, p. 194.

to the world that the Kingdom of God had come to them.[98]

The Community intended to keep knowledge of their new *practice* from reaching those outside the membership, since the latter would not understand the conscience of a redeemed man.[99] It was not long, however, before the secret was betrayed by one whose commitment they had misjudged.[100] By the Fall of 1847, public opinion was so incensed that John Noyes and several of the leading members were forced to flee Vermont under the cover of darkness. Those who remained behind found themselves the objects of hatred and reprisal.[101] This public reaction did not disturb Noyes. He consoled his fellow refugees by reminding them that the early Church had incensed their society by abolishing Jewish ordinances. They, too, must expect to be a stumbling block to the world. The nullification of the worldly ordinance of marriage was the offense against which the Gentile world

---

[98]George W. Noyes, *Putney Community,* p. 238. Noyes is reported to have said: "Yet we are certain that sometime within the limits of April, spring will have come. Such is our problem with reference to the coming of the Kingdom of God on earth. The evidence goes to show that the Kingdom of God will be established here not in a formal, dramatic way, but by a process like that which brings the seasonal spring." (George W. Noyes, *Putney Community,* p. 236). See also *Circular,* 14 September 1854, p. 487; Warfield, *Bibliotheca Sacra,* Vol. 78, p. 324.

[99]Jesus had taught in parables in order to reserve many things from the crowds; so the Community practiced "bible secretiveness". They reasoned that while it was their duty to present to the world the great matters of salvation, it was neither expedient nor prudent that they reveal all the lessons which had been revealed to them in the illumination of the Spirit. (*Spiritual Magazine,* 1 September 1847, pp. 120f).

[100]George W. Noyes, *Putney Community,* p. 182.

[101]Eastman, pp. 51-53.

of the 19th century was meant to stumble.[102]   The wife
of John Cragin gave birth to a son who was named Victor
Cragin Noyes.

The expulsion from Putney occurred at a time when
a fellow Perfectionist had purchased property at Oneida
Creek for the purpose of beginning a community modeled
somewhat on the Putney establishment.   Hearing of Noyes'
plight, he invited the latter to come to Oneida and take
on the leadership of the beginning association there. By
Spring of 1848, Noyes had gathered the original members
of Putney plus a large number of new disciples to what
was to be the site of the successful Oneida Community.
Within a few years of the foundation at Oneida, citizens
from central New York, horrified by the Community's "licentious" social policies, sponsored efforts to force
the Oneida Perfectionists to disband.   Fortunately the
Community was saved from a repetition of the Putney experience by the intervention of its immediate neighbors,
who, while hardly condoning the social practices of the
communists, testified to the Christian character of the
inhabitants of the Mansion House, and thus deflected the
force of attacks.   [A similar good will developed later
between the Wallingford Community and its neighbors, and
a motion to force its disbandment was rejected by the
local people at a public debate.][103]   Outsiders recognized in the Perfectionists of both settlements a people
who were scrupulously honest, conscientious in business,
modest in their dealings with outsiders, cultivated and
refined.[104]   Thus for the major part of its history, the

---

[102]George W. Noyes, *Putney Community,* pp. 118, 368.

[103]*Oneida Circular,* 6 November 1871, p. 356.

[104]*Circular,* 22 October 1866, pp. 253f.

Oneida Communities were free from persecution by the
law.[105] However, a new and more imposing effort to
force the Community to dissolve, or at least to abandon
their social practices, was initiated in the seventies,
and resulted in a major Convention being convened in
Syracuse in 1878. This Convention resolved: "that it is
an urgent duty of the people of the state to pass measures for the suppression of the moral practices of the
Oneida Community."[106] Because there was no law upon
the books which the Oneida Community was violating, the
Convention planned to push for legislation which would
force the Perfectionists to abandon their social experiment.[107] These plans never materialized for in August,
1879 the Oneida Community made public its decision to
voluntarily abandon the practice of communal marriage,
while continuing their life of shared property and education.[108] Thus came to an end the experiment in communal marriage.

The members of the Oneida Community insisted that
many of those who opposed communal marriage, as well as

---

[105]See *American Socialist,* 20 February 1879, p. 57
for history of legal efforts taken against the Oneida
Community.

[106]*American Socialist,* 20 February 1879, p. 57.

[107]Neither adultery nor prostitution were crimes;
there were laws against polygamy but these did not apply to Oneida since the situation there did not involve
multiple marriages. (*American Socialist,* 12 September
1878, p. 294; *American Socialist,* 20 February 1879, p.
60.)

[108]This new policy proved to be short-lived, and
in 1881 the members of Oneida completely abandoned communal life and shared property, converting the Community
industries into a joint-stock corporation--the Oneida
Community, Ltd. *American Socialist,* 4 September 1879,
p. 282.

many who thought themselves to be its allies, misunder-
stood the aspirations of its creators. Both groups
failed to take seriously the Community's insistence that
the system must be considered in the context of a radical
Christian concept of love. It would seem that some modern commentators, whether those condemning or those laud-
ing the experiment, likewise neglect to consider seriously the concepts of love which the system intended to incarnate. It is to a study of those concepts and their
institutionalization which we turn now.

CHAPTER TWO

ONEIDA'S THEOLOGY OF LOVE

PREMISES UNDERLYING ONEIDA'S UNDERSTANDING OF LOVE

A first reading of Oneida Community literature ac-
quaints one with the ambivalence with which the Perfectionists regarded "love". In certain passages, love is
compared to the bondage of slavery, degradation of nar-
cotics, the sinfulness of idolatry. Love is described
in terms of a self-indulgent, monopolizing spirit which
is hateful in the sight of God, and by which persons become bound and besotted, so that they cannot follow
Christ.[1] The Community members regarded most novels of
their day with scorn and horror on account of the romantic elements which inevitably pervaded their pages. Romance is the enemy of religion, of happiness, of God.
No intelligent observer could deny, Noyes concluded,
that the passion of sex is a fountain of corruption and
misery for the human race.[2]

But if the followers of Noyes were adamant in their
rejection of love as it was known in their world and
portrayed in popular writings, they were convinced that
there is a way of loving which must be exempted from

---

[1] "There is a sticky, self-indulgent, monopolizing spirit in
false love which is as hateful in the sight of God as bondage to
tobacco. In it persons become bound and besotted in their attention so that they cannot obey Christ or think of anything else."
(*Circular*, 24 September 1863, p. 119.)

[2] *Oneida Circular*, 12 July 1875, p. 218.

these charges, and which is, in fact, a source of grace,
peace and holiness for the Christian. There is a kind
of love which does not bring man into bondage or darken
his heart, but which helps him to seek and find God.[3]
The Oneida Community believed that this true love has to
be carefully distinguished from the romantic kind of
love, for the two, though radically different in kind,
appear to the unsophisticated to be the same.[4]

> ...hence it is very important that we discriminate
> between true and false fellowship, for there is a
> kind of fellowship that is as injurious a stimulant
> as alcohol...its effect in the end is disastrous.
> It destroys the soul. But there is a true fellow-
> ship, which God has provided for us, that produces
> a true vibration with no bad effects or painful re-
> action following. It warms our hearts in such a way
> that joy, health, and eternal life are its sequelae.[5]

The Perfectionists of Oneida were convinced that they
had succeeded in distinguishing the two, and, in the
pages of their journals, they explained to their readers the results of these studies.

In this chapter we will analyze this distinction
according to the following outline: first, we will consider three interrelated theological premises which form
the basis to Oneida's understanding of love. Second, we
will examine the principles which served the Perfectionists as guidelines in evaluating the purity of their relationships and distinguishing true love from the false
variety. Third, we shall consider specifically the

---

[3]Noyes was reported to have remarked in a "Home
Talk" given in 1868: "I believe there is a love that doesn't
bring us into bondage, that doesn't darken the heart and harden
it. I believe there is love between the sexes...that will help
the love of God...." (*Circular*, 12 October 1868, p. 234.)

[4]*Circular*, 11 July 1854, p. 376.

[5]*Circular*, 28 November 1870, p. 293.

nature of sexual love and its genital expression, according to Noyes' theories.

THE TRUE PRACTICE OF PLEASURE

To appreciate the distinctions which the Oneida Community made between true and false love, it is necessary to recognize several theological premises which determined their understanding of love, the first of which centers on the nature and use of pleasure. Noyes placed considerable emphasis on the doctrine that God is present within every created thing. The multitude of individual created things are like apertures onto the ocean of Divine being, through which man can reach and enjoy the beauty and love of God.[6] Properly used, he said, the world of creatures leads man to God: an attraction to matter is really the call of the Divine. "In reality the whole circle of our enjoyments--enjoyment of food, of intellectual pleasures, of love in all its forms--is the enjoyment of God."[7] Noyes believed that for the man who takes this elevated view of things, there is no monkish distinction between the good things of this world and the things of the Kingdom of God.[8] All are God-filled; all open upon infinite depths.[9]

---

[6]*Circular*, 26 September 1852, p. 186; *Circular*, 20 July 1854, p. 391.

[7]*Oneida Circular*, 27 November 1871, p. 378.

[8]*Circular*, 19 June 1856, p. 87. See also *Free Church Circular*, 26 March 1850, p. 67.

[9] "By giving yourself to any beautiful sensation, however small, you more than double it--every time you touch good and enjoy it, you touch God; and there are infinite depths there, however small the surface may appear." (*Circular*, 24 December 1853, p. 36.)

George W. Noyes, the founder's brother, and an important figure in the Community, wrote of the simple act of eating a peach in the following terms:

> My heart finds itself in the presence of God; and draws nourishment from his love. Thus the peach itself is but the shell and occasion of an interior pleasure which is eternal.[10]

Properly understood, then, man's use of external enjoyment becomes a method of interchange between his spirit and the Divine.[11] This, said Noyes, is the true meaning of the Lord's Supper: one faithfully celebrates Christ's ordinance when he learns to discern in every meal the presence of God behind pleasure. The act of eating, Noyes taught his followers, becomes an act of fellowship with God when one recognizes the Lord in the food one eats.[12] Noyes believed that for the man without spiritual perception, for whom eating is a mere animal exercise, love of food is idolatrous; but for the man who recognizes it as a medium of Christ, who seeks to meet Christ at every meal, food becomes the sacrament of His body and blood.[13]

---

[10] *Oneida Circular,* 12 August 1872, p. 258.

[11] "There is a way to use every form of external enjoyment, as a method of worship and interchange between us and the divine. On the other hand there is a way to use material pleasures as a medium of interchange between us and the diabolical...." (*Circular,* 27 November 1856, p. 177.)

[12] *Free Church Circular,* 25 April 1851, p. 130.

[13] "We love food; we cannot help it; it is a passion that is common to man; but going to this object as a mere animal exercise, without God, uninformed by the truth and unspiritualized, it becomes idolatry. Paul now shows us the way of escape with this passion, by pointing beyond the bare material character of the food and showing its significance as a *medium of Christ....* Let your souls meet Christ in the enjoyment. So your food becomes a communion of his body and blood, and your appetite leads to true worship." (*Circular,* 25 September 1856, p. 142.)

Noyes assured his followers that when matter is used in this way, i.e., when it is regarded as a medium of the Divine, it becomes a source of real pleasure. But paradoxically, when a man concentrates on the attraction of matter itself, failing to move beyond the attraction, and through it, to the source of pleasure, God, he will find little pleasure in the action. The object of desire fails to bring happiness, and leaves only emptiness and pain. Noyes insisted that man will never find true enjoyment in his use of the world until he seeks in it an intercourse with the other world. He must train himself to remember that what beauty he finds in the world is the reflection of God's presence there, and that the only way to possess that beauty is to seek fellowship with its source.[14] Noyes advised his readers that a man will succeed in gaining pleasure in things just so far as he learns to seek the soul of them and not the externals.[15]

Noyes' intent was not to turn men from seeking pleasure, but rather to set before them the only true

---

[14] "Here's how it works: whatever of value or beauty a person may see, conceive of, or aspire unto, he will say in his heart, this comes from God, the source of all beauty. However the value may seem to lie in the thing itself, still this appearance is but the reflection of God's goodness. The true way then to possess it is by seeking fellowship with the source." (*Spiritual Magazine*, 15 October 1849, p. 274.)

[15] The man who remains satisfied with the barren outside of things will starve and die. This was Paul's diagnosis, Noyes said, of the ailing members of the early Church: they were sick, weak or had died because they ate and drank unworthily; that is, because they did not discern the Lord's presence in their interactions with matter. See *Spiritual Magazine*, 15 May 1847, p. 10; *Free Church Circular*, 26 March 1850, p. 67; *Circular*, November 1856, p. 177.

way of finding it.[16] Like Solomon, who in seeking wisdom received honor and riches as well, the man who seeks
God first, receives in addition all the joy and happiness which the created world can provide.[17] The spiritual man, Noyes counseled, enjoys pleasure, not less so,
but more intensely than his idolatrous neighbor. When
Noyes rebuked his followers for the "pleasure-seeking
spirit", he was attacking their narrow-minded, paltry
satisfaction with a pleasure which was but a pale imitation of the true happiness waiting the man who seeks God
in all matters.[18] He exhorted his young community in
the following words:

> So that whether we eat or drink or sleep, work or
> play, we shall dwell in the interior truth...in
> the soul of things; and consequently shall be per-
> fectly happy without intermission.[19]

He encouraged the community members to cultivate their
senses and tastes, to increase the acuteness and range
of their powers to enjoy. He looked to the day when
circumstances would permit an even greater emphasis on
amusements, recreations--the playful part of life as
distinguished from its more weighty pursuits.[20]

---

[16]*Spiritual Magazine,* 18 September 1849, p. 253.

[17]"Solomon prayed for improvement--for wisdom, instead of
honor and riches; and God gave him all. This is the true way of
seeking pleasure. If we analyze the word improvement it is happiness, with this difference from the usual sense of the term, that
it is happiness which has continuance. Our theory does not turn one
from seeking happiness, but sets before him two ways of seeking--a
wise and a foolish." (*Spiritual Magazine,* 18 September 1849,
p. 253.)

[18]*Circular,* 16 July 1863, p. 80.

[19]*Free Church Circular,* 26 March 1850, p. 68.

[20]"We have already learned that true sport and pleasure do
not belong to the superficial and irreligious.... I think that in the
future, amusements, recreation, diversions, whatever you please to
call them--the playful actions of life, as distinguished from its
more weighty pursuits, will sustain a more prominent position."
(*Circular,* 26 June 1862, p. 79.)

Noyes felt that he had recovered in his doctrine of
pleasure a truth which nineteen centuries of false and
distorted Christian moral teaching had obliterated. True
Christianity, he said, was not the enemy of pleasure and
happiness, but its friend and champion. According to
Noyes, the orthodox churches strayed far from the true
teaching of the Primitive Church when they set themselves
as enemies of pleasure. Yet in doing this, they were
only following the lead of the "Church Fathers", who were
fervent lovers of renunciation and asceticism. The Fathers made death the finest and surest means of sanctification. Martyrdom became the way to perfection, and when
persecutions of Christians were no longer waged, this
fascination with death and negation, Noyes maintained,
was transformed into a glorification of the "virtues" of
self-torture, penance and sexual renunciation.[21] But
this asceticism of the patristic Church is false, untrue
to Christianity, and, Noyes insisted, a good example of
the discontinuity which occurred in Christian theology
at the time of the Parousia. With the ascension of the
truly justified saints, the only Christians left were
those tainted with the pride of false asceticism.[22]

This false asceticism was not the teaching of Jesus,
Noyes assured his disciples. Jesus had instructed his
disciples in the proper approach to the world: Seek first
the kingdom of God, and all things shall be given to you.
According to Noyes, this means that the man who seeks God
in every action, in every pleasure, in every attraction,
shall not only find God, but shall also find himself heir
to all the treasures which the material world can offer.

---

[21]*Oneida Circular*, 2 October 1871, p. 314.

[22]*Oneida Circular*, 2 October 1871, p. 314.

Noyes found Christ's promise of a hundredfold apposite
here: he who does not seek directly the pleasures of
family, home, lands and plenty shall receive them in an
abundance--in this life, not in the future kingdom only.
Jesus advocated an enormous expansion of all enjoyment
when he said that whoever forsakes the good things of
this world, i.e., whoever learns to seek the Divine in
material things, shall receive a hundredfold.[23]

But, Noyes maintained, as long as the orthodox
churches failed to honor the body and failed to guide
their parishioners in the ways of spiritualizing sense-
enjoyment, the search for pleasure would continue to be
misdirected, injurious and disappointing to man. By regarding the body as the devil's property and expecting
him to triumph in its appetites, Christianity had given
the temptor a great advantage.[24] The orthodox churches,
Noyes believed, attempted to suppress, even annihilate,
the passions of man, instead of suborning them into God's
service. Such measures were vertiginous, for sooner or
later, he said, these passions emerge--and then as enemies of Christ.[25] Christianity must learn again, Noyes
insisted, to value the passions as sources of great
strength and power, which, when properly controlled, aid

---

[23] "Christ's method is to take all these passions and make
them work for him. He says to them, if you will not seek your own
pleasure, I will give you a hundredfold." (*Circular*, 15 June
1853, p. 241.) "Jesus did advocate the enormous expansion of
all enjoyments when he said that whoever forsakes the good things
of this world for his sake 'shall receive a hundredfold.'" (*Oneida
Circular*, 14 July 1873, p. 230.) See also: *American
Socialist*, 9 November 1876, p. 258; *American Socialist*,
20 September 1877, p. 298.

[24] *Circular*, 13 June 1854, p. 327.

[25] *Circular*, 15 June 1853, p. 241.

a man in his search for holiness.[26]

Is there, then, no need for asceticism in the Christian life? Noyes would respond that there is. Man's passions are distorted by sin, and in order to ready them for service in the Kingdom, certain periods of renunciation may be necessary. But always, Noyes contended, renunciation should be valued as a temporary policy which looks to the day when the passions will be prepared for their proper role of leading men to God. If the Christian abstains from intercourse with the world, it must never be, Noyes protested, with the idea that matter is evil or that total abstinence is the end point in his spiritual journey.[27] Jesus exemplified this pattern: He, who spent forty days in the desert, fasting from food and drink, was in later life one who frequented feasts and banquets, was accused of being a wine-bibber, and sided with liberty against the restrictions of the Pharisees.[28] Jesus did not impose fasting on his disciples in the form of law, but he did foresee the day when they would fast, not in order to reject matter, but from the inclination of the heart which seeks to free itself from the evil spirit and come into a true relation with matter.[29] Noyes declared that Paul's rejection of the "flesh" was not a rejection of the body, but of the self-ish aspect of man (the old man) which interferes with the

----

[26]*Spiritual Magazine,* 15 October 1859, p. 273.

[27]"God being the interior of quickened matter, the attempt to escape from matter--to renounce its enjoyments--is precisely an attempt to divorce ourselves from God." (*Circular,* 23 November 1851, p. 12.)

[28]*Circular,* 6 January 1859, p. 197.

[29]*Circular,* 19 June 1862, p. 74.

proper use of matter.[30] Noyes advised his followers
that, while holding onto their Christian right to use
all things, they must be prepared to check the use of
the passions if the latter are under the control of a
selfish, evil spirit. But they must never make of
asceticism a final goal:

> Asceticism then, false everywhere, both as a philo-
> sophy and a religion, misleads man in his worship of
> God. Matter, united to God and blessed by him, should
> elevate and purify man, not debase him. Enjoyment of
> matter should attract him to God and to the worship
> of the Creator through his works....
>
> The intelligent follower of Christ while believing
> matter to be pure and holy, yet realizes that there
> is infused in human nature a spirit of incontinence
> in regard to the gratification of the senses and the
> enjoyment of material things, which needs crucifying.[31]

It is, Noyes protested, the selfish spirit of which the
world is full, and not the teachings of Jesus, that is
the deadly enemy of pleasure.[32]

Noyes recommended the books of Thomas a Kempis to
his readers as guides in learning to exorcise the passions. But he was quick to arm them against the monkish
spirit which permeated these writings, a spirit which
was satisfied with extinguishing evil passions rather
than hastening toward their rebirth.[33] Christ's gospel,
Noyes affirmed, does not teach us to cower away in
cloistered seclusion from the world, but to break through
the false partition which separates the sacred from

---

[30]*Circular*, 9 March 1853, p. 131.

[31]*Oneida Circular*, 22 May 1871, p. 166. See also:
Circular, 17 January 1854, p. 75.

[32]*Circular*, 18 April 1854, p. 232.

[33]*Circular*, 25 March 1854, p. 192; *Circular*, 1
April 1854, p. 202.

the secular, to view the whole world as the realm of God,
wherein all is sacred.[34] The fact that the passions as
they are practiced by most men tend to distract from God
does not warrant their annihilation. Both his study of
Scripture, and his reflections on experience convinced
John Noyes that, under the control of the Holy Spirit,
the passions are entirely different and can be trained
to take their place under the banner of holiness.[35]

INDIVIDUALISM AND POSSESSION

The second theological principle which plays an important role in John Noyes' teachings on social relationships concerns individualism and possession. Noyes
urged his followers to abandon the illusion of individu-
ality, to recognize that everything is part of a single
entity. Just as the same life flows in a man's arm as
in his leg, so too each man is part of something tran-
scending the individual. To recognize this is to be a
man of wisdom, to understand the truth of Paul's doctrine of the mystical body of Christ. Unfortunately,
Noyes admitted, recognition of this basic truth does
not come easily to man; there is a repugnance of the

---

[34] "This is the weak and feminine character of Christianity
of the present day. It baits mankind with the bare hook of human
obligation to a divine law, or with the dim vision of shadowy, unsexed and unhumanized ghosts, chanting the praises of God in a far
off future heaven, while it concedes to Satan the thousand-fold attractions of this life.... Christ's gospel teaches not that we must
cower away in cloistered seclusion from the world's enjoyments for
the fear of contamination of evil.... He breaks down the middle
wall of partition which separates the sacred from the secular and
merges this whole world into the great realm of the kingdom of God
wherein nothing is secular...." (Circular, 3 February 1859,
p. 7.)

[35] Oneida Circular, 25 August 1873, p. 274.

heart to the notion that each is not his own.[36] Noyes
urged his followers to be spiritually minded. They were
encouraged to frequently make a "confession of Christ",
for everytime they recalled their connection with Christ
and with each other, the "we spirit" would prevail over
the "I spirit", over that weak, sickly, unruly position
of individualism.[37]

One harm which Noyes contended would follow upon the
illusion of individualism is possessiveness. The man
who views his world, and other men, as separate entities
seeks to sequester, to own or possess, a multitude of objects and pleasures *for himself*. He views others as com-
petitors, whom he must exclude, outwit and outrun. Whenever men look upon others in the relations of separation
and isolation, Noyes attested, one can expect as a result
the spirit of selfishness.[38] Material pleasures, which
should be a means of holiness, become occasions of competition, envy, jealousy and pain when they are sought by
men imbued with a spirit of individualism and the consequent need to own and hoard the objects of pleasure.

But, in fact, Noyes insisted, ownership adds nothing
to the original enjoyment of something; rather it destroys

---

[36]*Spiritual Magazine,* 1 December 1849, p. 325.

[37]*Circular,* 29 January 1857, p. 5; *Spiritual Magazine,* 1 December 1849, p. 326.

[38]"Selfishness is that death of the spirit which looks upon
men only in their relations of separation as isolated beings--sep-
arated from God and our fellows, we necessarily breathe a spirit of
antagonism. This is the condition of the world just so far as it
is not affected by the resurrection principle. Our affirmation is
that the true position of mankind is one of union with God and each
other, and that this unity becomes revealed to the consciousness
and bears fruit in all unselfish action, when the resurrection
takes effect upon the spirit, by the faith and confession of Christ."
(*Circular,* 31 May 1860, p. 71.)

the true pleasure of it.[39] Ownership brings with it
cares and worries which are unhealthy and more than life
can bear; concern for property is a slow poison which
slowly kills the spirit of man.[40] But, Noyes taught,
when there is no ownership, no willful holding onto property and excluding of others, the pain is removed and
there remains only the unadulterated pleasure which the
world offers to those who do not try to possess its
treasures.

Christ said: "Except a man forsake all that he
hath...." This, according to the theology of Oneida,
was not intended as an indictment of enjoyment, nor intended to inculcate neglect or indifference to the good
things of this world. Rather, according to Noyes' interpretation, Christ was counseling men to forsake the desire to possess the things which they find pleasant.[41]
Christ himself possessed nothing, not even a place to
lay his head, because private ownership is inconsistent
with that kingdom he came to establish.[42] The Perfectionists were not enemies of pleasure but of possessiveness, the diacritical factor between healthful and un-
healthful enjoyment of pleasure. They maintained that
to say: "I enjoy this thing and I will have it for mine,

---

[39]*Circular*, 11 January 1852, p. 40.

[40]*Circular*, 5 November 1853, p. 406.

[41] "'Except a man forsake all that he hath', says Our Lord.
This certainly is not aimed at enjoyment, or intended to inculcate
mere neglect or indifference of the good things which God has provided for human use; but a radical principle is struck at--*viz.*
private possession.... Christ himself possessed nothing, not even
where to lay his head--not from asceticism, but because private
ownership is inconsistent with that kingdom which he came to establish." (*Circular,* 2 March 1853, p. 124.)

[42]*Circular,* 2 March 1853, p. 124.

and no one else shall have it" is counterproductive and
diabolical, because experience testifies that this stance
brings with it only disappointment and disgust.[43]

The desire to possess valued objects is natural to
man and difficult to overcome. Noyes and his brethren
at Oneida found that the only antidote to this is a correct perception of reality. One must come to see that
every pleasure leads to the same pervading principle,
God; that every pleasure, no matter how small its outward inducements, provides an opening into infinite depth,
mystery and joy.[44] There is no need, then, for disappointment when one particular pleasure, one object, one
honor, one love is not available; there are always other
objects which can give access onto the same source of
pleasure.[45] And because an access to pleasure is always
available, Noyes insisted, there is no reason for a man
to amass possessions for his private use. Noyes also
pointed out that, since all men are part of one whole,
it is possible for one man to share in the joys of another. He can experience the pleasure indirectly by mingling his passions with the corresponding faculty in another. Thus he participates in the pleasure of the other.
The man who is aware of this power of sympathetic enjoyment, and who works to develop it, finds no need for
ownership, no occasion for selfishness, envy or

---

[43]*Circular*, 19 January 1853, p. 75

[44]See *Circular*, 17 February 1859, p. 13.

[45]"It [the Gospel] teaches him that pleasure is an interior
spirit and therefore indestructible--that the only use of things is
to introduce him to that spirit; and that God has secured an everlasting supply of material for this purpose. Hence he has no occasion to appropriate and seclude anything to himself, but is free
simply to worship and enjoy." (*Oneida Circular*, 12 August
1872, p. 258.)

competition.[46] If the world believes it cannot enjoy
anything unless it is owned, the Oneida Perfectionists
believed that pleasure was better for being enjoyed with,
and through, others.[47] The Oneida people eschewed the
spirit of ownership, not only because it destroys true
enjoyment, but, more importantly, because it occupies
the heart and excludes one from fellowship with Christ.
They asserted that the failure to believe in Christ can
in most cases be attributed to possessive attachment.
"How hard for a rich man to enter the kingdom of God."[48]

INSPIRATION AND THE MALE-FEMALE PRINCIPLE

A third theological principle in the thought of John
Noyes which plays an important role in his theory and
practice of love concerns the concept of inspiration.[49]
As was indicated earlier, Noyes believed that the spirit
of one person can penetrate and take over the spirit of
another, so that the former can influence the thoughts,
words and actions of the latter. The model which Noyes
called upon to explain this phenomenon was magnetism.
Just as the magnet exudes an invisible force which can
control the action of objects with which it is not in

---

[46]*Circular*, 8 October 1853, p. 375; *Oneida Circular*,
2 September 1873, p. 306.

[47]"The little dirty acquisitiveness of the world is so small
that it cannot enjoy things unless they are 'mine'. Men's highest
ambition is to separate a little amount for themselves; but God
does not like that, he wants men to get their hearts large enough
to feel that property is better for being enjoyed with others;..."
(*Free Church Circular*, 25 April 1851, p. 131.)

[48]*Salvation from Sin*, p. 44; *Circular*, 5 March 1853,
p. 126; *Circular*, 5 November 1853, p. 406.

[49]This concept was introduced in Chapter I, pp. 18ff.
as a key to appreciating Noyes' theology.

physical contact, so too, the mind generates a kind of
force best compared to electricity or magnetism which
can permeate the senses, muscles and faculties of another, and can control them.[50] To Noyes, there was no more
mystery in the idea of a mind operating beyond the limits
of the body than in the fact of its operating in the
finger's end.[51] A man constantly generates a spiritual,
invisible influence which communicates his consciousness
to the minds around him, influencing in turn their
thoughts, actions and sensations, without the intervention of imagination, testimony, reasoning, or the senses.[52]
This theory was particularly credible in Noyes' day when
interest in mesmerism had captured the attention of Americans.

> Familiar experiments in biology show that one man can
> project his will or spirit into another so as to take
> possession of the latter's thoughts, feelings and emo-
> tions, making them respond in every respect to the mo-
> tion of his mind.[53]

Noyes termed the process wherein one man affects the
thoughts and actions of another in this way "inspiration".

There is a companion idea to be considered in con-
junction with inspiration: Noyes referred to one's re-
ceptiveness to the inspiration of another as the female
principle; the ability to "inspire" another, he called
the male principle. All men and women have within them
both the female and male principles--the ability to receive inspiration from those more powerful, and the

---

[50]*Circular*, 22 August 1864, p. 179; *Circular*, 27
April 1868, p. 41.

[51]*Perfectionist*, 3 May 1845, p. 15.

[52]George W. Noyes, *Religious Experience*, p. 396;
Circular, 19 February 1857, p. 17.

[53]*Circular*, 21 March 1864, p. 8.

ability to inspire or transmit power to those less perfect.[54] For reasons that will be considered, Noyes believed that spiritual growth depended upon a recognition
and acceptance of this dual nature.

John Noyes thought of salvation in terms of a chain
model. First, God the Father fills the Son with his
power; the Son in turn, having as female received the
Father's power within himself,[55] turns, and, now as male,
penetrates and transforms the souls of the Primitive
Church;[56] who in turn pass on their power to the faithful presently on earth.[57] Noyes taught his brethren at
Oneida that God intended a similar order should exist
among those living on earth. It was necessary for each
man to find his rightful place in this chain-like order,
to open himself to the influence of those closer than

[54] "All fellowship is of the nature of sexual intercourse.
Within ourselves, aside from the connection of the sexes, there
is a duality of male and female in our powers and passions. We
are, everyone of us, both male and female.... We shall find that
all our powers and passions are in these two forms--active and receptive." (Oneida Circular, 16 August 1875, p. 261.)

[55] Noyes conceived of the Godhead as a duality: a
"male" Father and a "female" Son. Commenting on Gen 1:
26f, Noyes wrote: "The critical reader will discover that the
language of the passages implies a plurality of persons in God...
and defines the plurality...as a duality by the terms of male and
female." (Circular, 28 March 1864, p. 10.) See also
Berean, pp. 78f. Noyes believed this also to have been
the doctrine of Paul who says that just as the man is
the head of woman, so God is the head of Christ (I Cor
II, 3). (Berean, p. 79.) See also George W. Noyes,
Religious Experience, p. 402. But, Noyes asserted, although Christ is to the Father the female or exterior
life, he is to man the interior or male life. (Circular, 12 July 1869, p. 129.)

[56] Circular, 14 August 1856, p. 118; Circular, 20
March 1865, p. 1.

[57] Circular, 6 June 1864, pp. 90f; Circular, 14
February 1861, p. 8.

himself to Christ, allowing these holier ones to mes-
merize and control him. In this way, his thoughts and
actions would ultimately be directed by God himself.
According to Noyes, this transfer of inspiration from
person to person is the way in which God intends to distribute his grace and power among men. The salvation of
the world, then, depends upon each person finding his
proper place in this chain of salvation. Like a cog,
each must receive and then transmit grace. But unless
men are aware of the dual nature of human life, unless
they glory in their receptivity as well as in their
ability to inspire, the grace and power of God will
never permeate the whole of mankind as intended. Every
creature must be female to life in advance of it and
male to life behind it.[58]

Noyes encouraged his followers to "cultivate" the
"female" part of their natures--to listen more than they
spoke; to be learners first and teachers secondly.[59] The
infirmities and weaknesses of their characters must be
seen as *receptacles* to the inspirations of others. Noyes
taught that Paul's reference to glorying in his infirmi-

---

[58]*Circular*, 26 March 1853, p. 149. The *Free Church
Circular*, 2 August 1850, p. 196, states: "God is dual, as
is man. But the devil is singular; therefore he cannot love, for
love implies duality or a twofold reciprocal life; it involves a
negative as well as positive action; and this we see in God and
ourselves." Noyes repeatedly asserted that a love for
the male-female principle was the first step necessary
in reforming society. Interestingly, his analysis of
the strife existent at the time between the North and
South was guided by this principle: the rupture had occurred because the idolatrous (slavery) South had refused
to be submissive to the North, which, because of its
closer relation with Christ through Revivals should be
the inspiring member of this particular duality. See
Circular, 30 May 1864, p. 81; *Circular*, 6 June 1864, p. 89.

[59]*Oneida Circular*, 16 August 1875, p. 261.

ties should not be taken to be merely poetical language,
but a confession that the power of Christ was able to
fill him precisely because he recognized his weakness
and need.[60]   The Oneida Perfectionists were convinced
that no amount of individual effort could make them holy
men.   They might resolve to do this or that, but the
strength to carry out that resolve depended upon their
willingness to open themselves to the strength of those
above.[61]   To some of Noyes' readers, this call to subordination meant an attack against the cause of individual liberty.   Noyes insisted, on the contrary, that only
through such humble submission could one attain the
strength and, consequently, the liberty of those who
possess real power.   Without power there can be no liberty for the individual.   Using the analogy of gears in
a machine, Noyes observed that the wheel's liberty and
power depend on its yielding to the wheels above it.
Just so, true power and liberty of the individual is the
result of subordination.[62]   The freedom and productivity
of the man who stands attached to the All is, Noyes as-

---

[60]See *Circular*, 5 April 1869, p. 18.

[61] "It is through our union and fellowship with those above
us that we are good.   No amount of individual effort will make us
good.   We may resolve not to do this or that thing, not to be
tripped up in that way again, but we shall only get strength and
good experience through the ascending fellowship."   (*Oneida
Circular*, 9 June 1873, p. 190.)

[62] "We shall never have peace or happiness, never feel at home,
till we have found our place, where we can receive and transmit
the action of God regularly and peacefully....   If we want to gov-
ern, we must first submit to be governed.   The wheel's liberty and
power of action on the machinery beyond depends on its yielding to
the wheels above it.   Power is the result of subordination; submission is the source of command."   (*Spiritual Magazine*, 1
December 1849, p. 331.)   See also *Oneida Circular*, 19
June 1871, p. 194.

sured his disciples, far greater than that of the man
who relies solely on his own resources. In taking this
position, Noyes clearly parted company with most Perfectionist groups of his day, who emphatically maintained
that the Christian should stand in a direct spiritual relation with God, needing no human teacher or interces-
sor.[63] Noyes argued that this kind of individualism was
incompatible with God's plan of salvation, and that the
man who attempted to stand independently and without a
master, would soon find himself bereft of both strength
and guidance.[64]

An understanding of the three principles we have outlined in this section--the nature of pleasure, the destructive effects of possessiveness, and the dynamic of
inspiration/receptivity--will prove to be important in
the analysis of Oneida's concept of Christian love, to
which analysis we now can turn.

THE CHRISTIAN WAY OF LOVING

ROMANTIC LOVE

As indicated in the introduction to this chapter,
the Community at Oneida considered "love", as commonly
understood in the world, to be a form of idolatrous, debilitating selfishness--a selfishness which they were
determined to exorcise from their lives. "Romantic
love", "narcotic love", "false love", "idolatrous love",
"sentimental love" were among the names they gave to
this affection, so idealized by the world and apotheo-

---

[63]George W. Noyes, *Religious Experience,* p. 203.

[64]*Spiritual Magazine,* 1 December 1849, p. 325.

sized in its novels.[65] Noyes insisted that romantic
love is like a narcotic: the initial experience of generosity and fulfillment prove to be bad counterfeit
symptoms. Ultimately, narcotic love degrades its user
and jades his appetite for the pleasures of true love.[66]
Noyes waged a battle through the pages of community publications against this amative drunkenness, so prevalent
in the world. Experience everywhere, he said testified
that this kind of love leads only to entanglements, torment and misery.[67] Noyes believed this false love to be
the source of most evils and disasters to which men and
women are subject, even disease, insanity and death at
an early age. Disordered amativeness, he said, is a
venom working everywhere in the world, and sending thousands to hospitals, insane wards and death.[68] But, if
the Oneida communists were adamant in their rejection of
romantic love, they were equally convinced that a kind
of love is possible which is beautiful and health-giving,

---

[65]Circular, 9 March 1868, p. 410.

[66]"What is the sentimental, exclusive, love-idolatry incul-
cated by novels, and generally thought by young people to be the
right thing between the sexes, but a refined kind of narcotism?...
sensation is not a safe guide in these things." (Circular, 3
October 1864, p. 225.) See also Circular, 10 April 1856,
p. 46.

[67]Oneida Circular, 27 April 1874, p. 137.

[68]"In regard to love: false love is unhealthy and productive
of disease, and wear and tear of body--is a medium for disease to
work in." (Circular, 12 January 1862, p. 71.) See also
Circular, 10 April 1856, p. 46. Noyes even suggested
that romantic love can be called "the venereal disease",
because it is the general spiritual infection of which
syphilis and gonorrhea are but partial manifestations.
(Circular, 2 December 1867, p. 299.)

wholly different from the disease of false love.[69]   To
differentiate that love from its parasitic imitator was
the goal which Noyes and his community set for themselves.

First, let us examine this false love which Noyes
found so damaging. What is romantic love? Romantic love,
in the eyes of John Noyes, is a relationship based upon
three unspoken principles. The first principle: love is
a force which should never be brooked; one must follow
its dictates wheresoever they lead. To attempt to modify,
control or suppress the movements of the heart is to med-
dle in areas Divine, and the outcome of such meddling can
only be unfortunate. Second, the one-love theory: for
each person there is one, and *only one,* person who is
able to satisfy all that person's needs. Thirdly, love
inevitably includes the concept of ownership, and the
jealous protection of one's "property" from the attention
of others. Noyes rejected romantic love because he believed each of these three unquestioned axioms, which
formed the concept of romantic love, to be essentially
false.

Noyes' disagreement began with the first of these
principles. He insisted that love--like any other pas-
sion--should be, can be, controlled; it is neither
inevitable nor uncontrollable, and it must be subjected
to enlightened self-control[70] Love depends upon atten-

---

[69]"We are not Shakers. Because we are deeply persuaded of the
mischief of false love we do not therefore abjure the true attraction and union of the sexes. We believe in true love, as the most
glorious and invaluable gift of God and the real life power of the
resurrection. But it is love that has religion in it, that is
purged of a selfish, egotistical will, that refuses to be intoxi-
cated and that leads the heart ever more in the ascending fellowship
that terminates in God."   (*Circular,* 10 April 1856, p. 46.)

[70]*Circular,* 14 January 1867, p. 350. The fact that
one does not fall in love with one's sister, or that a

tion, and attention is voluntary. Noyes believed that
one could learn to love almost any person, or one can
suppress any natural attraction simply by controlling
the attention. Noyes had no sympathy for the sentiments
expressed in the statement: "I fell in love, and could
not help it."[71] One of the few novelists who received
good reviews in the pages of the Oneida journals was Sir
Walter Scott, because the very nobleness of his heroes
was their fidelity to principles over the pressures and
allurements of romance. One of Scott's favorite plots,
as interpreted by his readers in Oneida Creek, was to
set up a tension between love and duty, allow duty to
conquer, and then bring in love as the reward of duty.[72]
Noyes assured his community that any love which moves beyond the control of reason is not worth anything. Love
is a valuable power; but any real use of power comes from

---

commoner does not fall in love with a princess--though
both of these relationships have occurred in cases where
true identity was unknown--shows, Noyes argued, that
knowledge can exert a control over the passion of love.

[71]"Love is the circulation of another's spirit in our spirit--
an influx; and it is connected with voluntary excitement on our part.
We can excite ourselves by attention to the matter so as to get in
love with almost any person; or we may suppress excitement, and even
excite ourselves against a person, so as to induce repulsion.... This
precludes our saying in any case, 'I fell in love, and could not help
it' and, on the other hand, it precludes our saying, 'I don't like
such a one, and cannot help it'. The flow and mingling of our life
between us and others we can invite or repulse by the voluntary
management of our excitements.... There is ever so much antinomianism in the views of love taken in the novels. All this talk about
falling in love, is antinomianism. When persons get desperately in
love pretty likely, if you go back into the secrets of their experience, you will find they voluntarily excited themselves." (*Free
Church Circular,* 6 March 1851, p. 39.)

[72]*Circular,* 16 April 1857, p. 51.

learning how to control it, how to turn it off, how to
direct it. The Oneidans set themselves the task of
learning how to control love by intelligence so that its
power would not be wasted.[73]

Noyes' objections to the remaining two principles
which informed the notion of romantic love--his objections to the one-love theory, and to the ownership concept of love--can best be understood by examining the
Oneida Community's description of true love, since among
its characteristics is the realization that love must
never be possessive, and that no one relationship can be
regarded as sufficient and irreplaceable. Our method of
studying Oneida's concept of love will be to examine
several, interlocking principles which guided the Community in its search for Christian love.

TRUE LOVE AND PLEASURE

The first principle of true love follows directly
upon the theory of pleasure introduced earlier in this
chapter.[74] As with the world of attractions in general,
so too in the matter of love: we must learn to seek the
Divine, to seek God, behind and within every fellowship.
In fact, according to Noyes, the attractions of fellowship provide the surest aperture by which the Christian
can come into union with the Divine. His love of another
person should be the means whereby he contacts his Creator. Anything short of this, Noyes protested, any love
which stops in forms and individualities, and fails to

---

[73]*Circular*, 1 March 1869, p. 393.

[74]See above, pp. 52ff.

perceive the universal, is blind, false love.[75]

Noyes compared the dynamic here to the situation of a farmer who takes the milk produced by a cow for her calf and uses it for a higher purpose, the nourishment of men. So, too, God excites man's heart by the attractions of human fellowship, but then teaches him to divert that excited love to Him.[76] God, Noyes believed, can lead the man in love to discern the Lord's body in the loved one, so that he learns to seek union with the Sacred in his affection for the lover.[77] The true Christian must strive to reach that stage wherein it becomes natural "to slip round back of the outward front of things and search out the interior, God-meaning of them.[78] Noyes constantly urged his disciples to avoid being seduced by externals and failing to seek God in all their loves. He encouraged them to that chastity which sees

---

[75]"We are bound in all things to rise from a special love to universal. Music should be a door through which we enter into the interior harmonies. The love of an individual person should introduce us to God, and bring us into rapport with the universal spirit of the sex,.... Anything short of this, any love of pleasure, which stops in forms and individualities, and fails to pursue it up to the universal, is blind." (*Circular*, 17 February 1859, p. 13.)

[76]*Circular*, 1 May 1856, p. 59.

[77]"Love cannot be pure, so long as we think of each other merely as human beings. We must rise to a higher platform, and discern the Lord's body in one another--think of ourselves as members of Christ. This is the only way we can fulfill the law--'Thou shalt love the Lord thy God with all thy heart.' With the common worldly view of human nature and of love it is impossible to do this. A man cannot love God with all the heart, and love a woman too. In order to fulfill the command, we must find a way in which the love between the sexes shall be found identical with the love of God: we must discern God and Christ in each other." (*Circular*, 29 April 1858, p. 55.) See also *Free Church Circular*, 21 May 1850, p. 123, and pp. 53f. of this book.

[78]*Free Church Circular*, 26 March 1850, p. 66.

God in all lovers and drinks in His Spirit in every relationship.

All new lovers experience awe, respect and a feeling of sacredness as a result of their relationship--a
feeling of depth and sublimity. This attitude arises,
Noyes declared, from a natural instinct which perceives
God behind the human being. But because the average man
wrongly assumes that these feelings of reverence are
caused by the object of his attention, he concentrates
all his energies on knowing that person. When boredom
and disappointment follow, when the sense of awe evapor-
ates--as it surely will when love is pursued in this
way--he concludes that he was mistaken in his first
vision. Not so, Noyes protested. This man's first in-
clinations were true. Each *is* an unfathomable mystery
to the other, because each is a *medium of God*. The
problem arises when a man fails to recognize and seek
God as the source of the awe and sublimity which is
being experienced. When the man centers all his attentions on the person loved, as if he or she were able to
bring the gifts of peace and joy, then that relationship
is bound to be disappointing and unfruitful.[79] Noyes
cautioned his disciples to develop a sense of reverence
in all their loves. The man or woman who recognizes the
Lord's body in all his relations will never lose the experience of beauty and sacredness which love brings to
the·Christian. Seeking beyond externals for the life
within, the lover becomes and remains an unfathomable
mystery, a bearer of the infinite riches of God.

Noyes insisted that he was not an enemy of love,
that he was the champion of the intensest kind of love.

---

[79]*Free Church Circular*, 22 January 1851, p. 365.

But he maintained that love becomes putrid and spoils
without the salt of reverence.[80] All that need be done,
he said, to prevent love from being destructive is to
graft it onto the element of worship. "A man may be
socially attached as deeply as ever lover was, and yet
be in a state of calm veneration and love of God."[81]
Noyes realized that the love which he advocated would
seem sterile and joyless to those uninitiated into the
world of the Spirit. But he assured them that this was
not the case. Quite to the contrary, only when love is
pursued in this way does pleasure result.[82] Christ, admitted into love, sweetens and strengthens it. Here more
than anywhere, Noyes attested, the promise of Christ is
borne out by experience: to those who seek the kingdom
of God first, all things are given.[83]

The principle "seek God in all things" has its negative corollary: avoid any relationship which would make
this singleness of vision impossible. Jesus told his
disciples: "Thou shalt love the Lord thy God with all
thy heart." And yet he gives immediately another commandment: "Thou shalt love thy neighbor as thyself." In
what way, asked Noyes, should the Christian reconcile
these two commands of the Master? Should he adopt a
"sharing" concept of love in which he loves things in
due proportion: God most and others in lesser degrees,
according to their worthiness?[84] No, responded Noyes.

---

[80]*Circular*, 17 June 1854, p. 335.

[81]*Circular*, 23 August 1869, p. 177.

[82]See above, pp. 54f.

[83]*Circular*, 7 November 1861, p. 159; *American
Socialist*, 4 April 1878, p. 109.

[84]*Circular*, 8 December 1859, p. 181.

The command is to love the Lord with one's *whole* heart, soul, mind and strength. God is a jealous God demanding not simply that we love him supremely, but that we love him alone.[85] He claims exclusive rights over the heart, and anything less than entire and exclusive devotion, any form of sharing, is idolatrous, a prostitution of heart.[86]

The two commands are properly reconciled, Noyes maintained, when a man learns to love God *in* his neighbor, so that his love for another person becomes identical with his love of God.[87] In the following reflections by Noyes, following the death of his brother, this problem is posed:

> We are required to love God with all our heart, soul, mind and strength. That would seem to leave no room for loving anything else;... If we love God enough to always turn back to him in our enjoyments, to make thankfullness the main part of the feast, then our loving other things does not interfere with our loving him. It is part of our love of God.... Thanksgiving carries love up into the worship of God; and the more we love the creatures of God in that way, the more we shall love God. I am led to these thoughts by this exercise: I was conscious that I loved George very much and desired to know how it was consistent with my love of God; and I began to feel thankful for him...thankful for all that he

---

[85] *Oneida Circular,* 8 January 1872, p. 9.

[86] "God...demands...no half-way allegiance, no partnership in affection distributed according to the popular theory of loving all things in due proportion, God supremely and other things co-ordinately--but the whole heart, soul, mind and strength, for himself alone.... The electric fluid of the human heart must first discharge itself exclusively and directly upward into God, and its action in all inferior beings must be only the 'returning stroke.'" (*Circular,* 8 December 1859, p. 181.) See also *Circular,* 1 December 1859, p. 176; *Oneida Circular,* 19 July 1875, p. 225.

[87] *Circular,* 28 November 1861, p. 171; *Circular,* 29 April 1858, p. 55.

> has been to me; and then I found that my love
> for him did not disturb my relations to God.
> Nothing can now prevent me from enjoying the
> thought of George Noyes...the remembrance of
> him. It is combined in my heart with thankful-
> ness and the love of God.[88]

The man who is pure of heart has a single object of love,
and he does not attempt to serve two masters. Christians, advised Noyes, are called to be single visioned,
to serve one master by seeking God in everything; for
only the pure of heart can see God.[89]

Noyes assured his disciples that any relationship,
in which one finds he cannot raise his heart to God, any
relationship, which demands one's full attention, is
sinful. Relationships which do not include God are opposed to the First Commandment: men cannot love God with
all their hearts, souls, minds and strengths as long as
they try to love a human without seeking God in that relationship.[90] This, said Noyes, is the true interpretation of the following New Testament dictum: "He who
does not hate father, mother, brother and sister...for
my sake is not worthy of me."[91] So convinced of this

---

[88]*Circular*, 1 August 1870, p. 156.

[89]*Circular*, 5 June 1856, p. 77; *Circular*, 18 July
1870, p. 137.

[90]"It is evidently a part of God's policy in his dealings
with men, to break up all social combinations which are based on
mere natural affinities and affections.... Combinations based on
natural affection are likely to be void of any reference to God and
opposed to the spirit of the first commandment. Men cannot love
God with all their heart, soul, mind and strength, so long as human
affections are blind and unsanctified." (*Circular*, 13 June
1864, p. 99.)

[91]*Circular*, 16 May 1864, p. 70. Even the "Song of
Solomon" was rejected by Noyes as imperfect, since it
describes a relationship between man and woman which
does not include God in the affections expressed. (*Circular*, 5 April 1855, p. 43.)

theory were the Oneida communists that they defined unbelief as "social relations without God". Unbelief,
they said, is never a direct refusal of God; rather it
is a positive attraction of one person for another which
causes one or both to withdraw his heart from God.[92] The
man who directs his attentions solely toward the person
by whom he is attracted is, they said, as inaccessible
to God and inspiration "as a man who hugs to his bosom a
clay image of the Buddha."[93] He who allows any fascination to draw his attention from the search for Christ is
indulging in a form of prostitution.[94]

Noyes admitted that it is difficult to resist the
attractions of "natural love". The temptation to eliminate God from a relationship, to allow concern for the
person loved to consume totally every other interest,
is not easily defeated. But then, Noyes reminded his
disciples, Christ came to bring a sword.[95] In his efforts to overcome the tyranny of natural love, the sincere man may have to refrain for a period from all love
relationships. But, if such measures are found to be
necessary, they must be only temporary.[96] Love is good--

---

[92]*Circular,* 4 September 1862, p. 118; *Oneida Circular,* 19 July 1875, p. 226.

[93]*Circular,* 4 February 1867, p. 369.

[94]"It is prostitution for a man to draw woman's heart away
from the Lord, or for a woman to draw a man's attention to herself.
The essence of prostitution consists in putting a thing to a use
below what it was intended for. We should set the Lord before our
face, and any kind of influence or fascination which tends to subvert that principle is prostituting us to lower and degrading purposes." (*Daily Journal of Oneida Community,* 3 March
1866, p. 161.)

[95]*Circular,* 13 October 1859, p. 150.

[96]Here Noyes is applying the general principles of
asceticism which were outlined above, pp. 58ff.

that premise must not be questioned. Nevertheless, one
may find it necessary, Noyes suggested, to remain apart
for a period of time, exorcising the spirit of false and
godless sociality, preparing the heart to love in a God-
centered way. This dormancy must be but a temporary
measure, however, observed only until the affections are
sufficiently disciplined and ready to be placed in the
service of worship.[97]

> You must not serve the lusts of the flesh, if
> you do you will be damned; you must not make
> monks of yourselves, if you do you will be
> damned; you must find a way to make your senses
> promote your spirituality.[98]

In summary, the communists of Oneida Creek believed
that while the external manifestations of love among
them might appear similar to those between others, yet
love at Oneida was quite different: the point of attraction was not to be found in externals, but far deeper
than anything visible. Love was the experience of those
whose hearts were drawn to Him who is "the chiefest among
ten thousands."[99]

TRUE LOVE AND DESIRE

The man, who realizes that the essence of love is
the happiness which contact with the Divine brings,

---

[97]*Free Church Circular*, 3 September 1850, p. 238;
Oneida Circular, 24 May 1875, p. 164. Such practices
of asceticism were necessary, Noyes confessed, even
among the Perfectionists, since they had been tainted
by the spirit of romantic love during the years of their
upbringing. But he urged them to strain towards the day
when strength would make such restrictions unnecessary.

[98]*Oneida Circular*, 27 January 1876, p. 26.

[99]*Oneida Circular*, 3 November 1873, p. 354.

knows that there is no reason for feelings of desire.
He knows that there is no reason to suffer when a particular lover is unavailable, for he realizes that the
identical joy can be found in whatever lover God sends
his way. He knows that the primary purpose of fellowship is to provide access to the interior spirit of
pleasure, and he knows that God has provided an infinite
supply of such relationships. Such were the contentions
of John Noyes.

> You say you love a particular woman and you
> think that you can not love anybody else; but
> if you analyze your feelings closely, you will
> find that you do not love her, you love happi-
> ness.... Is it certain that that woman is even
> the cause of this delectability of your heart?
> I say NO; God causes it. She is only a medium....
> One might as well think of loving some particu-
> lar tune and no other as to think of loving
> some particular woman to the exclusion of others.
> What we love in the particular tune is music,
> and what we love in the particular woman is
> love--and love is God.[100]

Desire arises when one fails to perceive that all
lovers are beautiful because they lead to God. A man
who does not think in this way, who fails to perceive
the truth about love, will expend considerable time and
energy comparing lovers and experiences. And should he
judge a particular relationship to be more satisfactory
than others, he will be distraught if circumstances make
it impossible for that relationship to develop. He will
worry, scheme, stoop to jealousy and revenge. Alter-
nating fits of depression and reassurance will character-
ize his life. Here one will find the advocates of the
one-love principle upon which romantic love is based.
Believing that one, and only one, person can bring

---

[100]*Oneida Circular*, 7 September 1874, p. 292.

complete happiness, they seek for their perfect lover,
wish to possess him or her when found, and feel justified in resorting to jealousy and reprisals when circumstances interfere.

Noyes told his community that this spirit of desire
must be exorcised from their lives if they were to be
happy and free. They were to strive for that maturity
in which an object can be totally enjoyed in the pres-
ent--without desire for greater pleasure, or fear that
the pleasure will terminate in the future.[101] As an exercise, the members of Oneida were encouraged frequently
to break any habit which they had allowed to develop.
By regularly withdrawing from one particular enjoyment,
and turning directly to another, they learned that pleasure was independent of particular circumstances. This
exercise prepared them to withdraw instantaneously without regret whenever a certain enjoyment was taken from
them, to be thankful for the pleasure enjoyed, and to
await openly the new pleasure which God inevitably provides.[102] "To be able to enjoy everything and yet be dependent on nothing but God for happiness" was a community
"common place" at Oneida.[103]

Noyes assured his disciples that these reflections applied with especial urgency to the matter of love. Accordingly, the wise man is one who never suffers when a
particular loved one is inaccessible because of circumstances, death, or affection for another. He knows that
no love is irreplaceable. He withdraws his attentions
without regret, grateful for the joy he has known, and

---

[101]*Circular*, 5 January 1853, p. 59.

[102]*Circular*, 5 January 1853, p. 59.

[103]*Free Church Circular*, 21 June 1850, p. 155.

waits, patiently, for the new loves that God will send
to him.[104]   True love gives rest; "love" that torments
is not love.[105]   When a man is unable to forget a former
lover, he knows that his affections spring from a sickly
spirit.[106]

TRUE LOVE AND OWNERSHIP

The world assumes that exclusivity is inherent to
love. The world assumes that a lover has a *right* over
the other, a right which excludes the possibility of
either one loving a third party. Noyes and the Oneida
Community were adamant in rejecting this theory. No one
ever has the right to demand love from another; no one
has the right to act as if he were the owner of another
person.

The Oneida Perfectionists questioned the notion
that the exclusive *pair* is the most perfect arrangement
for affection. Does it not make sense, they asked, that
multiple, open, and complex relations between many persons are more desirable than exclusive pairs? If isolation is bad, why has the world settled on duality as the
optimum arrangement?[107]   Man is gregarious, not dual; he

---

[104]Those are gravely mistaken, Noyes contended, who
attribute Jesus' weeping at the grave of Lazarus to regret and grief over his friend's passing. According to
Noyes, Jesus wept, not out of loneliness, but on account
of the oppressive unbelief which greeted him in the
friends and relations of the departed man. (*Perfectionist,* 1 April 1843.)

[105]*Oneida Circular,* 2 March 1874, p. 78.

[106]*Oneida Circular,* 30 March 1874, p. 105.

[107]Isolated pairing cannot be proven to be the
natural way, they maintained. Children know nothing of
such exclusiveness. They are fond of fellowship *en masse,*

ought, advised Noyes, to love whomever and whenever he
finds the lovable.[108]

The Oneida Community rejected the concept of ownership of persons, whether by legal or spiritual claim.
Any relationship which cuts off those involved from the
love of others is, according to their thinking, unchristian and to be resisted with vigor.[109] Noyes insisted
that true love cannot involve ownership or exclusivity.
It is possible to love, and to love passionately, without wishing to exclude anyone from the loved one's affections. The most beautiful kind of love, Noyes insisted,
is that between people who give each other perfect freedom to love any other person.[110]

Noyes assured the readers of the *Circular* that simple affection--love free from the tendency to own, hoard,
or exclude--is gentle and sweet and beautiful. But, he
added, possessive love is sharp, acrid, irritable and
nervous. The man who thinks that he owns another, or

---

and rarely play in pairs--and did not Jesus assure his
disciples that such were the natural inhabitants of the
Kingdom? (*Circular*, 23 August 1869, p. 178.)

[108]"Judging from the social character of the child, we may
affirm that man is not a conjugal animal; he was not made to associate in pairs. In the primary development of his nature, man is
a gregarious being. The conjugal instinct comes in with the second
growth of passion. The primary is the heavenly state.... All admit
that isolation is the lowest; then is pairing the highest? Is not
the gregarious state as much superior to the pairing, as that is to
the isolated?" (*Circular*, 16 May 1870, p. 65.) See also
Circular, 10 July 1865, p. 129.

[109]"We do not believe in ownership of persons at all, either
by spiritual claim or legal claim. We give no quarter to the 'marriage spirit', or to 'special love', or to any other fashion of
idolatry and appropriation that takes folks out of the family circle
of heaven and dedicates them to one another." (*Dixon and his
Copyists*, p. 31.) See also Estlake, p. 71.

[110]*Circular*, 4 January 1869, p. 330.

has exclusive rights to another, inevitably finds himself tormented by jealousy, and suspicion, which in turn
make love impossible. (Unfortunately, this jealousy is
never allayed by proofs of good conduct or faithfulness.)
This rancid love renders men tenacious, breeds discord,
and excludes all hope of harmony. It leads to a "rooster
spirit", by which all others become rivals to one's affections for the beloved and thus potential enemies.[111]
This same love fathers that insanity which results in
badgerings of the "beloved", threats and fumigations
against imagined rivals, and even the distortion of conscience which justifies murdering "out of love". The
Oneida Circular reported, with horror, cases from real
life as well as fiction of men who killed unfaithful
wives or their suiters, and then claimed they did this
because of their "love". The same paper observed that
while love delights that all should share the beauty of
the beloved, lust would rather that the object of its
affections be hated and injured before he or she be
shared with others. Lust prefers to prey upon its vic-
tims in *solitude* "like the tiger in his jungle by night."[112]
The thing, however, which horrified the people at Oneida
most was that society condones these crimes of jealousy:
not only is society prepared to exonerate these tyrants
from murder, it lauds the depth of feeling which led them
to these extremes. Not many men allow jealousy to lead
to these violent acts, the Community at Oneida admitted,
but many honor as virtuous a feeling which is cruel,
selfish and harmful--and call it love.[113]

---

[111]*Circular,* 27 March 1856, p. 39.

[112]*Circular,* 9 October 1865, p. 233.

[113]*Circular,* 15 March 1869, p. 410; *Oneida Circular,*
26 January 1874, pp. 36f; John Noyes cited the following

Unfortunately, Noyes observed, most men and women,
nurtured from youth on possessive love, believe it to
be natural, and are naively unaware of the possibility
of any other kind of love.[114] But the man who is wise
according to Noyes' criteria realizes that love is good
and wholesome only when there is no attempt to own or
possess. His approach in love is that of the beggar to
whom a rich man opens his house: he neither demands a
particular room, nor claims exclusive right to any room
in the house. He learns to enjoy, with gratitude whatever love comes his way, with no desire to claim ownership. He seeks to retain that simple love, free from
possessiveness, which insures health, warmth, energy
and life.[115]

Noyes realized that love is not easily purified of
this spirit of possessiveness. In a sense, it is "natural" to develop feelings of ownership toward those one
loves. Jesus' Mother, Mary, according to Oneidan the-

---

examples of false love in a hometalk given to the Community: "I say to myself, this woman is so exceedingly pleasant
to me, I *will* have her. She is mine. I will appropriate her to
myself.... I must keep it away from everybody else; I must forget
God owns this beautiful woman;.... William S. Hatch once said...
'I would spear the tallest arch-angel if he would undertake to med-
dle with my wife!' And Clifford Clark said 'I will have my Sally
if I go to hell for her'.... The love in the beginning is angelic
but selfishness at the end is diabolical." Noyes urged his
brethren to "resolve to have no love which does not give you
rest. Love that torments you is not the true kind." (*Oneida
Circular,* 2 March 1874, p. 78.)

[114]"All the turbulant forms of love that render man tenacious,
and breed discord, and exclude all hope of harmony, are supposed to
be natural, constitutional and incurable. Simple love by itself is
not conceived of. Love in the greedy, excessive, appropriating form
is considered the correct style." (*Circular,* 22 November 1869,
p. 281.)

[115]*Circular,* 5 September 1870, p. 193; *American
Socialist,* 20 June 1878, p. 198.

ology, had to be weaned from this spirit. Noyes noted
that the only interviews between Mother and Son recorded
by the evangelists involve occasions when Jesus denied
the claims which she would make on him in view of their
relationship.[116] In the temple, he reminded her that
his first allegiance was to Something beyond family ties;
this lesson was repeated at Cana; and again when Jesus
responded harshly to the message that his Mother and
Brethren were waiting to see him. In each of these in-
cidents, Noyes saw Jesus reminding his Mother that she
had no claim upon him by right of relationship; no right
to take him from that which he had come to do. And lastly, on the cross, Jesus took the opportunity to remind
Mary that there was no cause for sorrow, because there
were other "sons" whom she could love in his absence.[117]
Noyes often cited the promise of Jesus that those who
give up Father, Mother, Sisters, Brothers, Wives for his
sake would discover a hundred-fold of Fathers, Mothers,
Sisters, Brothers and Wives. By this is meant that the
true disciple of Jesus should not limit his love to those
with whom he is bound by legal or blood ties, but should
learn to discover in every man and woman a potential parent, lover or child.[118]

Thus far, we have seen that Noyes opposed those exclusive relationships wherein the partners, out of a

---

[116]"It is remarkable that the Evangelists only notice those
interviews between Christ and his mother in which he took occasion
to deny the claims of natural relationship, and confess his heavenly
birth. It is evident that he was obliged to resist in her the claim
of a mother; and there is reason to believe that this crucifixion of
her motherly feeling was the 'sword' which Simeon said should pierce
through her soul." (Circular, 13 December 1853, p. 14.)

[117]Oneida Circular, 5 April 1875, p. 106.

[118]Circular, 16 May 1864, p. 70.

sense of possessiveness, forbade one another any other
lovers. But Noyes opposed as well that exclusiveness
which arises, not because either partner selfishly refuses to grant necessary freedom to the other, but because both are content to look solely to one another for
affectional needs. Though Noyes could understand the
tendency to perpetuate a delightful relationship, to
settle comfortably into a proven love, he argued that
even this gentle exclusiveness was contrary to God's plan.

Noyes' position here reflects his general conviction
that healthy life demands frequent change of pace, a
shifting of persons, activities, and things. Noyes believed that whenever a person settles into one way of
doing things, there is a tendency for the very familiarity to destroy the spirit. He insisted that God wanted
men and women to constantly enlarge themselves, to entertain new experiences rather than resting content in any
one experience. Similarly, Noyes urged his disciples to
resist the temptation toward habitual love.[119] By this
he meant that relation which is continued simply because
it is comfortable and does not demand the effort to meet
and love new persons. Habit, he said, is the essence of
romantic love:

> I don't care how much special love there is in
> the sense of warmth, ecstasy, devotion; but
> when love becomes a habit and loses its in-
> spiration, it is hateful.[120]

---

[119]"There is sometimes a disposition in us to claim that a
certain form of love, which is delightful to us, should be perpet-
ual--that we should be allowed to arrest ourselves there, and...
[retard] progress. This of course brings us into difficulty at once;
for such is not the plan of God--his plan is to enlarge us, to con-
tinually bring us into new places, and give us new experiences. It
is no part of his plan to allow us to get into a settled stationary
condition...." (*Circular*, 12 June 1856, p. 83.) See also
Oneida Circular, 14 December 1874, p. 402.

[120]*Oneida Circular*, 27 April 1874, pp. 138f.

Habitual love lulls its devotees into an inertia which
prevents growth. Once one becomes accustomed to habitual fellowship, there is a tendency to stay with that
relationship, no matter how dull and uninspiring it may
be.

Noyes utilized the model of molecular bonding in
order to explain his concept of healthy love. He urged
his companions to sever the bonds, the attachments,
which enthrall the heart and thus bind one in place.
They must be like fluid--contacting, without adhering
to, many other molecules. Love should be fervent, but
not adhesive.[121] A poem by one of the Oneida communists,
reprinted in the Oneida journals many times over the
years, describes love among the angels as being perfectly fluid, fervent but not adhesive:

> This was the strain
>   that still anon
> His silver tones
>   would dwell upon
>   "Meet and pass on"
>
> "Meet and pass on";
>   Though love is sweet
> You still must part
>   If you would meet
>   and loving greet
>
> The other hearts
>   that coming haste,
> Love's banquet free
>   with you to taste
>   no time to waste.
>
> One moment touch
>   heart's fullest tone--
> Its deepest thrill--
>   Then swift go on:
>   Meet and pass on.[122]

---

[121]*Circular*, 10 April 1865, p. 34.

[122]*Circular*, 27 February 1865, p. 397.

The goal, Noyes told the Community, is to achieve
detachment such that one can enter into intimate fellowship with a person for a day or for a minute, and then
part with him outwardly, perhaps forever, and think
nothing about it. To love with all the ardor of the
soul, and then move on without regret! But this can be
done, Noyes would add, only if one remembers that in
each person he is finding Christ, to whom he needs no
introduction and from whom he can never be parted. [123]

LOVE AND THE ECONOMY OF SALVATION

The next important principle which shaped the practice of love at Oneida is a direct corollary of the theory of inspiration introduced earlier in this chapter.
Because men are influenced by the invisible spiritual
powers emanating from others, [124] it is important that
they seek the companionship of those who will influence
them toward goodness and holiness. It is the *duty* of
every man serious about salvation, Noyes declared, to
seek the companionship of those who are wiser in the
knowledge of God than himself. He must keep his heart

---

[123] "We must not be content with ourselves till we do not need
an introduction to any person that belongs to the family of God; till
we can pass right into intimate fellowship with such a person, without an introduction, for a day or for a minute, and then part with
him outwardly for the ages of eternity, and think nothing about it--
learn to love them with the bliss of heaven, and then not see them
again for time out of mind. How are we going to mingle with and enjoy the whole society that we are part of, if that cannot be done?
It can be done; but only by recognizing Christ in all his members.
We feel acquainted with Christ, and we find him in all his members;
so that we may pass into any degree of fellowship with them, and for
any time, without...any hankering for future and special attention.
For the fundamental fellowship, which his life dwells in, remains
eternally." (*Free Church Circular*, 20 March 1851, p. 70.)

[124] See above, pp. 64ff.

and ways open to their inspection and inspiration, so
that, being possessed by their spirit, he should become
like them.[125] The basic principle to be kept in mind is
that a man's spiritual life develops only to the extent
that he associates and mingles with superior life.[126]
Noyes insisted that no improvement can be expected from
the companionship of two people on the same level. In
fact, experience showed him that such fellowship mili-
tates *against* growth in the life of the Spirit. Those
for whom holiness is a priority should, Noyes advised,
resolutely court the society of those who possess the
virtues in which they are themselves deficient, that
they may become attractive to God.[127]

Therefore, Noyes counseled the person choosing a
companion to be guided primarily by criteria of inner
beauty, closeness to Christ, nobility of spirit. He
urged the members of the Community not to allow themselves to be swayed by external inducements, but to seek
a knowledge of the inner person. This, he pointed out,
is the real meaning of modesty: to be reserved with
others, not in order to avoid acquaintance, but in order
to allow the spirits to meet one another first.[128] For

---

[125]"The law which controls us in regard to these is that it
is the duty of each one to seek to rise in the scale toward those
who are wiser in the knowledge of God than himself; to keep his
heart and ways open to their inspection; to bring his will and desires into accord with theirs, and to pass into close connection
with those below him only so far as he is sent and can be controlled
by those who are in the higher position of ascending fellowship to
him." (*Oneida Circular*, 5 August 1872, p. 252.)

[126]*Circular*, 14 August 1856, p. 118.

[127]*Oneida Circular*, 3 November 1873, p. 354.

[128]"Whatever inducements to fellowship appeal primarily to
the outer senses, attracting the attention by external persuasions,
we may be sure that such fellowship is of the nature of alcoholic

this reason, the sincere lover avoids too much conversa-
tion, frivolity and petty escapades, for these prevent
the interchange of inner life.

A criterion which Noyes suggested by which to test
the purity of one's love is its openness to truth. The
man who loves with true inspiration, he said, is able to
recognize the faults of the beloved, does not hesitate
to confront the other with these faults, and is constant
in his efforts to help the beloved overcome them.[129] It
is the selfish, pleasure-seeking spirit of idolatrous
love which seeks approbation rather than the good of the
other, that shrinks from telling the beloved the truth
by which he might improve.[130] Noyes believed that any
friendship which does not allow the Truth "to come and
salt it", is a corrupt thing. "Love and criticism", he
said, "go together in the present state of human
character."[131]

Not only would Noyes place the passion of love in
the service of personal spiritual growth; he assigned to
it an important role in the economy of world salvation.
As explained above,[132] Noyes believed that the only way

---

stimulant...the true source of fellowship is within." *(Circular,*
28 November 1870, p. 293.) See also *Free Church Circular,*
5 July 1850, p. 170; *Free Church Circular,* 22 January
1851, p. 355.

[129]*Circular,* 9 October 1865, p. 233.

[130]"Any friendship that does not admit the truth to come and
salt it is a corrupt thing. Love and criticism go together in the
present state of human character.... It is a selfish, pleasure-
seeking spirit that shrinks from telling a friend the truth, when
he might improve by it; we do not seek the friend's good but we
seek our own enjoyment in his approbation." *(Circular,* 26
March 1863, p. 15.) See also *Circular,* 19 June 1865,
p. 109.

[131]*Circular,* 26 March 1863, p. 15.

[132]See above, pp. 66ff.

in which God's power and grace can reach all men is by means of chains of life stretching from Jesus Christ to the most unsanctified member. Each man receives inspiration from those above him, and then, in turn, he inspires persons less spiritual than himself. An analogy which Noyes utilized to impress his point was the heating of a metal bar: though only one end of the bar be placed in the fire, eventually the heat is transferred throughout the metal. So too with mankind: the union of God with his holiest ones begins a process of receiving and passing on heat energy.

For Noyes, love is one way in which a person may place himself under the influence of his superior or himself inspire those less advanced. Therefore, in choosing people to love, Noyes instructed the members of Oneida to keep in mind the important role which love could play in the economy of salvation. They should, he advised, choose as companions those through whom God's grace could be received, or to whom his strength could be given. As we shall see later, this principle is a key to understanding many of the social practices at Oneida.[133] Noyes directed his disciples to cultivate that humility which willingly accepts its rightful place in these chains of salvation, submits with docility to the inspiration of those above, and is careful that its relations to those less advanced is prudent and always motivated by desires for their advancement in grace. They must recognize, he said, that in their love relations they have an opportunity to either receive or transmit the power of Christ; they must realize that to love others is to participate in God's plan of salvation.

---

[133]A longer discussion of these positions will be given in Chapter III under our treatment of the "ascending fellowship".

By encouraging men to enter love relations with
those in need of their strength, the "chain principle"
seems to contradict Noyes' earlier injunction to avoid
the influence of those less spiritual than oneself.
Noyes would answer that wisdom lies in being sure that
the influence of the "ascending" fellowships outweigh
the "descending". In his own case this would mean that
more energy and time should be put into his relations
with the saints of the Primitive Church (now in heaven)
than with those who came to him in search of strength.

SUMMARY

The members of the Oneida Community maintained that
whereas true love, which seeks God and the good of the
community, is like a fire in the hearth, and a source
of cheerful comfort to the household, "the love of the
flesh, the love which most people would call natural, is
likely to burn the house and all."[134] But this true
love, they would add, is possible only for men willing
to "crucify the flesh"--that is, to eliminate selfishness, exclusive ownership, uninspired passion from the
relationship. The goal of the Oneida Communists was
neither the idolatry of novelists' love, nor the death
of monkish celibacy, but love as intended by God, which
works to man's true pleasure and happiness. This true
love, they found, ministers a hundredfold more of pleasure than the sensualist enjoys in his solitary, possessive and frantic search for happiness. The Oneida Community thought of itself as a witness to the possibility
and beauty of life lived without romantic love.

In this section we have considered the principles

---

[134]*Circular,* 27 March 1856, p. 39.

which John Noyes applied to every kind of love-relation-
ship, not just to those involving love between man and
woman. Noyes' caveats against exclusive, habitual,
pleasure-seeking ties were intended by him as guidelines
in evaluating all of one's friendships, family bonds, relations to offspring as well as sexual loves.[135] The
next section will consider specifically love between the
sexes, or "amativeness", in the thinking of John Noyes.

LOVE BETWEEN MAN AND WOMAN

John Noyes considered it a direct and indisputable
principle that:

> God made mankind in the beginning male and female,
> and has given no intimation that this original
> constitution will ever be altered, but on the con-
> trary has declared by the mouth of Paul that 'the
> man is not without the woman, neither is the woman
> without the man IN THE LORD'.[136]

Noyes was convinced that love between persons of the
same sex can be valuable and healthful, but that it can
never replace the invigorating relation between man and
woman. Man needs to be united with woman, and without
that experience, Noyes believed, he is doomed to incom-
pleteness and aridity. Noyes argued that

> No union of mere man with man can at all compare
> with that between the sexes. To do away with
> the sexual relation would be to blot out the
> very sun from the heavens.[137]

Noyes encouraged men to include women in every part of
their lives. Woman, he said, belongs to man's side

---

[135]See *Free Church Circular,* 17 August 1850, p. 214.

[136]*Spiritual Moralist,* 13 June 1842, p. 1.

[137]*Circular,* 19 March 1857, p. 36. See also *Circular,* 11 December 1865, p. 308.

during work, recreation, sport and discussion, for her
presence changes these activities into occasions of
growth, joy and spirit. He looked to the day when there
would be no institution in which men and women would not
be found together as collaborators. Noyes believed that
once Christ's precept of brotherly love had been digested
by mankind there would be need for another commandment: man must love woman.[138]

Noyes' insistence in these matters followed upon his
theory of sexual complementarity. God has created man
and woman so that they complement and complete one another in a union which is more joyful and more creative than
that possible between two men or two women. Noyes utilized several images to convey this complementing dynamic
in sexual love. He used the analogy of chemical combus-
tion: the human elements have been arranged by God in the
dual form of masculine and feminine, and their combination, like that of the elements in gunpowder, produces
power and strength.[139] He turned to the myth of Plato's
androgynous man as another apposite image of the complementing principle: male and female are the two severed
parts of the original whole man, and they seek one another in order to regain a lost completeness and peace.[140]
A third model used by Noyes to convey the nature of sexual love was to contrast the unity of an interlocking

---

[138]"I don't know but there will be a third commandment.
Christ says: 'A new commandment give I unto you, that ye love one
another', that provides for the sphere of brotherly love. Still
another new commandment I think must come, that man shall love woman. Brotherly love was perfected in the Primitive Church.... But
we must not think that God's work is going to stop with the experience they had in this world." (Circular, 11 July 1861, p. 90.)

[139]Circular, 7 January 1867, p. 337.

[140]Circular, 6 April 1868, pp. 23f.

ball and socket to that of two plane surfaces in contact.
Just as man and woman fit together physically in an interlocking relation, so they are spiritually capable of
greater unity than is possible between people of the
same sex. In this regard we read:

> What is the difference between the love of man
> towards man, and that of man towards woman? At-
> traction being the essence of love in both cases,
> the difference lies in this, that man and woman
> are so adapted to each other by the difference
> of their natures, that attraction can attain a
> more perfect union between them than between man
> and man.... Attraction between the magnet and
> the steel is the same whatever may be the forms
> of the surfaces presented for contact. If the
> tangent ends are plane surfaces, the steel ad-
> vances to plane contact. If the tangent ends
> are ball and socket,...the steel, seeking by the
> law of attraction the closest possible unity,
> advances to interlocked contact.... Love between
> man and man can only advance to something like
> plain contact; while love between man and woman
> can advance to interlocked contact.[141]

Noyes saw in the sexual attraction an instance of
a great cosmological mystery: dual principles attract
one another into energy-producing unities. Noyes invited his readers to scan the boundless plane of nature
and see there sexual duality informing every kind of
life. This duality, he assured them, would be found in
the world of the invisible as well: in the ranks of
angels, principalities and powers--even in God, the
source of all.[142]

Some confusion occurs at this point because Noyes
uses the concept of a male-female duality in two differ-

---

[141][Oneida Association), *First Annual Report of the
Oneida Association: Exhibiting its History, Principles
and Transactions to January 1, 1848* (Oneida Reserve,
New York [1849]), pp. 22f. Hereafter cited as *First Report*.

[142]*Circular*, 28 March 1864, p. 10.

ent senses. First, as we saw earlier, he refers to the
dynamic in which one person "inspires" a "receiver" as
a male-female duality. Because every person has within
himself both a male and female aspect, everyone can re-
late to others either in the role of male or the role of
female.[143] On the other hand, Noyes uses the terms of
male and female in their usual sense to apply to the
sexual nature of mankind, to the fact that mankind is
divided into the masculine and feminine sexes. And much
that Noyes says about the importance of the sexual relation parallels what he says about the male-female duality.

One possible explanation, and one for which there is
supporting evidence, is to suggest that Noyes saw the
man-woman relationship to be the most important manifestation of the more general male-female principle. Accordingly, *for Noyes the male-female dynamic is most in-
intensely operative in the love between man and woman.*
Consider the following:

> The distinction of the sexes is one of the
> various methods that God has established for
> the circulation of life. A difference in
> constitutional characteristics offers advan-
> tages for fellowship. This is true between
> man and man, and *only more intensely so between
> man and woman.* The distinction of the sexes is
> to be accounted as a circumstance favorable to
> the circulation of friendship or universal love
> and nothing more.[144]

According to this statement, the man-woman relationship
is not essentially different from other relationships
by which God's grace is transmitted to the world. In

---

[143]For example, Christ is the female in the relationship between himself and the Father, but he assumes
the male role in his relations with the Church. See
above, pp. 66ff.

[144]*Circular,* 31 January 1870, p. 362. [Emphasis
added.]

other words, it is not essentially different from relationships in which the inspirer-receiver dynamic is operative. In both instances "difference in constitutional characteristics" is necessary. While such a difference is possible between man and man, it is more intensely so between man and woman. Elsewhere, Noyes observes:

> In other words, love between the different sexes
> is peculiar, not in its essential nature but be-
> cause they are so constructed with reference to
> each other, both spiritually and physically (for
> the body is an index of life) that more intimate
> unity, and of course more intense happiness in
> love, is possible between them than between per-
> sons of the same sex.[145]

Further corroboration of this hypothesis is found
in Noyes' repeated insistence that the subject of the
sexual relationship deserves far greater study, because
in settling rightly the problems between man and woman
lay the solution to many of the problems besetting the
world.[146] Noyes' position here is understandable if one
accepts the hypothesis that for him the relationship between man and woman is the most important manifestation
of the general male-female principle which pervades all
man's relationships. In learning to conform to the male-
female dynamic present in the sexual relation, men would
discover the key to many other problems as well:

> The great question for the whole nation...to
> study, is the question of the relation of man
> and woman.... Settle this truly, and everything
> else will be settled...people...will be called
> to study the great constitution of the universe,
> which is imaged in the two-fold relation of man

---

[145]*First Report,* p. 23.

[146]*Circular,* 30 May 1864, p. 82; *Spiritual Moralist,*
13 June 1842, p. 5.

and woman.[147]

Noyes claimed that all civil disorders result from an
ignorance or rejection of the Creator's plan; they arise
because men refuse to subordinate themselves to their
rightful superiors. And in Noyes' mind, this weakness
began with the improper and uninspired relations between
man and woman. Speaking of civil disorders, he wrote:

> If they are the result of an attempted reversal
> of the law of duality, which is the law of male
> and female relation throughout the universe, does
> not the plainest common sense and common logic
> point to the individual social relations of the
> man and the woman of the nation as an underlying
> cause of the whole trouble? *The dual relation of
> man and woman is the source and type of all the
> dualities of human society.* Its discords must
> therefore be the source of discords in all human
> combinations.[148]

In the sexual relation is manifested the dynamic which,
when applied to other situations, can save the world.
When reformation begins in the sexual relation, when women learn to accept the female role and when men become
conscious that the power to inspire a woman depends upon
their subordination to others and to Christ, then, said
Noyes, there will be hope that men and women will carry
an appreciation of this principle into all their dealings. A major reason, then, for Noyes' insistence that

---

[147]*Circular,* 30 May 1864, p. 82. Compare this interpretation of Noyes' insistence on the importance of
restoring true relations between the sexes to Warfield,
who says that Noyes believed that through the abolition
of marriage--"that is to say the institution of promiscuity in the relation of the sexes"--all the world's problems, and even death, would be abolished. (*Perfectionism,* Vol. II, p. 326.) This, I believe, is an unfair
misreading of Noyes' position.

[148]*Circular,* 5 September 1864, p. 193. [Emphasis
added.]

the study of the sexual problem be given priority was
his belief that the latter is a type and source of the
all-pervasive male-female principle.[149]

---

[149]This explanation does not completely eliminate
the confusion which exists about this issue. For example, consider the following: "What is it that is good and
beautiful and interesting when a man and woman love each other?...
It is the element of sexual attraction. This is always good and
beautiful--the love of man and woman. It is the old, divine mystery,
which has its source in God, and is in everlasting manifestation between the Father and the Son and all heavenly beings. (*Circular*,
26 June 1865, p. 116.) Does Noyes mean here that sexual
love is a reflection of the Godhead because it is a prime,
perhaps *the* prime, image of the male-female, inspirer-
receiver dynamic which exists between the Father and Son?
Or does he understand the sexual nature of man to be a
reflection of some universal principle of sexuality over
and above this particular dynamic? Some other puzzling
questions present themselves. For example, if the interpretation given in our text is correct, one wonders
whether in man-woman relations the man always has the
role of male inspirer. In his book, *Free Love and its
Votaries* (New York, 1970), p. 196, John B. Ellis cites,
without reference, a quotation in which Noyes states that
Adam was created especially in the image of the Father
and Eve in the image of the Son. Does this imply that it
is man who must always be the inspirer in man-woman relations? Or did the founder of Oneida expect that in some
situations the man should place himself in the position
of receiver to woman? Another way of asking the question: Should one think of the chains of salvation as
one-link chains, in which men and women alternate positions (thus implying that women are in some circumstances the inspirers of men), or is the woman always
to look to man as her head? In diagram form, the question
is posed as follows:

In creating mankind in duality, God intended that the
two forms would participate in his life by loving one
another; to refrain from this, Noyes thought, would be
"monstrous" and unnatural.[150] It would be to condemn
oneself to a half-natured existence. Noyes warned that
the man who denies his sexual nature--that which makes
him most completely to be in the image of God--does so
at his peril.[151]

The Perfectionists of Oneida could not hold these
views on the importance of love between man and woman
without assuring themselves that their founder, Jesus,
had been among the great lovers of the world. Though
recognizing that he neither married nor practiced genital

Later, when studying the polity at Oneida, we will see
that the young men were taught to seek older women as
lovers in fulfilling the principle of ascending fellowship. This would suggest that diagram A best reflects
Noyes' understanding of the situation. This interpretation is supported by an early text from the *Free Church
Circular*: having pointed out that a woman can be daugh-
ter (subservient), sister (equal) and mother (superior)
to man, the author notes: "And the fact that all three of
these characters are developed on both sides, does not interfere
with the general fact that man is superior to woman. But because
man is the head of the woman, it does not follow that woman cannot
be the mother of man." *(Free Church Circular,* 20 December
1850, p. 325.) This text (though it is the only one like it
that this author has located) would suggest that the Community interpreted Paul's admonition about woman being
submissive to man to represent a description of the *general* relations between woman and man. Woman as a sex
must look to man for strength, though in the case of
the individual, she may take the part of the superior
party in a relationship.

[150]"There is no doubt that love itself is natural; that it
is provided for in the human constitution. God evidently intended
it, and men and women would be monstrous if they did not love each
other." *(Circular,* 22 November 1869, p. 281.) See also
Oneida Circular, 23 December 1872, p. 410.

[151]*Circular,* 13 February 1865, p. 377.

sexual relations,[152] they saw in Jesus' relations to
Mary of Bethany indications of warm intense sexual love.
In fact, as the Oneida Community read the account of the
miracle at Bethany, it was the power-releasing effect of
the sexual love between Jesus and Mary which was responsible for the miraculous return to life of the dead brother.[153] Finally, the Christians of Oneida saw in Jesus'
ascension from Bethany a symbol that his love for Mary
had outlived death and would bloom again in heaven.[154]
Who, they asked, could doubt that this love, which was
the cause of Jesus' death (resurrection of Lazarus was
done in response to Mary's plea) was consummated in
heaven?[155]

Next we will consider Noyes' position with regard
to genital sexual relations. Noyes believed that genital
sex is good, a valuable helpmate in promoting love between the sexes. He considered physical sexual relations
to be "a fine art", intrinsically more pure and aesthetic
than singing, eating or drinking. In Noyes' eyes, to rob
the body of its sexual functions would be worse than to
rob it of its voice, hearing or sense of taste.[156] Noyes
believed that love should normally be expressed in a physical way. He felt that those who accept the principle

---

[152]*Circular*, 6 January 1859, p. 198.

[153]"By his meeting with Mary, the volumes of feeling between
them, like the electric surfaces of a thunder cloud, were made ready
for discharge. In him it took the tremendous form of omnipotent
vitality recalling her dead brother from the grave." *(Circular,*
24 September 1866, p. 218.)

[154]*Circular*, 1 August 1870, p. 155.

[155]*Circular*, 24 September 1866, p. 219.

[156]*Bible Communism*, p. 53; *Circular,* 2 January
1865, p. 329.

that one should love all men, but then restrict physical
expression of that love to one person, or perhaps to
none at all, "strain at a gnat and swallow a camel."[157]
He argued that the burden of proof in this matter lay
with those who would deny the rightness of sexual relations between lovers.

   Noyes taught his followers to regard bodily sexuality as a sacrament: a means of union with God; a channel
by which his grace and power could be shared; a source of
growth and joy. During sexual relations, he argued,
every spiritual person is conscious of being drawn near
to the Divine source, of being wrapped in a "nimbus" of
sacredness, purity and infinite beauty.[158] There was no
doubt in the mind of John Noyes that sexual genital love
was intended by the Creator as a passion which would
bring man into communication with himself. In every

---

[157]*First Report,* p. 21.

[158]"But I will say finally, that there may be no mistake between us, that so far from regarding the act of sexual enjoyment as
in itself unholy, I am sure that there is no sacrifice except that
of the heart, that is more acceptable to God." (Letter to Harriet
Holton by Noyes at time of engagement, cited in *Circular,*
10 September 1866, p. 204.) "...sexual intercourse is in its
nature the most perfect method of 'laying on of hands' and under
proper circumstances may be the most powerful external agency of
communicating life to the body, and even the Spirit of God to the
mind and heart." (*Bible Communism,* p. 45.) "It [sexual love]
is a passion which is peculiarly allied to religion, in which the
devout heart, holding the body within bounds of chaste control,
rises into communication with God." (*Circular,* 4 June 1866, p.
92.) "My impression is that in the exaltation of sexual fellowship
all good persons are conscious of being drawn near to the divine
source. A sense of sacredness and purity--...infinite joy super-
venes on such occasions. What is this but the enwrapping nimbus of
the Divine Being?" "That which symbolizes the union of the Eternal
Bridegroom and Bride and springs from it is not rightly associated
with shame: it is not an orgy, but a sacrament." (*Circular,* 1
January 1866, p. 330.)

sense of the word, it is a Sacrament of love. Who, he
asked, would dare to view it with disdain, or to counsel
men--in the name of religion--to refrain from sex or to
curtail its practice to a frugal diet?

Asked whether the "sacrament of sexual love" could
be practiced publicly, Noyes steadfastly insisted that
the day would come when a regenerated humanity would include sexual manifestations as an important part of ritual.[159] His reasoning was as follows: (a) since man is
a composite of flesh and spirit, he should worship God
in body as well as in spirit; (b) since man is a dual
being, incomplete in himself, perfect worship should
entail his praising God as a complete man--that is united
to woman in body and spirit.[160] Noyes was willing to
concede that this policy might not be possible at the
present time because of the lack of perfect selflessness
in man. Just as the new convert finds it difficult to
pray publicly because he is self-conscious, so men and
women are at the present time unable to "pray" sexually
before one another. For now, Christians must obey the
injunction of Christ who told his followers to withdraw
into their closets and pray to the Father in secret.[161]

By way of conclusion: Noyes was not unaware of the
dangers of undisciplined love between the sexes. He
realized full well that amative love can easily lead
one away from God, from spirituality and from the community. Perverted and turned to bad ends, it can carry
man to destruction with whirlwind violence.[162] But sex-

---

[159]*Circular*, 4 June 1866, p. 92.

[160]*Circular*, 7 August 1865, p. 161.

[161]*Circular*, 4 June 1866, p. 92.

[162]*Circular*, 15 March 1869, p. 409.

ual love can be redeemed. When properly disciplined,
amative love, far from being an enemy, plays a key role
in man's search for holiness and God. Wild, natural,
vigorous, amative love can be civilized when grafted onto the delicate spirit of charity, its strength adding
power to a man's growth in love and benevolence. Noyes
and his community placed great importance on love between the sexes: to be whole, they believed a man must
come into loving relations with woman.[163] In an early
home-talk, Noyes observed:

> There is tremendous importance in the action of
> sexual passion. Perverted and turned to bad ends,
> it will carry us to destruction as will a whirl-
> wind. There is terrible strength in it, and
> given up to godless powers, there is nothing so
> destructive to peace and happiness in individuals
> and communities. The same passion, governed by
> God, mixed with benevolence, sweetened by the
> Spirit of heaven is productive of unbound happi-
> ness and improvement.[164]

SOCIAL INSTITUTIONS AND ONEIDA'S THEOLOGY OF LOVE

ONEIDA AND MARRIAGE

John Noyes viewed marriage as an institution which
sanctions and intensifies all the evils of false love.
Behind the closed and "sacred" doors of marriage is, he
insisted, "a world of selfishness, idolatry, and licentiousness...that cries to heaven for judgement."[165] In

---

[163]See *Circular*, 28 November 1861, p. 171; *Circular*,
2 September 1858, p. 128; *Oneida Circular*, 14 July 1873,
p. 230; *Circular*, 19 June 1856, p. 87; *Circular*, 11 July
1861, p. 90.

[164]Cited in *Circular*, 15 March 1869, p. 409.

[165]*Oneida Circular*, 10 August 1874, p. 260. See
also *Circular*, 28 November 1870, p. 292.

short, for all the reasons that Noyes opposed romantic
love, he opposed marriage, seeing in that institution
an incubator of false and foolish affection. Marriage
transforms the heavenly passion of love from a vehicle
of God's grace into a drudge devoted to the most menial
of services.[166] It introduces man and woman into a
state where it is all but impossible to resist the tendencies of idolatry and sickness. The *Circular* once
quipped that if married love was permitted to Adam and
Eve in Eden, there would have been no need for Satan to
have taken pains for any further temptation.[167] Specifically, Noyes opposed marriage for the following reasons:

First, marriage amplifies the innate tendency of
romantic love to evolve into a stance of ownership.
Marriage supposedly gives the man the right to demand
love and service of his partner, regardless of his conduct or worthiness. Marriage makes love and all its offices a habit and a duty, rather than an inspiration.[168]
Noyes believed that in marriage the average man comes to
think of his wife as an object, something owned and to
be used for his pleasure.[169] At its worst, he said, marriage shelters acts of cruelty and violence which the law
could never allow except within the sanction of wedlock.
Whatever care, affection and concern the man felt toward
his wife during the days of courtship gives way to a relation that might better be called slavery: odious ob-

---

[166]*Circular*, 18 September 1856, p. 138.

[167]*Circular*, 16 May 1864, p. 66.

[168]*Oneida Circular*, 13 January 1873, p. 20

[169]*Oneida Circular*, 12 April 1875, p. 113.

ligation on one side; sensual recklessness on the other.[170]

Secondly, marriage feeds the natural tendency of
love to become idolatrous. Inevitably, Noyes maintained,
care for one's family becomes the ruling passion of a
person's life: every energy is devoted to the task of
providing life's necessities in a world where the nuclear
family system makes sharing impossible. Marriage encourages a sickly dependence of the partners on each
other, and an unhealthy concentration on children. All
these pressures leave little time or energy for God or
the search for improvement...and such a state, Noyes
concluded, can only be termed idolatry.[171]

Thirdly, Noyes contended, marriage chains persons
in pairs for life, even though there is no reason to
suppose that such pairing is natural or to be desired.
Marriage is based on the assumption that love must be
exclusive, that any form of non-exclusive love is prodi-
gal and false. Society recognizes the right of marriage
spouses to demand the complete attention of their mates,

---

[170]*Circular*, 13 February 1865, p. 377. Nor is it
always the woman who is the victim in marriage, Noyes
pointed out. In many cases, it is man who becomes the
slave of woman. She, by tears and tantrums, can force
his heart against his better judgment. (*Circular*, 8
May 1865, pp. 61f.)

[171]"Marriage on the worldly plane of things, deteriorates
persons invariably, drawing them away from God, away from improvement, and absorbing them in each other. As a rule, husbands and
wives live for each other and for their children--they live in the
element of horizontal fellowship--in a combination in which God
and the spiritual world are taken very little into account."
(*Circular*, 14 August 1856, p. 118.) "One radical fault of
marriage exclusiveness is that it induces a sickly dependence of
the partners, one on the other.... When human fellowships monopo-
lize my attention and consciousness, so that my faith in a present
available Christ is obscured, then are they open to serious objection
and criticism." (*Circular*, 28 February 1861, p. 14.)

even exonerating murder when performed under the aegis
of outraged honor. Yet human nature repeatedly testifies, Noyes maintained, to the fact that the need for
love cannot be satisfied by one lover. The secret
history of the human heart, he said, bears out the assertion that a person is capable of loving any number
of persons and that the more he grows in love, the greater his desire to love many. This, insisted Noyes, is the
law of nature, suppressed and denied by common consent,
and yet secretly known to all.[172]

Fourthly, Noyes asserted that marriage is responsible for many unnecessary evils: it actually "provokes to
secret adultery"; ties together unsuited natures; keeps
apart matched natures; gives the sexual appetite only
scanty or monotonous fare; and condemns adolescents, who
are ready for sexual intercourse but too young for marriage, to a period of unhealthy waiting, with the attend-
ant temptations to fornication, masturbation, and other
perversions.[173] Lastly, marriage is a barrier to insti-
tuting a system of scientific breeding, and therefore
makes impossible needed steps toward the improvement of
the human race.[174]

In the eyes of Noyes and his community, then, marriage must be judged narrow, selfish, contemptible and
mean; a breeder of tyranny and oppression; a shield of
all manner of wickedness. It is a closed, pent-up

---

[172]"All experience testifies...that sexual love is not naturally restricted to pairs.... On the contrary, the secret history
of the human heart will bear out the assertion that it is capable of
loving any number of times and any number of persons, and that the
more it loves the more it can love." (*Bible Communism*, p. 35.)
See also *Circular*, 11 August 1852, p. 158.

[173]*Bible Communism*, p. 37.

[174]*Circular*, 14 March 1870, p. 414.

concern where light cannot enter and where non-improve-
ment reigns. It sets mankind against one another in
competitiveness and exclusive ownership.[175] The time
has come, proclaimed the *Circular*, to cease all this
"sentimental twaddle about a system that is about as
defensible as the beautiful patriarch institution that
has lately ceased to exist in the South."[176]

In view of this strong rejection of the institution of marriage, it may be surprising to find that
Noyes did not advise his readers to abandon their married lives. The root problem, he explained, was not
the institution, but the selfishness which flourished
within the system of wedlock. Marriage only augmented
a disease present within the world: selfishness.
There was no point, he counseled, in annihilating marriage until some headway had been made in eliminating
selfishness from the practice of sexuality. True reform was not to be found with those who simply rejected
marriage without providing a plan to restructure amativeness. In fact, until man transformed his concept
and practice of love, until he learned to place sexuality in the service of the Spirit, Noyes declared that
the institution of marriage must be tolerated as the
best means of controlling a perverted amativeness, which,
if left alone, would destroy all in its way. Before
considering this last point in detail, however, it is
well to consider the theological, and especially scriptural, arguments which Noyes used to support his attack

---

[175]"We wish then to disavow all fellowship with selfish
love whether in marriage or out of it. There is a world of selfishness, idolatry, and licentiousness in the marriage system that
cries to heaven for judgement, and is becoming intolerable to
earth." (*Oneida Circular,* 10 August 1874, p. 260.)

[176]*Circular,* 14 March 1870, p. 414

on the system of marriage.

John Noyes always maintained that the primary reason for his rejection of marriage was the authority of the Scriptures. He said that a careful study of the Bible and of Jesus' ethic had convinced him that in the perfect Christian society there is no place for marriage.

First, he argued that, according to the Gospel of Matthew, Jesus clearly taught there would be no marriage in the kingdom of heaven. When the Sadducees attempted to trick Jesus by asking to which of her many husbands a hapless bride would be married, Jesus responded that in heaven there would be no giving or taking in marriage (Matt. 22:23-30). This pericope, Noyes maintained, says nothing with regard to sexuality or love; it is solely concerned with the fact that in heaven there is no ownership of persons, no rights to exclusivity.   The kingdom of heaven, Noyes maintained, would witness the joys of love and sexual passion cleansed from the contamination of marriage.[177]

Secondly, Jesus gave the command that Christians should love one another. Yet, said Noyes, the marriage spirit makes such a commandment impossible to fulfill,

---

[177]"In the kingdom of heaven, the institution of marriage, which assigns the exclusive possession of one woman to one man, does not exist. Matt. 22:23-30. 'In the resurrection they neither marry nor are given in marriage.'   Note.--Christ, in the passage referred to, does not exclude the sexual distinction, or sexual intercourse, from the heavenly state, but only the world's method of assigning the sexes to each other, which alone creates the difficulty presented in the question of the Sadducees. The constitutional distinctions and offices of the sexes belong to their original paradisaical state; and there is no proof in the Bible or in reason, that they are ever to be abolished, but abundance of proof to the contrary." (*First Report*, p. 19.)

by breaking mankind into isolated, excluding pairs.[178]
The family institution is manifestly a spirit that is
totally at war with the Spirit of the Gospel.   It is
one of the old bottles into which new wine cannot be
placed.[179]

> The abolishment of sexual exclusiveness is in-
> volved in the love relation required between
> all believers by the express injunction of
> Christ and the apostles; and by the whole tenor
> of the New Testament.   The new commandment is
> that we love one another, and that, not by pairs,
> as in the world, but *en masse*.[180]

What is more, Noyes insisted, Jesus intended that this
teaching should be implemented in *this* world.   He taught
his disciples what social relations pertain in the kingdom of heaven, and then instructed them to pray that the
kingdom would come, that his ways would become a reality
here on earth just as they were in heaven.

The enemies of Noyes would point out that neither
Jesus nor Paul instructed their disciples to abandon
marriage.   Noyes admitted that, for many reasons, Jesus
and Paul did not themselves forbid Christians to marry,
or condone any practices of free love.   He admitted that
the apostolic band, and later the Primitive Church, sub-
scribed to a community of goods, but never extended the
principle "all things in common" to persons.[181]   He admitted that Paul did not encourage the churches to anything like free love, but defended the married state,

---

[178]"Then again, the unity which is the glory of a perfect
state [see John 17] is out of the question with the marriage system in existence.   That all may be one, there must be no private
ownerships."   (*Circular*, 23 October 1865, p. 252.)

[179]*Oneida Circular*, 14 April 1873, p. 122.

[180]*Bible Communism*, p. 31.

[181]*Circular*, 19 March 1866, p. 4.

assuring his disciples that it was an honorable way for
the Christian. He admitted that Paul condemned divorce,
adultery, and polygamy.[182]

But, Noyes argued, if Jesus and the early Church
did not forbid marriage or advocate a community of persons, they carefully and adamantly established the *principles* which in the proper time would subvert marriage
and lead to a full life of community.[183] According to
Noyes' reading of Scripture, the Christian who dies with
Christ and who rises into a new resurrection state is
beyond death, and hence is free from sin and law and all
the temporary relations of the human state.[184] Noyes

---

[182]In admitting that no precedent to free love could
be found in the early Church, Noyes rejected the positions advocated by some of his contemporaries who cited
the *agape* of the Primitive Church and Paul's reference
to his "spiritual wife" (I Cor 9:5) as evidence that the
early Church had in fact embarked on the course of free
love. [Some scholars of Noyes' day apparently interpreted Paul's question in this passage of First Corinthians ("Have we not...the right to take a Christian woman
round with us like all the other apostles and brothers
of the Lord....") to mean that Paul was living with a woman. But Noyes rejected this interpretation on the basis
of other passages. *Circular*, 24 February 1868, p. 394;
Dixon and His Copyists, pp. 28-31.] Although such a theory would have strengthened his position, Noyes resisted
any temptation to sponsor what he considered poor exegesis.

[183]"We admit that Christ and the apostles, with wise reference
to the transitionary necessities and hostile surroundings of the
church of their time, and to the purpose of God to give the Gentiles
a dispensation of legal discipline, abstained from pushing the war
against worldly institutions to the overthrow of marriage. Yet we
insist that they left on record *principles* which go to the subver-
sion of *all* worldly ordinances, and that the design of God was and
is, that, at the end of the times of the Gentiles, the church should
carry out these principles to their legitimate results." (*First
Report*, p. 24.)

[184]"They [Paul and Christ] adhered to the principle of marriage *for life* without any essential exceptions. But they found a way
to introduce what may be called a post-humous state into this world

maintained that expediency alone was responsible for the
decision of the Primitive Church not to attack the institution of marriage, and not to exercise their rightful freedom from earthly ordinance in the matter of sexual relations.[185] Noyes maintained that because the
early Church concentrated its efforts in combatting sin
and preparing themselves for the Second Coming, they did
not feel that they had the time or energy to be concerned
with less important issues.[186] For the same reason, the
Primitive Church did not attack the many other institutions which would have to be destroyed in time if Christ's
kingdom were to tome. The imminence of the Second Coming
suggested that their policy should be one of walking soft-
ly and avoiding efforts to overthrow the institutions

---

by the application of the death of Christ. Their doctrine was that
by believing in Christ we are crucified with him." (*Circular*,
19 March 1866, p. 2.) See also: *Bible Communism*, pp.
34, 86f.

[185]"The abolishment of worldly restrictions on sexual intercourse, is involved in the anti-legality of the gospel. It is incompatible with the state of perfected freedom towards which Paul's
gospel of 'grace without law' leads, that man should be allowed
and required to *love* in all directions, and yet be forbidden to
express love in its most natural and beautiful form, except in one
direction. In fact, Paul says with direct reference to sexual
intercourse--'All things are *lawful* for me, but all things are not
expedient; all things are lawful for me, but I will not be brought
under the power of any;' (I Cor. 6:12;) thus placing the restrictions which were necessary in the transition period, on the basis,
not of law, but of expediency, and the demands of spiritual freedom, and leaving it fairly to be inferred that in the final state,
when hostile surroundings and powers of bondage cease, all restrictions also will cease." (*First Report*, p. 22.)

[186]*Bible Communism*, p. 77. As was seen earlier,
Noyes, in his reading of the New Testament, understood
that the Primitive Church lived in the expectation of
the imminent return of Jesus, an expectation which Noyes
believed proved to be quite correct. See above pp.
30ff.

which dominated the world.[187] For example, the apostolic Church tolerated slavery, enjoining slaves to be submissive to their masters--not, Noyes hastened to point out, because the Church was insensitive to the evils of slavery--but because there were other more important things to be done in a short period of time. Noyes suggested that marriage and slavery occupied the same position in the mind of the early Church.[188] Just as slavery, an obviously unchristian institution, was to be tolerated until the tide of battle against sin had been turned, so the Primitive Church did not oppose marriage.[189] But, Noyes insisted, the attitude of the Primitive Church to both slavery and marriage was intended as a temporary policy which would give way to a more perfect social organization when the major work of converting men to the Christian message was significantly well grounded. Unfortunately, said Noyes, the Christian world canonized these *pro tem* policies and established them as permanent and unquestioned parts of the Christian tradition. In so doing, Christianity entirely abandoned the absolute goals toward which Christ and Paul were directing their followers.[190]

---

[187]Henry J. Seymour, *The Oneida Community, a Dialogue*, p. 20.

[188]In *Ephesians*, in *Colossians*, and in *First Corinthians*, said Noyes, we find the two associated, and similar advice being given with regard to both institutions. (See *Bible Communism*, p. 79.)

[189]Noyes placed considerable emphasis on similarities between marriage and slavery in debating opponents. The newly arising, popular sentiment against the latter was easily suborned into the battle against marriage.

[190]*Bible Communism*, p. 69.

If Paul did not forbid marriage, argued John Noyes,
neither can he be made out as a champion of the state.
Noyes insisted that Paul knew Christ's teaching of the
marriageless resurrection state, and on this account refrained, as did his master, from marriage.[191] But Paul
also knew, said Noyes, that the full practice of communal love was something for the future, and thus he resisted in every way any attempt to embark prematurely on
the program of free love. If a man could not remain
celibate, then Paul advised him to marry and follow the
laws of marriage until the kingdom of God arrived.[192]
According to Noyes' interpretation, Paul urged those who
were married, or found it necessary to marry, to be
mindful that marriage was but a temporary institution
which was about to pass away: "Those who have wives
should live as if they had none...because the world as
we know it is passing away" (I Cor. 7:29).[193] Noyes insisted that it is useless to try to make either Christ
or Paul or the Gospel to be the humble servant of marriage. It is as plain as can be, Noyes wrote, that the

---

[191]*Circular*, 24 March 1859, p. 34.

[192]*Circular*, 24 February 1868, p. 394.

[193]"Paul expressly places property in women and property in
goods in the same category, and speaks of them together, as ready
to be abolished by the advent of the kingdom of heaven. 'The time,'
says he, 'is short; it remaineth that they that have wives, be as
though they had none;...for the fashion of this world passeth away.'
(I Cor. 7:29-31.) On the day of Pentecost, 'they that bought were
as though they possessed not.' The fashion of the world passed
away in regard to property, for the time being. It is fair to in-
fer from Paul's language, that the fashion of the world in regard
to wives was, in his view, to pass away in the same manner; i.e.
that exclusiveness was to be abolished, and free love or complex
marriage take its place in the heavenly state into which the church
was about entering." (*First Report*, pp. 20f) See also:
Bible Communism, pp. 30, 109f; *Oneida Circular*, 10 August 1874, p. 260; *Oneida Circular*, 28 June 1875, p. 202.

vision of Christ and Paul was that "all may be one"--
not two and two--and that they attacked marriage just
as hard as they could with safety during the Church's
transition-pilgrimage.[194]

Noyes believed that the time had come when Christianity could at last complete the work begun by Jesus
and Paul. Just as 19th century America had taken up the
long overdue battle against the institution of slavery,
so Noyes and his Community saw themselves as Crusaders
against the institution of marriage. In the members of
the Oneida Community, who had spent years disciplining
themselves in the ways of unselfishness, Noyes saw men
and women prepared to experiment in the Christian social
state.

Noyes did not suggest that this course was open to
the majority of men. Only those who had overcome selfishness, who had entered the state of perfection, were
fit to attempt the dangerous life of free love. Noyes
maintained that for the majority of men, the law of marriage was still necessary. The exclusive family had
been instituted by God after the fall of men from grace,
and it should not, Noyes contended, be put aside by anyone until he was sure that he was living in the state of
grace. Noyes insisted that for those who were not yet
perfected, Paul's policy must remain the rule: celibacy
preferred; marriage allowed; polygamy, adultery and divorce opposed.[195] As long as men were unsanctified,

---

[194]*Oneida Circular*, 26 May 1873, p. 169.

[195]*Circular*, 12 March 1866, p. 411; *Circular*, 19
March 1866, p. 1

Noyes insisted, as long as they were unable to resist
the degradation of idolatry and selfishness in their
social lives, better that these vices be kept in bounds
by the limitations and shackles of marriage.[196]

The above remarks partially explain the seeming ambivalence one finds in the positions taken by Oneida on
the subject of marriage: at one time, marriage is attacked; at another, it is defended. In two contexts,
Oneida attacked marriage. First, in response to the
position that marriage is the ideal Christian state, instituted by Christ, Oneida maintained that marriage is,
if anything, the antithesis of Christianity. Secondly,
when, by marriage, men mean marriage as understood by
the world, full of idolatry, exclusiveness and jealousy,
Oneida maintained that it is a state *absolutely* incompatible with the spiritual life. In two contexts, Oneida
is found supporting marriage. First, as an institution
valuable in a world as yet unchristianized, as an institution curtailing the animal amativeness still existent
in the world, marriage is to be respected and defended.
Secondly, when purified and cleansed of exclusiveness,
jealousy and idolatry, when transformed by the principles
of true Christian love, it is a state in which a Christian can grow in the spiritual life. A man and a woman
can transform marriage into a holy state, learning to
love God and their brethren in and through conjugal love.[197]

---

[196]"It is not in concentrating upon one the love that should
flow to all that idolatry consists, but in placing one creature
where alone the living God should be enthroned. As well have one
idol as many, and better too, for the former is less debauching.
While men are in a state of alienation from God and consequent
idolatry, limitation is their best condition...." (*Circular,*
24 July 1865, p. 145.) See also *Bible Communism,* p. 78.

[197]*Circular,* 12 March 1866, p. 411. In several
articles, Noyes even championed the possibilities of the

Noyes explained to his disciples that for most of them circumstances were such that it was more *expedient* to remain in marriage, though, of course, in marriage cleansed of much which the world identifies with wedlock. Noyes insisted that he was not opposed to this decision. It was the same decision which the Primitive Church had reached in similar circumstances. Indeed, he reminded his readers that it was never his intention to woo readers away from marriage and into community life.[198] His purpose in publishing a paper concerned with life in community was, among other things, to teach the doctrine of true love so that people could apply this new concept to the life situations in which they found themselves.

It was not, then, the intent of Noyes to argue that marriage should cease among men of his day, even among perfected Christians. It was only when Oneida was attacked by the righteous who uncritically accepted marriage as *the* Christian state that Noyes lashed out with tirades on the evils of marriage. He simply wished to argue that there was no absolute commitment of Christianity to marriage and that, in fact, if there were any

---

state of marriage. He described the family as a school of love and of community principles. No one, he said, who could not love in marriage would be able to live in community life. Community of goods and love was the essence of family life, and though limited to a few persons, this sharing introduced men and women to the concept of Christian detachment. See *Circular*, 8 August 1864, p. 161; *Circular*, 17 October 1864, p. 241; *Circular*, 26 December 1864, p. 321; *Circular*, 18 January 1869, pp. 345f; *Oneida Circular*, 16 January 1871, p. 20.

[198]Noyes pointed out on one occasion that the policy of the Community toward estranged couples, who wrote seeking advice, was to urge them to work for reconciliation, and to remove the causes of discord. (*Circular*, 6 September 1855, p. 130.)

commitment, it would be to non-marriage for the redeemed.[199]
Though Noyes opposed marriage vehemently as it was practiced and understood by his contemporaries, he recognized
the redeemability of marriage and the contribution it had
made, and would continue to make until the day came when
the majority of men were prepared to move into responsible free love.

ONEIDA AND CONTEMPORARY ANTI-MARRIAGE EFFORTS

The Oneida Community was not the only movement in
nineteenth century America which demanded alternatives to
the system of marriage. Surprisingly, John Noyes rejected the platforms of these other movements with the
same fervor he manifested in his crusade against idolatrous marriage. For example, the writings of Swedenborg
and others on "spiritual affinities" had captured the
interest of many Americans. According to this doctrine,
God has created for each man and woman a natural mate, a
partner with whom to spend eternity. Only with this
particular person could a man or woman find the true
love to which they are called. Accordingly, life consists in faithful, eternal marriage once the natural

---

[199]There was apparently something of an anti-marri-
age movement on the mid-nineteenth century American
scene. See *Circular,* 25 December 1852, p. 46; *Circular,*
23 March 1868, p. 4; *Circular,* 23 August 1869, p. 183.
Many Christians were worried about the future of the
family and of marriage. Noyes pointed out to them that
Christianity must not consider itself wedded to the marriage system. Marriage was giving way to something in-
comparably better; the small seedlings of communism
found in family life were about to germinate into full
community. The Christian, Noyes said, must not cling
to the past, but turn his efforts toward finding a better future. See *Circular,* 2 March 1868, p. 405; *Circular,* 11 October 1869, pp. 233f; *Circular,* 27 December
1869, p. 324; *Oneida Circular,* 10 August 1874, p. 260.

mate has been found. But before this marriage can begin, there must be a period of searching, of temporary
relations.[200] Consider the following excerpt from a
diary, cited by Dixon:

> ...my mind was made up never to marry, when a
> Bible Spiritual Medium came some miles to meet
> me, sent, she said, like Peter to Cornelius...
> and she told me that believers must enter in
> pairs, and that among the things lacking in my
> case was a wife--that I must and would soon find
> MY mate...that I would know her soon, as we should
> meet.... I met with a young music teacher...
> strange as it may appear, I felt that she was to
> become my wife as soon as I heard her name spoken;
> and two days later, at the foot of Niagara's reef
> of rainbows, baptized by the mists of heaven, we
> pledged ourselves to unite our destinies and work

---

[200]*Circular*, 3 February 1868, pp. 370f; William H.
Dixon, *Spiritual Wives* (London, 1868), pp. 356-359. The
doctrine taught that many, perhaps most, will not recognize their affinity until they reach heaven. But some
are fortunate enough to discover the destined partner in
this life. Nothing should prevent them from consummating
that relationship as soon as it is discovered. These reformers opposed marriage as a man-made institution which
kept apart those destined by God to be with one another.
They maintained that regardless of one's state of life,
a man or woman, upon discovering his true affinity,
should follow that inspiration. Apparently Swedenborg's
writings had been circulating feebly in this country for
many years before the era of Socialism. According to
Noyes, nothing of a popular interest had been shown in
them until the ideas were advocated by the Community at
Brook Farm, and by allied Transcendentalist writers.
(See *American Socialisms,* pp. 539ff. In his book *Spiritual
Wives,* pp. 389ff, William H. Dixon states that support
for the doctrine grew due to the writings of a respected
Old Testament scholar from Dartmouth and Princeton,
George Bush. He in turn introduced his disciple Andrew
Jackson Davis, who later separated from his mentor and
wrote his own *Great Harmonia.* "The Harmonial Philosophy
[of Davis] teaches in effect that persons who are not
'affinitized' are committing adultery in living as man
and wife" (p. 398). Later in the same work, p. 401,
Dixon states that there were four million who followed
the doctrines of Swedenborg in one form or another in
America at the time of his writing (1868).

> together for human welfare as long as it was
> mutually agreeable.[201]

This movement found no ally in John Noyes. It was in
essence, he attested, the very antithesis to what he
professed. Its idolatrous emphasis upon the importance
of a particular person in one's life opposed his belief
that individual persons are but the replaceable occasions through which one reaches the source of happiness.[202]

Originally, Noyes had adopted the term "free love"
as descriptive of his own system, but as a free love
movement grew within this country, Noyes was forced to
abandon the term.[203] Almost weekly, the *Circular* would
publish a repudiation of any association with the various
free love organizations across the country. Noyes rejected these groups because (a) there was no sense of
care or dedication on the part of the men toward the women they loved; and (b) there was a disregard concerning
the consequences of bringing fatherless children into
the world.[214]

Noyes also took issue with the celibate life-style
proposed by the Shakers (though he felt that the latter
came closest to the Christian ideal of love which he was
promoting). The Shakers rejected the idolatrous trap of
marriage; they refused to participate in a free love
ethic which would work havoc; they recognized the importance of associating men with women. But by their

---

[201]*Spiritual Wives*, pp. 386f.

[202]*Circular*, 23 October 1854, p. 562; *Circular*, 25
October 1855, p. 158; *Circular*, 8 September 1859, p.
131; *Circular*, 3 February 1868, pp. 370f.

[203]*Circular*, 27 June 1870, p. 116.

[204]*Circular*, 27 February 1862, p. 11; *Circular*, 14
May 1866, p. 72; *Oneida Circular*, 21 August 1871, p. 268.

strictures against any special love between man and woman, and their horror of any genital sexual expression
of love, the Shakers had separated themselves from a
great source of grace and joy. On this basis, Noyes rejected their policies.

In summary: Noyes repudiated marriage as the optimum social institution for the Christian, intent on following the principles of true love outlined in this
chapter. Likewise, he rejected the alternatives to marriage which were advocated by his contemporaries: the
celibacy of Shakerism; the ethic of free love; the philosophy of spiritual affinities.

So far we have studied those writings of Noyes and
associates which dealt with their theology of love.
From scattered writings on the subject, we have con-
structed an ordered analysis of Noyes' concept of love,
discerning and applying its underlying philosophical
principles, differentiating and explicating the basic
aspects of the theory. Further insight into Noyes' theory of love could be gained by posing and answering the
question: "How would this theory actually be implemented
in real life?" Any theory is better understood when we
know how its author would apply it to the actual living
situation. In the case of John Noyes' theology, we are
fortunate, for Noyes--unlike most theorists--attempted
to put his theory into practice. In the institution of
the Oneida Community, we have Noyes' attempt to apply
his principles to real life. By studying the application, we should better be able to understand the theories that Noyes was proposing. In the next chapter,
we will turn to an intensive study of the polity of the
Community with regard to love and relationship as reported in their journals. Our purpose in this study
will be to better understand Oneida's theory of love by

studying an application of that theory.

A methodological problem may seem to present itself
here: can one construct a valid picture of life at
Oneida based on documents which, because of their prose-
lytizing nature, may well have idealized, edited, and
distorted the actual events at Oneida? This problem is
obviated, however, as soon as one remembers the intention of this chapter: to ask John Noyes to deepen our
udnerstanding of his theory by explaining how he would
put it into practice. If our intention were specifically historical--to ascertain what did in fact occur within the walls of Oneida, to determine to what degree
Oneida was successful or unsuccessful in its efforts--
then it would be necessary to validate the reports of
Community journals. But since our interest is only to
flesh out our understanding of Noyes' *theory,* we need
not be concerned with this problem. Even were we to
suppose that the reports given in the journals were completely idealized, even fantasized, they would still
fulfill our present intention: to increase our understanding of Noyes' thinking by asking how *he would carry
out* his theories in practice.[205]

---

[205]In point of fact, the present author believes
that the picture to be gathered from the pages of the
Community journals gives a fairly accurate impression of
life at Oneida. The people at Oneida did not publish
their papers with the intention of attracting new members
to the Community. Within a few years of their foundation, they had reached what they considered to be full
membership, and thereafter their main efforts in this
regard were to discourage people from applying for admission. Regularly they reminded readers that the purpose behind founding the Oneida Community and publishing
a circular was to exemplify the possibility of a new way
of loving, a way of loving which they hoped their readers
would integrate into their own life styles. See *Circular,*
30 December 1867, p. 332. It would seem from a reading

of the journals, that the Oneida people did not try to
gloss over whatever shortcomings existed within the Community.   The pages of the *Circular* contain stories, reports, and feature articles which make it quite clear
to the reader that life at Oneida was far from perfect:
that compromise was necessary; that men and women were
often guilty of smallness; that renewal and reform were
regularly needed.   Perhaps, then, the halo effect is not
as operative within the pages of the Community publications as one might at first assume.   However, the ac-
curacy of these observations does not affect our proposal to rely on these documents for an understanding of
the principles of love advocated by Oneida, and the
polity which they as a model for the implementation of
those principles.

CHAPTER THREE

POLITY OF THE ONEIDA COMMUNITY

ONEIDA: A COMPROMISE

Complex Marriage was the name which Noyes used to
describe the social system at Oneida Community. Noyes
considered this social system to be an original contribution to Christian morality: while others before him
had taken stands against marriage, they had been content
simply to destroy the golden calf of wedlock, or had
erected in its place the doctrines of spiritual wivery
which Noyes considered to be more idolatrous than marriage. Complex Marriage represented an attempt to replace marriage by a system which was consonant with the
highest of Christian ideals about love. All of the members participating in that system were to consider themselves married to one another, joined by a bond which
was as solemn and as permanent as that of any marriage.[1]
All pledged themselves to love and care for one another.
Each member was to love every other member--there was to
be no place for exclusiveness, cliques or animosity at
Oneida. Children were to be thought of as the offspring,

---

[1] "Free love with us does not mean freedom to love today and
leave tomorrow.... The tie that binds us together is as permanent and sacred, to say the least, as that of marriage, for it is
our religion.... We are not free lovers in any sense that makes
love less binding or responsible than it is in marriage." (*Circular*, 14 May 1866, p. 72.) See also *Oneida Circular*
5 May 1873, p. 150.

not of one couple, but of the whole Community. And,
Noyes never tired of reminding them, these goals would
be possible only if each member sought God in every relation and depended upon His power.

Complex Marriage was not intended by Noyes to be an
exact imitation of the social system which he believed
existed among the saints in heaven. That could not be.
Noyes believed that even the generous and noble men and
women who had embraced Perfectionism were not able to completely practice the heavenly state of love immediately.
Imbued from youth with concepts of false love, coming
from a world which was unaware of true love, they would
require much re-education before they would be fit to imi-
tate the heavenly society. As perfected Christians, Noyes
believed these men were indeed beyond the law, no longer
bound by the usual ordinances of marriage and morality.
But at the same time, because of their backgrounds, there
was need for a certain curtailment of their freedom--at
least until they had overcome the influences of their upbringing. For this reason, Noyes saw the need to insti-
tute guidelines, structures, and restraining forces to
the amative passion. Estlake, a former member of the
Oneida Community, wrote in this regard:

> The first Perfectionists found it expedient to
> adopt some modification of the angelic mingling...
> in the establishment of a new system of sexual in-
> termingling would be a material departure from the
> fashion of the world, and at the same time contain
> within itself sufficient restraining influences to
> check any who may be tempted with selfishness. This
> new system they called complex marriage.[2]

According to their journals, the Community at Oneida accepted the idea that there was a need for guidance in
matters of the heart, expecially for the younger and

---

[2]Estlake, p. 85.

newer members.[3] Therefore, they developed regulating,
curbing principles, based upon experience, designed to
educate the passion of amativeness. In the *First Report*
of the Oneida Community, we are advised that the Community
had developed many "prudential" but "transitory" principles which governed the members in the practice of their
social system.[4] Furthermore, the Community believed that,
when necessary, it must take upon itself the responsibility of seeing that each member observed these principles.
Just as a child will never wean itself, so the beginner
may require help from wills other than his own if he is
to be weaned from false attachments and improper love,
the Community reasoned.[5] Noyes warned the Community
that there was certain to come a time in each member's
life when he would be called upon to abandon his own will
in the matter of fellowships because spiritual growth
was being impeded by false amativeness.[6] Complex

---

[3]*Daily Journal of Oneida Community,* 23 March 1866,
p. 224.

[4]P. 17. As Warfield, *Bibliotheca Sacra,* Vol. 78,
p. 323, points out, Noyes saw the need for the system
of Complex Marriage (rather than complete free love) to
be a temporary condition. He viewed Oneida as a school
where men and women would experiment with those principles which were eventually to be practiced by everyone.

[5]Speaking about the need to separate from attachments, the *Circular* observed: "Weaning only begins when the
child ceases to nurse. It is a life time process, and we are not
sure but that it will be continued beyond this life. The word
weaned implies a separation from certain objects of attachment,
and with the separation comes a spirit of hearty reconciliation
and thankfulness.... The child, unless aided by other wills and
influences than its own, would probably never wean himself.... In
stepping up from the lower to the higher help from above is necessary." (*Circular,* 18 July 1864, p. 141.)

[6]*Circular,* 28 June 1860, p. 87. The Community
journals tell us that this outside "help" was administered

Marriage was, then, something of a compromise. If, in
the heavens, the saints interpose no barriers whatsoever
to the free interchange of affections, this was not yet
possible for their associates on earth.

According to Community journals, it was understood
that the elder members of the Oneida Community would
play the major role in this task of discerning and root-
ing out the cancer of idolatrous love. Just as the
world does not leave the running of important businesses
to the immature, neither should it assume that the young
have the wisdom to take complete responsibility in matters of the heart.

> They [the Oneida Community] believe the whole
> matter of love and its expression should be sub-
> ject to enlightened self-control and should be
> managed for the greatest good. In the communi-
> ties, it is under the special supervision of the
> fathers and mothers, or in other words, of the
> wisest and best members, and is often under dis-
> cussion in the evening meetings, and is also
> subordinate to the institution of criticism.[7]

Love, it was argued, should not be left to the impulse
of the young and immature; it should be under the super-
vision of wisdom, for upon the proper government of love
depends the future character of the human race.[8]

SPECIAL FRIENDSHIP AT ONEIDA

It can be gathered from Community publications that

---

when necessary, often in the evening meetings, when ses-
sions of criticism would regularly center on the matter
of false love. (*Circular*, 7 February 1856, p. 11; *Circular*, 9 April 1857, p. 47.)

[7]*Handbook of the Oneida Community: Containing a
Brief Sketch of its Present Condition, Internal Economy
and Leading Principles* (Oneida, New York, 1971), p. 50.
Hereafter cited as *Handbook, 1871.*

[8]*American Socialist*, 18 April 1878, p. 125.

the matter of special friendship was one which the members were encouraged to scrutinize regularly. Any fellowship which offended the principles of non-exclusivity,
any attempt to hold persons in the way of ownership, any
relationship which appeared to be replacing the love of
God in the life of a member--was to be condemned.[9] How
sad it would be, Noyes observed, if, having escaped the
idolatrous system of marriage, the members of the Community should allow themselves to be enticed into a bondage more damaging than wedlock. It was the purpose of
the social system of Oneida to make all free to attend
upon the Lord without distraction, not to facilitate a
new system of idolatry.[10]

Community policy insisted that a general love for
every person in the community must be the first concern
of a member after his love of God. The paramount affection which was to reign within the walls of Oneida was
that of brotherly love--the family love which a child
has for all the children of his father.[11] Those activi-

---

[9]*Circular,* 14 January 1867, p. 351.

[10]"The object that I have, and that God has in establishing
through me our present social system, is not to put us in such relations to each other that our bondage and distractions and divi-
sions should be increased and become worse than they are in the
world, but, on the contrary that we might get *free* from the distractions of the world. It is the object of our social theory to accomplish just what Paul...could not accomplish, that is to make all
the object of Communism." (*Circular,* 12 October 1868, p.
233.) Noyes warned his followers to be on the watch for
even subtler forms of bondage. Love for the Community
itself, or for its founder, could invidiously substitute
for faith in God. These subtle forms of idolatry must
be resisted, for nothing must take the place of total
dependence on God. See *Oneida Circular,* 19 July 1875,
pp. 225ff.; *Circular,* 4 September 1862, p. 118.

[11]"...the paramount affection of the household is not
sexual, but <u>brotherly</u> love, an affection that grows directly out of

ties which favored group participation were to be encouraged, while those unsuited to participation by large
numbers were to be given a second place.[12] The Community was wary of affections which withdrew members from
this general circulation into special relationships. Any
fellowship which took precedence over the universal fellowship of brotherly love was to be regarded as a weak-
ening influence on the spirit and health of the whole
community, and was to be rooted out without delay.[13] It
was not just special loves between the sexes which were
to be regarded as harmful: any friendship that excluded
others came in for censure. A member of the Community,
writing many years after Oneida's demise, recalled that
as a child he was taught to regard "partiality" as something seriously wrong if not sinister, and that he was
often separated from his cousin for several days because

---

the common relationship to the Father, and, of course, is as universal as that relationship, and as appropriate between male and
male as between male and female." (*Bible Communism*, p. 28.)
See also *Circular*, 13 March 1856, p. 29; *Circular*, 16
December 1858, p. 187.

[12]*Circular*, 14 June 1860, p. 79.

[13]"Any condition of our affections that withdraws us from the
general circulation into a special home of our own--a special love,
a special friendship, a special circle from the Communism which
constitutes the circulation of the whole body, goes to weaken the
body, and is a bad kind of love. The effect of it is not only to
weaken us in spirit, but physically--to hinder the generation of
life and health among us, and to hinder us from becoming mediums of
life to the world." (*American Socialist*, 13 January 1876,
p. 14.) See also *Circular*, 28 June 1860, p. 87. One
reads, for example, in the following report of a member
being criticized because she failed to associate with
the community at large: "She is preoccupied with a few select
friends while the mass are excluded from her associations.... Less
devotion to her particular friendships and more to the whole was
recommended." (*Circular*, 16 April 1863, p. 27.) See also
Circular, 23 April 1863, p. 31.

he had fallen into the error of partiality.[14]

The beginning student of Oneida might understandably conclude from reports like these that Oneida policy
admitted no place for friendships based upon affinities
of nature. One expects that a policy which insisted
that a man must love every member of the community, and
which called for uprooting the tares of exclusivity,
would forbid any preferences, any speciality, based on
attractiveness. The reader who is familiar with the efforts at Oneida to spiritualize love, and especially the
reader who is familiar with the tradition against particular friendship within Roman Catholic community life,[15]
might assume that by this repeated prohibition of special
friendship, Noyes was forbidding the brethren at Oneida

---

[14]Pierrepont B. Noyes, *My Father's House: An Oneida Boyhood* (New York, 1937), p. 49.

[15]The tradition which has dominated much of Roman Catholic religious life over the decades is one which regards
special friendship as inimical to true spiritual devotion and to the cohesiveness of the community. Actually,
there is an older tradition in the history of religious
orders which, without denying the dangers of carnal or
evil relationships, insists that friendship, individual
and intimate, is a treasure and grace perfectly consonant
with the religious life. See: St. Basil, *Ascetical
Works,* trans. Sr. M. Monica Wagner (New York, 1958), p.
245; Louis Bouyer, *The Cistercian Heritage,* trans. Eliza-
beth Livingstone (Westminster, Maryland, c1958), pp. 33,
138, 159f; Jean Bremond, *Les pères du désert,* Vol. II
(Paris, 1927), p. 392; Columban Browning, "Particular
Friendship", *New Catholic Encyclopedia,* Vol. VI (New
York, 1967), pp. 205f; A. Fiske, "Cassian and Monastic
Friendship", *The American Benedictine Review,* 12 (1961),
pp. 190-205; A. Fiske, "Aelred's of Rievaulx Idea of
Friendship and Love", *Citeaux,* 13 (1962), pp. 5-17, 96-
132; Gerald Kelly, *Guidance for Religious* (Westminster,
Maryland, 1956), pp. 67f; Adolphe Tanquerey, *The Spirit-
ual Life,* trans. H. Banderis (Westminster, 1930), p. 287;
Sr. Teresa, "Friendship among Religious", *Cross and Crown,*
5 (1953), pp. 311-322; G. Vansteenberghe, "Amitié",
Dictionnaire de Spiritualité, Vol. I, cc. 501-530.

to single out any person in the community for especial
affection. Based on what we have seen so far concerning love at Oneida, one might expect to find that Noyes
discouraged any relationship in which a person showed
more affection for his partner than for other members
of the community. One might expect that the people at
Oneida were taught to love each and every member with
equal love, showing no preferences, avoiding those relationships in which there was a tendency to love with an
affection which could not be extended to every other
person.

And yet, this does not seem to have been the intention of Oneida's founder. While recognizing the danger
of idolatry in intense personal love, while insisting on
care and at times renunciation in matters of the heart,
while ever vigilant to detect signs of exclusivity, ownership, habit, or pleasure-seeking in relationships,
Noyes maintained that one could love another person, intensely, more than others, without offending the principles of true love. The *First Report* of the Community
expressly states that the principle of perfect community
of interest "does not exclude...special companionships,
founded on special affinities of nature and position; it
only denies exclusive appropriation."[16] The Oneida Perfectionists insisted that, although brotherly love was
the affection which must be cultivated before all other
social affections, and although they must love one another first as members of Christ, there still was a place
for special friendships and loves based upon the affinities of nature.[17] Apparently, the Community believed it

---

[16]P. 20.

[17]George W. Noyes, in *Putney Community*, p. 117,
cites from an unnamed pamphlet published by Noyes in

is possible and necessary to distinguish those fellowships which are special without excluding (and therefore
are to be encouraged) from those which isolate the
couple from the general flow of communal life (and must
therefore be avoided). Even in Noyes' first statement
of principles, the "Battle Axe Letter", the attack on
exclusivity does not involve an attack on *particularity*.
One important sentence in that letter reads:

> The guests of the marriage supper may have each
> his favorite dish, each a dish of his own pro-
> curing and that without the jealousy of exclu-
> siveness.[18]

In an article published by the *Circular,* the writer makes
the following comment:

> The community spirit, which includes all, irre-
> spective of special attraction, is the paramount
> principle in a true society and subordinates all
> others to it. But it is not right to say...that
> there is NO room for the play of special affini-
> ties.... There is no need whatever of separating
> the two things and putting them in such direct
> antagonism. The true method is to reconcile them
> and make the love of beauty SERVE the community
> spirit.[19]

Noyes did place great emphasis on the need for, and
the beauty of, brotherly love: the care and affection
of a man for each member of the communal family. He

1849: "In the Kingdom of God the intimate union that in the world
is limited to the married pair extends through the whole body of
communants; without however excluding special companionships
founded on special adaptability...." Confusion can occur here
because Noyes uses the term "special friendship" in two
different ways. Sometimes he uses it to refer to exclusive, idolatrous love which he condemns; in other
places, it refers to those closer associations which,
without offending by exclusivity, naturally occur in
the lives of men. As will be shown, he both expected
and encouraged the latter.

[18]*Oneida Circular,* 24 August 1874, p. 275. On the history
of the "Battle Axe Letter", see above, pp. 38ff.

[19]*Circular,* 11 September 1856, p. 135.

urged the Community brethren not to allow special love
to usurp in importance that brother-love which should
exist between every member of the community. Likewise,
Noyes looked to the day when the love of brotherhood
would eclipse in importance the special love which most
men and women estimate so highly. But if Noyes thought
that brotherly love is, or should be the most important
human relationship, he never denied the rightful place
of special affections. One cannot, he would insist,
love all equally.

Actually, Noyes maintained that there need be no
antagonism between brotherly love and special love.
Special love should engender general love. The affection one feels toward an individual, far from undermining
one's affection for the larger community, can increase a
person's love for his brothers. The wise man, said
Noyes, finds in his love for another an occasion for
gratitude, not only to God, but to the community which
nourished the individual, and is responsible for forming
whatever beauty the loved one generates.[20] He insisted
that the true purpose of specific affections is to lead
a person increasingly into brotherly love for the community. In a hometalk, Noyes remarked:

> All specific affections are subordinate to and
> feeders of general affection--they have no
> other rightful existence.[21]

In fact, Noyes advised, when the emotion arising from a
special friendship is not ultimately directed toward the
larger community, it only torments the persons involved.[22]

---

[20]*Circular*, 11 September 1856, p. 135.

[21]*Circular*, 28 November 1861, p. 171.

[22]"Love between the sexes in this Association should be a
stimulus to love for the whole Association; and it will be if it

The Oneida communists were convinced of this theory: that special loves need not offend the universal spirit of brotherhood; rather they could nourish love for the Community. Perhaps the most startling manifestation of this understanding is a pseudo-marriage ritual which reportedly took place at Oneida. When a certain man, having lived as an associate for several years, was accepted for membership, the Community decided to symbolize his "marriage" to the Community by means of a wedding ceremony. The candidate chose a "bride", one particular woman to be his bride and to represent the Community's acceptance of him. Obviously, the Oneida people thought it appropriate that this man's vow to love the Community as a whole should be symbolized in his vowing love to one particular member.[23] The fact that the policy of the Community was to retain the title of "Mrs." for those who had been married previous to association is another significant detail. One might expect that a group wishing to emphasize communal love would eliminate all such titles which indicated special relationship. Yet this was not the case.[24] The Community did not wish to deny the special relation which existed between those who were formerly married; that relation perdured into

_____

is intelligent love.... Every specific love I have toward woman makes me love the whole race of women...my love ascends from the individuals to the sex, from the sex to society, and from society to God.... This is their [the specific affections] true destiny, and if they do not go on to this they will torment us." (*Circular*, 28 November 1861, p. 171.)

[23]*Oneida Circular*, 5 May 1873, p. 150. The author found no other reported incident of this ceremony. Nonetheless, it serves as testimony to the spirit of the dwellers at Oneida.

[24]See, for example, *Circular*, 16 January 1865, p. 346; *Circular*, 5 August 1867, p. 166.

their new lives. (Of course, within community that relation had to be transformed, purged of any idolatrous
elements; the partners had to allow one another the freedom to love others, perhaps even more than they loved
one another.) The Community thought it quite proper to
celebrate the anniversary of the wedding of John and
Harriet Noyes: the special love which existed between
them, far from being jealously resented by others, was
seen as a valuable source of life for the whole association. In 1871, the *Oneida Circular* observed:

> People...would have to look the world over to find
> two who are more united, who have a truer love or
> more genuine respect for each other than JHN and
> HAN. The unity between them is perfect...flowing
> on like a river year after year, it has grown so
> wide and deep that it is a reservoir of life to the
> whole community.[25]

An incident, reported by Estlake about his first days in
the Community, illustrates well how the Oneida people
meant their policy of non-exclusive love to be put into
practice. Estlake, being a new member, had made every
effort to conceal from "C" the fact that he was seeing
"B", who was an ardent lover of "C". Yet when "C" became aware of their feelings, he showed no jealousy, ex-
pressing pain only over the fact that his relations with
"B" were such that they had curtailed the freedom of
others with her.[26] In a reported criticism, John Noyes
cited a particular couple as being a model of proper
intimacy. He pointed out that it was apparent to everyone that there was not a couple in the Community who
were more fond of each other, more sweetly united and
affectionate than this particular couple. Yet, he added,

---

[25]*Oneida Circular,* 17 April 1871, p. 125. See also
Circular, 7 July 1859, p. 95.

[26]Estlake, pp. 76f.

they were independent of one another and perfectly free
from exclusiveness and jealousy. No man, he observed,
would worry about being an intruder in loving Mrs. L,
for Mr. L. would be glad of it. Noyes summed up his observations by stating:

> The closest and most sacred love between pairs
> united in the way of special companionship will
> be found in those who give each perfect freedom
> and who have hearts for the whole Community.[27]

Specific, intense attachments, then, were not only
permitted at Oneida--they were encouraged. Noyes was
well aware of the tendency of special loves to offend
against community love, and to involve the participants
in idolatrous exclusivity, jealousy and loss of spiritual sensitivity. But his solution was not to forbid all
special affections. Rather he schooled his followers in
the spiritual value of special affections, in the methods
of utilizing the power released by special friendship as
a gateway to communal and celestial loves.

The vow which the communists of Oneida made to love
one another and to avoid exclusiveness should not, they
insisted, be interpreted as a claim to *equality* in love.
Communism is not, they said, a great leveling institution. It does not place upon members the responsibility
of loving all equally, or of repressing those depths of

---

[27]*Circular,* 4 January 1869, p. 330. The following
reflections also suggest the ideals which the members at
Oneida sought to attain: "If the object of my affection found
pleasure in the society of other men, it made me happy to think
that she was free, and that no act of mine had been the means of
placing impediments in the way." (Estlake, p. 72.) "The love
of God certainly makes it easy in Bible Communism for two or more
men to love the same woman and love each other none the less.... I
have heard men in the Community say, when their hearts were strongly drawn out in love for a woman, that it pleased them to have her
beloved by other men...." (*Oneida Circular,* 26 January
1874, p. 37.)

feelings which they feel for a few, simply because they are not able to offer this same forceful love to all. To try to make a perfect democracy of love, Noyes and his community believed, is a vain endeavor.[28]

Noyes taught that the essence of love is attraction. And while volition can concentrate and quicken congenial elements and thus increase love, it cannot *create* congeniality and thus it cannot create love. The Oneida Community insisted that all the rights of the affections and antipathies should be respected, and that there should never be compulsion in the matter of love.[29] Noyes wrote:

> No one can love truly merely because it is his duty; to a great extent it is not at the disposal of his will. It is the result of attraction and is, in its very nature, founded on a perception of beauty in its object.... They therefore who feel the want of love from others should not fret and complain, but be content with what they can merit. They should study to increase their real attractions. We are entitled to just so much love as our intrinsic value and beauty will draw.[30]

Noyes argued that the morality (often advocated by the orthodox churches) which maintains that one should love others out of a sense of duty is advocating patronage, not love: love cannot be demanded, forced or made an

---

[28]*Circular*, 21 October 1858, p. 155; *American Socialist*, 28 December 1876, p. 313.

[29]Consider the following guideline: "You may sincerely love a woman in your heart, and be joined to her in eternal faithfulness, and yet if she is not externally attractive you are not to be blamed for not particularly enjoying her external society. In such a case love ought not to be forced..... We should not try to bridge this chasm, but fill it up, and make the breach a stimulus of improvement." (*Circular*, 5 April 1869, p. 18.) See also *Circular*, 8 August 1864, p. 164; *First Report*, p. 22.

[30]*Spiritual Magazine*, 15 Feburary 1847, p. 180.

object of duty. Because amativeness can only arise when
two spirits are attracted to one another, love can never
be demanded. The Oneida Community said that it could
promise each member equality of opportunity, but that it
could not guarantee each member that he would find persons who would welcome his special attentions. Each
member within the Community had the right to expect from
every other member that general, brotherly love so important to community living. But, the Community taught
its members, they must never presume to require special
love as something owed because of membership in the Community.[31] The Community advised the person who found
that others did not seek his special affections or respond to his overtures of friendship to attribute the
fault to himself and his own lack of attracting spirituality. They believed that the only fruitful course of
action for such a person was to work at perfecting himself, at achieving that union with Christ which is the
only true source of attractiveness.[32]

---

[31]This policy is illustrated in a detailed case
history, reported in the *Circular* of 9 January 1865, pp.
337ff., of a Mr. Mills whose insistent overtures of love
were repeatedly rejected by the woman of his desires.
The Community approved this woman's action and defended
her right to choose for special lovers those to whom she
was attracted. While she had an obligation to love each
person with a general love, she was not required to accept as a special friend this man toward whom she felt
unmoved.

[32]"No one can love truly, merely because it is his duty. To
a great extent it is not at the disposal of the will. It is the
result of attraction, and is in its very nature founded on a perception of beauty in its object.... They therefore who feel the want
of love from others, should not fret and complain, but be content
with what they can merit...study to increase their real attractions.
We are entitled to just so much love as our intrinsic value and
beauty will draw.... As it is Christ within us that makes us love-
ly, our great object should be to be filled with him. By union
with Christ, every individual may draw on the treasures of his

There were, however, two qualifications to this
policy of non-obligation in the matters of love which
should be mentioned. First, while one would not be
forced to show special love to those to whom he is not
attracted, it is his duty to maintain an openness, a
susceptibility, to the attractive influences of others.
No person at Oneida would ever be castigated for refusing
the advances of another. But the member who failed to
give others a chance, who arbitrarily armored himself
against others, would be accused of unfaithfulness to
his obligations to community.[33] Secondly, the Community
insisted that a man or woman in choosing a lover must
make his evaluation against the criteria of spiritual
quality. Not outward inducements but the attractions of
the inner person must be the magnet to which one allowed
himself to be attracted. He must consult and be guided
by the spirit of truth in choosing lovers. The Community
insisted that the Christian can learn to sense the wisdom
of God at work within him, which shows the way in the
selection of lovers.[34] The obvious question which poses
itself is: "What of the unattractive?"...those toward
whom no one is receptive or attracted? The Community
insisted that in such cases they would not resort to
compulsion of any kind, but rather would urge the neg-
lected member to examine his own lifestyle, his own

---

loveliness, and thereby at length enjoy the affection of others to
an extent beyond all that he can conceive." (*Spiritual Magazine,* 15 February 1847, p. 180.) See also *Spiritual
Magazine,* 11 August 1849, p. 209; *Free Church Circular,*
20 December 1850, p. 335.

[33]*Spiritual Magazine,* 15 February 1847, p. 180.

[34]*Circular,* 12 September 1861, p. 127; *Oneida Circular,* 15 January 1872, p. 18; *Oneida Circular,* 28
September 1874, p. 316.

union with Christ. The Community was convinced that no
person is hopelessly unattractive. Lack of lovers merely indicated the need for internal, spiritual surgery.

> It is true that communism finds its subjects
> very unequal as to their social attractiveness,
> but it begins with repudiating the idea that
> any member is hopelessly unattractive, and sets
> criticism to work.... Faith and patience are
> necessary on the part of the unattractive, but
> the miracles of criticism are so common amongst
> us, there is nothing but encouragement for the
> brave of heart.[35]

Earlier it was shown that Noyes dedicated himself to a war against "stickiness" in relations.
The poetic line: "Love and pass on" was seen to summar-
ize his insistence upon the virtues of variety and fluidity in social relations.[36] Again, the reader can easily
be misled: he can understandably conclude that the
Oneida Community encouraged a "love them and leave them"
attitude among its members—an irresponsible rejection
of commitment.[37] Yet, as so often with Oneida, there
was a balancing principle: in this case, it is important
to recognize that Noyes juxtaposed to his principle of
fluidity a principle of fidelity.

In his early correspondence with Harriet Holton before their marriage, Noyes included the following words

---

[35]*Circular,* 18 June 1866, p. 109.

[36]See above, pp. 87ff.

[37]For example consider the following statement:
"Special intimacies—should we seek to make them perpetual? The
course of discussion of this evening tended to show that Providence
and the nature of things are opposed to the continuance of special
one love intimacies.... Special external intimacy is good and desirable in its time, and for certain objects, but when its uses
are fulfilled it becomes a hindrance rather than a help. It is as
much the dictate of benevolence for a mother to wean her child at
the proper season as it is for her previously to nurse it." (*Circular,* 23 May 1861, p. 63.)

to dispel any fears she might have that his principles
excluded the virtue of fidelity:

> Take heed to his spirit and let none deal
> treacherously against the wife of his youth;
> for the Lord the God of Israel saith that HE
> HATETH PUTTING AWAY.[38]

The Oneida Community was insistent that, once a man loves
a woman, he must remain faithful to her forever. There
is, they argued, no such thing as a temporary relationship.[39] But this principle did not mean that a man was
to love only one person. The world believes that one
true love necessarily precludes all other loves; Noyes
thought this theory to be quite perverted.[40] Addressing
the young Community in 1848, Noyes said:

> We must not turn from one to another. God will
> forbid it. But our coming into relations of
> love with more does not divorce us from our
> first love. Faithfulness to one does not pre-
> vent our loving a great many with equal ardor.[41]

In fact, Noyes insisted, the love a man has for a particular woman is enhanced, rather than excluded, by his
learning to love others.[42] From this principle, the Community developed the following guideline: a test of true
love is its ability to be integrated into a person's life
without excluding previous loves. Noyes wrote:

> The true principle in the case is something like
> this: We should in the first place commence by
> seeking a legitimate love--see to it that our
> first love has the sanction of God and religion

---

[38]Cited by Parker, p. 63.

[39]*Circular*, 19 May 1859, p. 66; *Circular*, 8 September, 1859, p. 131.

[40]*Circular*, 4 December 1856, p. 182

[41]*Circular*, 16 May 1870, p. 66.

[42]*Circular*, 4 December 1856, p. 182; *Circular*, 19
May 1859, p. 66.

> and truth. The next rule is that all subse-
> quent attractions and movements in love shall
> be organized into the first one, be helpers
> to it, in the position of the secondary to the
> primary.[43]

When one finds a new love crowding out previous affections and demanding all the attention, then one knows
that he has fallen into false love. If one finds himself
concealing his love for one person from the other people
he loves, then he knows that his love is not true. If
such a policy seemed unreasonable to outsiders, if they
thought it impossible that a man or woman could acquaint
one lover of a relationship with another, it was, the
Community maintained, because tradition and education
had ingrained in them the erroneous notion that every
new love must crowd out its antecedents.[44] The *Circular*
cited as illustrative of this principle the following excerpt from Stowe's novel, *Dred*:

> Neither do I love anybody BETTER THAN YOU, Anne.
> The love I have for you is a whole, perfect
> thing, just as it was. See if you do not find
> me every way as devoted. My heart was only
> opened to take in another love, another wholly
> different; and which, because it is so wholly
> different never can infringe on the love I bear
> to you.[45]

Thus, while Noyes found it necessary to insist on the
evils of habit, and to encourage his followers towards
freedom, he maintained that this thrust had to be balanced by notions of faithfulness, of fidelity and of

---

[43]*Circular*, 21 February 1856, p. 19.

[44]*Circular*, 21 February 1856, p. 19.

[45]*Circular*, 4 December 1856, p. 182. The protagon-
ists in this incident were actually brother and sister,
rather than lovers. But the Community saw in their
story an illustration of a principle which they would
apply to every relationship.

commitment. If one finds the latter concept less often
than the former in Noyes' writings, it is because the
idea of fluidity in love needed constant emphasis, and
the idea of fidelity very little emphasis, among a people
who had been nurtured from youth on ideas of permanence.

THE ASCENDING FELLOWSHIP

The term, "ascending fellowship", represents another
important policy of the Oneida Community with regard to
love. Briefly, this policy directed members of the Community to seek out the companionship of those more
spiritual than themselves. This principle formed an important guideline used by the Community members and the
elders in evaluating the rightness or wrongness of their
relations. Writing many years later, Pierrepont Noyes,
son of the founder, recalled hearing men and women intensely discussing whether their relations were ascending
or descending (a query, he added, whose answer often
brought them face to face with the dilemma of self-denial
or an uneasy conscience).[46]

The institution of the ascending fellowship was a
direct corollary of two principles outlined in Chapter
Two: first, men and women radiate spiritual powers by
which they influence the thinking and actions of those
with whom they associate, so that a man takes on the
spiritual image of those with whom he is intimately related.[47] Secondly, the power of Christ can be distributed

---

[46]Pierrepont Noyes, *My Father's House*, p. 133.

[47]*Circular*, 20 January 1873, p. 26; *Mutual Criticism*,
pp. 57f. The *Oneida Circular* observed:
"If you follow up the ascending fellowship you will find
that it will make you not only greater than you can be
by yourself, but greater than you can have any conception of while

through the world only if there is formed a chain of persons in right order, that is from the holiest to the unregenerate, each link of which receives grace from above, and then passes it to those below.[48] The ascending fellowship refers to the efforts of the Oneida Community to form only those relationships which conformed to these two principles. Community policy directed that members should seek the companionship of those who were closer to God than themselves, so that they might share their holiness and power. In addition, the communists were taught to be mindful of the necessity of "organization" if the Oneida society were to become truly holy, and to engage in fellowships which would contribute to this organization. In John Noyes, the Oneida Community believed they had a man who, through his special relation to St. Paul, was extremely close to God. Each member hoped to share in that unction. By organizing themselves in an ascending chain--each man finding his place--every person could partake indirectly, but with full benefit, in the grace entering the world through Noyes, without putting the drain on his time and energies which would occur if each person were to seek direct fellowship with him.[49]

Thus, in overseeing the love relations within the Community, the elders were guided by the principle that special love must not only be free from exclusiveness and ownership, but that it must be placed in the service of individual and community improvement. The Community

---

in the selfish, isolated state. Your destiny will be proportioned, not to your own greatness, but to the greatness that you are joined to, that has taken possession of you and flows through you." (25 March 1872, p. 101.)

[48]*Circular,* 10 April 1856, p. 45. See above, pp. 66ff, 92ff.

[49]Pierrepont Noyes, *My Father's House,* p. 132.

members were urged to examine their fellowships, and to
be sure that a predominence of ascending relations existed.[50] The key was to be certain that a greater emphasis was given to seeking ascending fellowships, and
that whatever descending fellowships were permitted were
under the direction of the ascending relation.

Because this principle of ascending fellowship was
so important in Oneida's attempt to practice true Christian love, it will be well to backtrack and consider this
policy in greater detail. First, the different kinds of
fellowship. By horizontal friendship the Community meant
one between two persons who had attained approximately
the same spiritual development. Without completely re-
pudiating these, the Oneida Community believed that such
friendships contribute little towards individual or collective improvement,[51] and, in fact, tend towards degradation and deterioration.[52] Far more valuable, the Community believed, are those relations in which one party
is more advanced in faith, spiritual experience, sincerity, conservatism and wisdom. Only in these relations
where the more spiritual inspires the other is there op-

---

[50]Predominence, because, quite obviously, if there
was to be ascending fellowship there had to be descending as well.

[51]Noyes maintained that when two persons on the
same level associate, no improvement occurs. In fact,
he said, experience shows that the effect is to destroy
aspiration for advance into the spiritual life. (*Circular,* 14 August 1856, p. 118.)

[52]"Mere horizontal fellowships and combinations, whether individual or collective, degrade and deteriorate. It is the Ascending Fellowship alone which can elevate, refine and save."
(*Circular,* 14 August 1856, p. 118.)

portunity for spiritual growth.[53]   Every member at the
Oneida Community was encouraged to seek this latter type
of relationship, to form fellowship with those more
spiritual, submitting to their direction.[54]   To do this
demands humility and goes against the natural tendency
of the heart--Noyes recognized this.[55]   But, he assured
the Community, only by submitting to this rule of fellowship would they advance in the spiritual life. What is
more, every person, when sufficiently transformed by the
inspiration of his ascending fellowship, might well expect that others would come to him in an attitude of submission and receptivity, seeking his inspiration in their
lives.

The Community recognized that the person whose inspiration is sought by those less spiritual than himself
should enter into such relations. But they cautioned
him to be wary. He must never forget that such relationships (as good and necessary as they might be) represent
"expenses", a loss of resources. Such relations drain a
man of his strength. Therefore, all care had to be taken
not to go spiritually bankrupt, not to over-estimate
spiritual strength. To prevent this bankruptcy, Community

---

[53]"The mating together of persons of the same age and class,
the young with the young, and the inexperienced with the inexperienced, is no good. All intimate relations, whether between persons
of the same sex, or of different sexes, should be such as to have
on the one side or the other faith, spiritual experience, sincerity,
conservatism, and wisdom for guidance. And if there is any relation in which this is not the case, it is not only unprofitable
but will lead to positive loss." (*Circular*, 7 February 1856,
p. 11.)

[54]Noyes himself followed this principle by seeking
the inspiration and guidance of Saint Paul and the members of the Primitive Church.

[55]*Circular*, 3 April 1856, p. 43.

members were advised to always maintain a balance of ascending fellowships over descending.[56] Unfortunately,
they were told, the natural tendency is in the opposite
direction: to over-extend oneself in favor of the descending fellowship, to prefer those relations with the
less-spiritual, and to allow the ascending fellowship to
be smothered by the descending.[57] The main problem with
family life in America, Noyes often argued, is that the
descending fellowship eclipses the ascending. Parents
spend all their energies on their children, and allow
their relationships with one another and with God to
fall into desuetude.[58]

Noyes counseled his Community to resist a false
sense of altruism. Their primary responsibility was to
save their own souls; and that selfishness which insists
upon self-preservation was to be lauded, despite the advice of the unspiritual who think altruism to be the
only virtue.[59] Self culture is the primary business of

---

[56]*Circular*, 7 September 1868, p. 193; *Circular*, 23
August 1869, p. 178.

[57]Harriet Worden in her *Old Mansion House Memories*,
p. 22, tells about the instruction given to new members
joining the Community: "They were recommended by the committee
to seek the ascending instead of the horizontal or descending fellowship. Fellowship flows downward with facility, and it needs patience
and endeavor of will to turn our hearts to those above us."

[58]"The unstudied fondness and fancy which obtained in marriage
is concentrated toward the children which follow;...the parents love
their children--and this is right--but it does not stop here; they
surrender themselves to that love." (*Circular*, 15 August 1864,
p. 174.)

[59]"If you find yourself struggling in the water,...it is not
your duty to let somebody else drown you. If you can save yourself,
but cannot save somebody else, don't let sympathy drown you--NEVER!
There is an instinctive tendency in those who are drowning to seize
hold of somebody and sink both." (*Oneida Circular*, 12 January 1874, p. 21.)

believers. The greatest disease in life (though a common malady among religious zealots) is to be salt without savor--to try to inspire others when one has exhausted
his own spiritual resources.[60] The Community advised
members that they must say "no" to those demands for affection, time and labor illegitimately placed upon them;
because the responsibility in controlling fellowship lies
always with the "superior" member. The Community taught
that it is the "inspirer" who must determine the rightness, the intensity and the longevity of each relationship, and that he must base these decisions on an awareness of his own resources.[61] Aware of his strength, he
must terminate or refuse relationships which are demanding more time and energy than he can afford. He must be
sure that time and energy remain for the pursuance of the
ascending fellowship, such that at all times he maintains
a healthy balance in favor of the ascending fellowship.[62]

---

[60]*Circular*, 16 March 1854, p. 176.

[61]"If we can get love working according to this rule--ascend-
ing fellowship first, and then descending fellowship as much as the
ascending fellowship allows and sanctions--no matter how much love
there is going, nor how much special love, I would not set up a
distinction of right and wrong between general and special love,
except that special love, when false, makes more mischief. I insist that all love, whether general or special, must have its authority and sanction and inspiration from the ascending fellowship." (*Circular*, 23 November 1868, p. 281.)

[62]There are several statements which could be interpreted to mean that a man was to engage only in those descending fellowships which were sanctioned by his inspir-
er--that he should obtain some form of permission for
every new relationship. The following is an example of
a statement which is open to this interpretation: "You
may have just so much descending fellowship as the ascending fellowship directs and allows...." (*Circular*, 23 November 1868, p.
281.) However, there is evidence which suggests an interpretation of this kind of statement which is less re-
strictive in intent. According to this interpretation,

It is easy to be deceived in this matter. The key is to
avoid that false "baby-benevolence" which hurries to save
others, while self remains in ruins.[63] One must evaluate
the spiritual condition of other persons and avoid long
contact with those whose presence can only be debilitating. There is, Noyes assured his listeners, no value
in pretending that all are saved, all are lovable, or all
are deserving of our affection. John Noyes saw no wisdom
in that false "tolerationism" which would have men con-
sort with all, regardless of their spirituality. This
easy, good-natured, ethic "which fellowships any and
everything that comes along, is nothing but a...counter-
feit of the true public spirit."[64] The true disciple of
Jesus will not hesitate to label as evil any fellowship
which is antagonistic to Christ's Kingdom, and to avoid
further intercourse with the person involved.[65] Of
course, the Oneida Community was criticized for these
elitist policies. Who were they, it was asked, to judge
others, to ignore Jesus' command to love sinners? Noyes
confessed that he himself, when younger, had shared this
zeal for tolerance and service of the weak, had suffered
his heart to bleed for reprobates till he was too weak
to do any good for God's people. Such mis-instructed

---

the counsel to indulge only in the fellowships which the
ascending fellowship allows means that one can indulge
in descending fellowships, as long as they do not de-
tract from one's love of, and submission to, the ascending fellowship. It is this interpretation which has
been given in the text. See *Oneida Circular,* 16 August
1875, p. 261; *Circular,* 7 September 1868, p. 193.

[63]George W. Noyes, *Religious Experience,* p. 239.

[64]*Circular,* 26 September 1852, p. 185. See also:
Spiritual Magazine, 15 October 1849, p. 276.

[65]*Perfectionist,* 22 March 1845, p. 4.

benevolence, he had learned, accomplishes nothing but
the desolation of its subject.[66]

The elders at Oneida sought to inculcate the principles of the ascending fellowship within the Community.
Their children were taught the importance of the principle from earliest years and were encouraged to seek
the company of those more advanced than themselves.
Pierrepont Noyes recalls, in his writings, that one of
the most serious and frequent charges voiced in children's meetings was that of "too much horizontal fellowship." The children were admonished to avoid clubbing
together in peer groups, and to seek out the company of
their elders.[67] As the children matured, they were
taught to find their companions among the older and better and to resist the temptation to foster the fellowship of their peers solely, because it was axiomatic
that young people were at a stage where all their relations should be ascending--that is ones where they sub-
mitted themselves to the inspiration of those holier
than themselves. In their spiritual state there was
little place for either horizontal or descending fellowships.[68] The principle of seeking the companionship of

---

[66]"By reason of ignorance and false education, I have suffered my heart to bleed for reprobates, till I was almost too weak
to do any good to God's people. Such benevolence accomplishes
nothing but the desolation of its subjects. It is a breach in the
spirit by which the heart's blood is poured out not a sacrifice
unto God, but a libation to that mother of abominations, who is
described as being 'drunk with the blood of the saints.'" (George
W. Noyes, *Religious Experience*, p. 347.)

[67]*Circular*, 21 June 1855, p. 87; *Circular*, 3 April
1856, p. 43.

[68]"The young in the community are trained to seek the ascending fellowship, to find their companions and lovers among the older
and better. There is nothing so destructive to a girl's modesty

those *more spiritual* than oneself gradually, and perhaps
imperceptibly, was glossed to read: seek the companionship of those *older* than oneself.[69]   The children were
taught not only to seek the companionship of their elders, but to do so in a spirit of receptive humility.
Otherwise they would not reap the values which these associations should bear.   They were taught to respect the
wisdom of their elders and to cultivate a spirit of obedience and modesty with regard to them.[70]

The practice of ascending fellowship had an added
advantage, the Oneida Community advised.   It enabled
them to avoid one of the traps which often threaten community: the tendency toward peer cliques and "generation gaps".   One effect of a policy of ascending fellowship, quite obviously, is that it encourages young and
old to mingle and associate.   In the Oneida Community,
those activities which could be shared by the young and
old alike were favored.   Elder members were urged to
join the younger in sport, fishing and swimming, while
the younger were allowed to take a place among the older
in the shops and during special visiting hours.[71]   In-

---

and sweetness as unrestrained association with those of her own age."
(*Circular*, 18 June 1866, p. 109.)   See also *Circular*, 23
November 1868, p. 281.

[69]*Handbook, 1871*, p. 50.

[70]*Free Church Circular*, 20 December 1850, p. 334;
Circular, 12 June 1865, p. 97.

[71]The Oneida Community claimed that, unlike most
families where unity is blighted by generation gaps,
Oneida was a place where young and old were respectful
of one another, and shared much.   In an article based on
interviews at Oneida during the 1930s, Carl Carmer, "A
Reporter at Large; Children of the Kingdom", *The New
Yorker*, 12 (March 28, 1936), p. 46, reports that many
decades later the influence of this principle could

terestingly, the elders, as well as the children, were
admonished to avoid the temptation to group with those
of their own age. The Communists said they had found
that the old need the society and sympathy of the young
as much as the young do that of the old, lest they suc-
cumb to the sins of old age: indolence, criticism, loss
of enthusiasm and fault finding.[72]

The principle that the young ought to in general associate with the older was applied by the Oneida Community with especial emphasis when the passion of amativeness
was involved. The Community believed that faithfulness
to this great principle was the only way to keep love
safe and healthful. Boys and young men were encouraged
to turn their attentions towards women older than themselves; and the girls were instructed in a similar policy. Among the principles by which the elders guided the
social organization of the Community was the following:

> It is regarded as better for the young of both
> sexes to associate in love with persons older
> than themselves and if possible with those who
> are spiritual and have been some time in the
> school of self control, and who are thus able
> to make love safe and edifying. This is only
> another form of the popular principle of con-
> trasts. It is well understood by physiologists
> that it is undesirable for persons of similar
> character and temperaments to mate together.
> Communists have discovered that it is not desir-
> able for two inexperienced and unspiritual per-
> sons to rush into fellowship with each other;
> that it is far better for both to associate with
> persons of mature character and sound sense.[73]

---

still be recognized in Kenwood (home of many Community
descendents), where anything from tea parties to golf
foursomes would consist of people ranging from twelve
to seventy years of age.

[72]*Circular*, 23 August 1856, p. 127.

[73]*Circular*, 14 January 1867, p. 351.

In this way, the relations between the sexes were open
to the instruction of the most spiritual and experienced
members. The elders of the Community believed that without this proper education, the passion of amativeness
would suffer almost irreparable distortions. Left to
their own devices, the young would inevitably and inno-
cently warp the passion of love. The Community believed
that correct education in the ways of true love had to
be begun at the time of the first awakenings of amativeness. The Community hoped to foster a generation of men
and women whose concept of love would in no way be influenced or shaped by distorting notions of romantic
love.[74]

Not unexpectedly, commentators on Oneida's history
have not scrupled to attribute invidious motives to the
originators of this system which pressured the young to
direct their romantic passions toward the older members
of the Community. Ellis for example has only disdain
for the practice, seeing in it the cunning of old roués
desirous of the favors of the fresher members of the

---

[74] "Youth of both sexes: all are brought up to be subordinate
in all things. At the age when liable to be subject to the prompt-
ings of a false amativeness, they are looked after, taught to walk
in the light in regard to this part of their experience; and under
the guidance of the wiser and older are instructed and not left to
ignorance, starvation and the devil...." (*Circular*, 4 June
1866, p. 93.) "The great principle by which love in the Community is made safe and healthful is that of the ascending fellowship.
In other words it is the mingling in love of the young and old.
Boys and young men are taught to turn their attractions towards
persons of the opposite sex older than themselves. Girls and young
women are also instructed in the same manner. In this way the relation between the sexes is open to the instruction of the central
members, and love does not assume that passionate uncontrollable
character depicted in novels, as the height of terrestrial feli-
city." (*Circular*, 2 December 1867, p. 301.) See also
Circular, 28 June 1860, p. 87.

Community.[75] Such charges seem unfair in the light of
the general sincerity and integrity which characterized
life at Oneida. But, without calling into question the
motivation of Noyes and his fellow members, one can still
question the effects of this system when put into practice. Noyes argued that they are uninformed who insist
that love between persons of disparate ages is unnatural
or without lustre. The examples of Ruth, Mary of Nazar-
eth, Jane Eyre were put forward as illustrative of a
tradition of love relations between young and old.[76] If,
on a purely natural order, the old cannot compete with
the young in attractions, Noyes assured his interrogators
that, for those with spiritual sight who seek the inner
spirit, the elder has far greater attraction.[77] Noyes
argued that the man who denies the possibility of love
between young and old should likewise deny the possibility of loving God, or of rising into any fellowship with
Christ.[78]

The principle of maintaining the ascending fellowship was also applied to the question of family relation-

---

[75]Ellis, p. 178.

[76]*Circular*, 24 June 1867, p. 114.

[77]*Circular*, 29 May 1856, p. 72.

[78]*Circular*, 1 May 1862, p. 47. It would be interesting to know to what degree pressure was brought to
bear upon the young to seek the fellowship of older members. Ellis, pp. 142f, (whose prejudice in this matter
should not be overlooked) reports of a rather chilling
criticism of a young man who was castigated for not
showing enough fondness for the older women. On the
other hand, the *Circular* (whose potential prejudice we
have already noted) assures the reader that there was no
compulsion in this direction, and that the pictures of
forced, detested combinations of young and old were without basis in fact. (*Circular*, 24 June 1867, p. 113;
Circular, 2 December 1867, p. 301.)

ships. Community members were taught that it was important to avoid too much fellowship with outside relatives,
especially with those who were unsympathetic to the religion of Perfectionism.[79] Applicants were advised that
a condition of acceptance into the Community was a willingness to break contact with unbelieving relations, because such intercourse was unprofitable to the sincere
Perfectionist, and would slowly drain away whatever
spiritual strength he might attain.[80]

In summary, the principle of ascending fellowship
was one which the Oneida Community considered essential
to the success of communal marriage. It was an organ-
ized machine which constantly kept its levers in opera-
tion in order to uplift character and draw all toward
the plane of goodness attained by the most Christlike
and therefore most central members.[81] It was not an
easy principle to put into practice, that was admitted.
It kept out many who would have otherwise sought admis-

---

[79]*Circular*, 21 March 1864, p. 4.

[80]*Circular*, 22 January 1863, p. 199. Much of John
Noyes' early correspondence with his own family reflects
his decision to cut himself off from them, at least until he had attained strength enough to withstand the
siphoning effects of their influence. In a letter to
his family, Noyes wrote: "I am as free for God's service, as
if I had never known father, or mother, or brother, or sister; and
now I am ready to turn and bind up the wounds I have given in the conflict that is past. 'The wisdom that cometh from above is first
pure, then peaceable'; not first peaceable, and then pure. During
my spiritual infancy I have been compelled to fight for purity.
Now I am strong enough to proclaim peace, and to keep the peace,
whether my proclamation is heeded or not." (George W. Noyes,
Religious Experience, pp. 232f.) See also letters cited
in the same work on pp. 174, 175, 239.

[81]*Encyclopedia Britannica* reprint, n.d., n.p.

sion to Oneida.[82] The *Circular* admitted that the principle was questioned by some members within the Community
at different times,[83] but assured readers that the con-
sensus of opinion testified that, difficult as it might
be, faithfulness to the principle brought peace, happiness, unthought of improvement, and the only guarantee of
continued success in the communal venture.[84]

WOMAN AT ONEIDA COMMUNITY

John Noyes counted the recognition of the true dignity of woman, and the defense of her rights, as among
the most important contributions which the Oneida Community made to society. According to Noyes, a woman in the
world of his day had no more freedom than would a slave:
the prisoner of marriages which were often loveless, she
was expected to submit to the sexual demands of her husband regardless of personal feelings or moods. She was
condemned to a life of household drudgery, with no opportunity to develop her talents and avocations. Although her health was often destroyed by repeated child-

---

[82]*Oneida Circular,* 30 September 1872, p. 316. In
fact, the Community found from experience that the direction of a prospective candidate's fellowship provided a
reliable predictor of his chances for success in community life. See *Circular,* 30 September 1867, p. 226.

[83]*Circular,* 20 May 1867, p. 76; *Circular,* 11 November 1867, p. 275.

[84]"True circulation requires that love should take an upward
direction.... In this way a circulation may be set going from the
very bottom of society toward the Primitive Church. The dissolution and ruin of the Association is involved in any but that order
of circulation." (*Circular,* 7 February 1856, p. 11.) See
also: *Spiritual Magazine,* 1 December 1849, p. 331; *Circular,* 30 September 1867, p. 226; *Oneida Circular,* 25
March 1872, p. 101.

bearing, she was never given the right to refuse this
task. Noyes was determined that this would not be the
situation of women at Oneida. There, women were to be
free: free from the possessiveness of men; free from
compulsory sex; free from compulsory child-bearing.[85]
At Oneida, no man was to have the right to *demand* the
love of a woman; no man could *claim* sexual privileges as
a right; no man could impregnate a woman unless she gave
her consent to the possibility of pregnancy.[86] The institutions which the Community developed to protect the
woman against both unwanted pregnancies and sexual demands will be discussed in the next two sections of this
chapter. Here, we would look at the policies of the
Oneida Community to remove the barriers between the
worlds of men and women; to include women in all business,
social and intellectual ventures.

First, according to reports in the *Circular,* Community women were respected as co-workers with men. It was
a Community policy to place men and women side by side
in many industries. Community policy urged the women to
keep indoor work to a minimum, and to join the men in
the garden or at the workbench as often as possible.
Every effort was made to integrate the sexes during times
of labor.[87] The Community reported that, given the opportunity, women proved to have both the talent and the
endurance of body necessary for important business positions.[88] The Community was convinced that:

---

[85]*American Socialist,* 20 February 1879, p. 63.

[86]*Circular,* 14 April 1859, p. 46.

[87]*Circular,* 26 May 1859, p. 71.

[88]The *Circular,* 14 January 1867, p. 352, reported
that in 1867 two of the most important departments were
supervised by women. Several times in its history, the
office of editor for the *Circular* was filled by a woman.

> One of the greatest inventions of Communism
> is its method of making women (much to their
> satisfaction) effective co-workers in pro-
> duction with men.[89]

Not only would this policy of co-sexual labor provide
Oneida with a new source of talented workers, but, Noyes
contended, it would improve the quality of the men's
work as well, because the mingling of the sexes at labor
makes work attractive and enjóyable. Noyes was convinced
that by introducing women into the shops he had found a
great secret to successful industry.

Secondly, with regard to social barriers, Noyes exhorted the men and women of Oneida to share all social
gatherings together. There was to be no activity from
which women were barred because of sex. The Oneida
founder was convinced that every activity would be far
more enjoyable and beneficial when among its participants
were members of both sexes. "If we are going to have
fun, the men and women must have it together."[90] He pro-
phesied that the next generation would share his conviction in this regard and would expurgate any institution
which did not bring the sexes together. The *Circular*
cited a story which is apposite here: when it was noticed that, quite by accident, the Community band's
membership had fallen into the 'bad old-fashioned way of
sexual separation' a cry of horror was voiced--this was
hardly in keeping with their constitutional principle:
the sexes together in all the cares of life.[91]

Thirdly, women at Oneida were encouraged to take

---

[89] *Circular,* 14 January 1867, p. 361.

[90] *Oneida Circular,* 22 June 1874, p. 207.

[91] *Circular,* 1 March 1855, p. 27.

their places beside men in intellectual endeavors. The
popular theory that woman is affectional by nature and
therefore unsuited for intellectual development, Noyes
discarded as a false myth. Whatever truth there is to
the charge that women are uncomfortable with ideas and
logic must be attributed to the social conventions which
suppressed their native intelligence. If men were reared
under the same prejudices and circumstances as women,
Noyes suggested, they would demonstrate an equal irra-
tionality.[92] Actually, Noyes informed his congregation,
woman's proper sphere was in the forum of the intellectual, and given the opportunity to expand into that realm,
Noyes predicted that she would naturally take over the
department of education.[93] The men were admonished to
take seriously the advice of the women in matters of
spiritual improvement, for their femininity gave them
access to wisdom not always available to the male mental-
ity.[94]

But Oneida's studied efforts to defend the rights
of women should not be identified with those movements
which would obliterate completely distinctions between
the sexes. As before, we find a balancing principle

---

[92]*Free Church Circular,* 20 December 1850, p. 324.

[93]It should be noted that while Oneidan policy encouraged women to take up many roles traditionally assigned to men, the men at Oneida were encouraged to develop those aspects of personality usually considered
peculiar to women. In a reported criticism, a man was
criticized for his over-emphasis upon the strong manly
side of his nature without a corresponding development
of the "gentle" side of his nature. He was told that
the two phases of character are not irreconcilable.
(*Mutual Criticism,* p. 54.) Later, a man was criticized
because "there is not woman enough about him." (*Mutual
Criticism,* p. 62.)

[94]*Circular,* 29 January 1866, p. 365.

which modifies the simplistic picture which might take
form. Oneida's insistence on the rights and importance
of woman was not understood by them to mean that man and
woman were equal. A review of a book by John Stewart
Mills, having lauded the latter's exposé of the evils of
the marriage system, comments in concluding:

> But when he tries to prove the equality of the
> sexes--at least to deny their substantial in-
> equality--one has a vague feeling that he is
> proving too much. You wonder how it was that
> man got ahead of woman so; did he get up earlier
> in the morning? or did he lie abed plotting?[95]

While championing the rights of woman to freedom, dignity
and responsibility, the Community maintained the principle that woman is always to approach man as her inspirer. The proper relation of the sexes, the Community
argued, was stated by Paul when he said: "the head of
every woman is the man". This was God's plan: that woman receive inspiration from man; and Oneida was uninter-
ested in tampering with that design.[96] Perhaps surprisingly, the Oneida Community refused to support the women's right movement which was gaining popularity in mid-
nineteenth century America. They opposed it--not because
they did not feel women's plight in the world was unjust;

---

[95] *Oneida Circular,* 4 December 1871, p. 389.

[96] *Circular,* 16 July 1863, p. 79. In Chapter Two,
mention was made of the unanswered questions which remain in regard to the relationships between men and women. One wonders how the Community integrated the principle that man must be the head of woman with that aspect of the principle ascending fellowship which encouraged the young men to seek as lovers the older and
more spiritual women. A possible explanation suggests
that the Community meant that in *general* women must look
to man for inspiration, even though, in individual relationships, roles might be reversed on account of age
or other circumstances. This was the interpretation advanced above. See pp. 101f, 153ff.

not because they did not agree to the justness of the
liberties that the women were seeking--but because they
were fundamentally opposed to the way in which these women were seeking dignity. The latter sought dignity by
setting themselves up in opposition to man--by relin-
quishing their feminine, receptive, subordinate role,
and attempting to play man. This setting of the sexes
against one another, the Oneida Community viewed as
fundamentally contrary to the heavenly organization.
This wrong-headed effort could only result in confusion
and despair: it would result in the destruction of the
feminine personality, and consequently the dual nature
of the human race. In the eyes of the Community, a woman trying to act like a man, breaking her subordinate
connection with man, and setting up for independence,
was odious.[97] The Community contended that the women at
Oneida had achieved all the freedoms and opportunities
for which the advocates of women's rights fought, but
that they had gained these without abandoning Paul's
principle that the head of every woman is the man.[98]

---

[97]"Woman must make sure of establishing the only legitimate
and natural channel through which the life and beauty of God can
flow to her; and that is her connexion with man. If she breaks
that connexion she becomes unattractive. A woman unsexed, or trying to be and act like man, is odious.... In breaking their subordinate connexion with man, and setting up for independence, and
assuming a masculine character they infallibly lose the beauty and
bloom of womanhood." (*Circular*, 12 March 1863, p. 6.) The
following point was made during the criticism of a Community woman: "One of her radical faults is insubordination to
man...she does not sufficiently respect man--does not give him his
due as a spiritual being, and as an essential link between herself
and God." (*Circular*, 16 April 1863, p. 27.)

[98]"Apropos to this subject, the women of the Oneida Community
are under reproach among the advocates of women's rights as not
being progressive in their lives. We choose reproach rather than
to dishonor Paul, who says that "Man is the head of the woman",
but we shall retain our self-respect while we know that practically

SEXUAL PRACTICES IN THE ONEIDA COMMUNITY

It is perhaps unfortunate that the Oneida Community
is remembered, not as a Community which challenged con-
ventional concepts of romance and love, but as the group
which practiced sexual abberations. Throughout its history, the Community insisted that the sexual freedom
which they had initiated was neither the most essential
aspect of their social theory, nor was it anything like
the imaginings of observers. Noyes believed that sexuality had been distorted in importance by both puritan and
licentious personalities. He urged his readers to imi-
tate the Oneida Community who had learned to view sexuality through balanced eyes: to view it as one important
passion of man.

Oneida was circumspect in reporting details about
sexual activities within the Community, not because of
prudishness, but because: (a) they did not wish to upset or enrage public opinion and repeat the history of
Putney; (b) government restrictions against "obscene"
literature could have been applied to the *Circular* if it
was not careful to draw a cloak of secretiveness about
their private lives; and (c) they soon recognized the
need to protect themselves against the morbid curiosity
of outsiders whose requests for information about social
life at Oneida were motivated by anything but an appreciation of the spiritual aspects of the program. For all
these reasons, detailed knowledge concerning the sexual
aspects of communal marriage is not to be found in the

---

we are enlarging woman's sphere every day, not by usurping authority, but by the help of our lords."   (*Circular*, 10 August
1868, p. 164.)   See also *Handbook of the Oneida Community,
1875* (Oneida, New York, 1875), p. 26; *Circular*, 22 May
1865, p. 77.

pages of Community journals. However, Oneida publications
did part the curtain of secrecy on occasion, and these
scattered insights enable us to form a rough sketch of
the sexual aspects of communal marriage at Oneida, to
which we now turn.

First we must consider the practice of Male Continence. Without this method of sexual intercourse, Noyes
could never have responsibly proposed the practice of
Complex Marriage. Noyes claimed to have discovered this
method quite independently of other writers.[99] In the
early years of their marriage, Harriet Noyes had borne
five children for John, four of which had been born prematurely and had died. As her health would have been
endangered by any further pregnancies, Noyes decided to
abstain from sexual intercourse, rather than expose her
life to danger. Under these circumstances, Noyes was led
to ponder the nature and meaning of sexual intercourse.
He concluded that there are two quite separate movements
in sexual activity, and that the second of these, orgasm,
need not be practiced every time one wishes to express
physical love.[100] As Noyes explained it:

> The sexual conjunction of male and female no
> more necessarily involves the discharge of the
> semen than of the urine. The discharge of the
> semen, instead of being the main act of sexual
> intercourse, properly so called, is really the
> sequel and termination of it. Sexual inter-
> course, pure and simple, is the conjunction of
> the organs of union, and the interchange of
> magnetic influences, or conversation of spirits,
> through the medium of that conjunction.[101]

---

[99]*Circular,* 4 December 1865, p. 301; John H. Noyes
Male Continence (Oneida, New York, 1872), pp. 10f.

[100]*Male Continence,* pp. 10f.

[101]*Male Continence,* p. 12.

The practice of this "simple" sexual intercourse in which
the man avoids the discharge of semen, Noyes termed Male
Continence. Noyes experimented with this technique in
1844, and in 1848 published his theory. He maintained
that it is possible for a couple to practice Male Continence in sexual intercourse without strain to either the
man or the woman. He assured his readers that the practice of this method was not difficult to master and that
most men were capable of it.[102] Noyes pointed out that
Male Continence reverses the standards of sexual morality.
In the world, it is woman's responsibility to protect
herself from unwanted pregnancies, to stop the man from
exercising his natural desires. Male Continence, on the
other hand, places upon man the moral responsibility to
restrain himself and to avoid impregnating his partner.
Let men assume that restraint is pre-eminently a masculine virtue, said Noyes, and the world will have a far
stronger front against unwanted pregnancies.[103]

Just as a kiss or an embrace has a value that is
complete in itself, and does not necessarily lead to
further acts of intimacy, so sexual intercourse without
emission of seed is a full action in its own right, and
need not be connected with orgasm. This analysis paral-

---

[102]Noyes admitted there might be a few men of nervous temperament, those men for whom the slightest excitement causes involuntary emissions, who would find Male
Continence impossible. But these, he said, would be
rare exceptions: "...in the normal condition, men are entirely
competent to choose in sexual intercourse whether they will stop
at any point in the voluntary stages of it, and so make it simply
an act of communion or go through to the involuntary stage, and
make it an act of propagation." (Male Continence, p. 8.)
See also Dixon and his Copyists, pp. 33f.

[103]Circular, 28 February 1856, p. 21; Circular,
14 January 1867, p. 351; Circular, 18 April 1870, pp. 38f.

leled thoughts Noyes was considering on the nature of
love. Noyes believed that the primary purpose of love
between the sexes is the mutual benefit and joy of the
two parties. While love could be involved with the desire to procreate, it need not be so. Amativeness and
propagation are two separate aspects of love between the
sexes, and the former of these, Noyes believed, is the
more important. Eve was given to Adam--not primarily to
be mother of his children--but to be a helpmate, a companion to assuage his loneliness.[104] Noyes suggested
that these two aspects of love coincide perfectly with
the two aspects of sexual intercourse. Sexual intercourse
without emission is designed to express the amative aspects of love; and sexual emission of seed is proper when
the intentions are propagative. Noyes suggested, therefore, that orgasm should be indulged in only when the
partners are specifically interested in conceiving children.

Noyes maintained that the practice of Male Continence "vastly increases" the pleasure and benefit of
sexual intercourse for both the man and the woman.[105]

> In contrast with all this, lovers who use their
> sexual organs simply as the servants of their
> spiritual natures, abstaining from the propaga-
> tive act, except when procreation is intended,
> may enjoy the highest bliss of sexual fellowship
> for any length of time, without satiety or ex-
> haustion; and thus marriage life may become
> permanently sweeter than courtship or even the
> honey-moon.[106]

Male Continence introduces men and women to the joys of

---

[104]*Spiritual Magazine,* 25 June 1842, p. 11, *Circular,* 1 January 1866, p. 330.

[105]*Male Continence,* p. 14.

[106]*Male Continence,* p. 14.

the first steps of sexual enjoyment which usually go unnoticed by people taught to rush over the first stages
of sexual union and to hurry on to the abyss of sexual-
ity--orgasm.[107]   Noyes wrote in this regard:

> I appeal to the memory of every man who has had
> good sexual experience to say whether, on the
> whole, the sweetest and noblest period of inter-
> course with woman is not that FIRST moment of
> simple presence and spiritual effusion, before
> the muscular exercise begins.[108]

Noyes compared sexual intercourse which includes orgasm
to a banquet which finds its participants drunk beneath
the table at its conclusion. With Male Continence, the
participants never lose control or awareness of themselves.[109]   Noyes insisted that the practice of Male Continence raises sexual intercourse to a "fine art", the
culminating flower of true refinement:

> ...so amative intercourse will have place among
> the "fine arts." Indeed, it will take rank above

---

[107]*Circular*, 25 July 1870, p. 146.

[108]*Male Continence*, p. 8. Noyes' insistence that
men and women learn to notice and enjoy the first stages
of sexual intercourse is illustrative of a more general
principle which he applied to many aspects of life: do
not rush immediately to the final stages of any action,
but learn to savor and respect the initial stages. Noyes
applied this theory to the matter of love, indicating
four distinct stages in its development, each with its
peculiar beauty and joy: (a) inarticulate love or unac-
knowledged love; (b) expressed love or courtship; (c)
consummated love (sexually expressed); and (d) propagation. While not rejecting the importance of the latter
stages, Noyes advised his followers against the tendency
to rush quickly from the first to the fourth stages without savoring the other steps. (*Circular*, 1 May 1856,
p. 59.)

[109]In cases where a couple wished to conceive a
child, Noyes advised that the loss of control which ac-
companies orgasm should be endured as the price one pays
for the object in view. (*Male Continence*, p. 8.)

> music, painting, sculpture, etc.; for it combines
> the charms and benefits of them all. There is as
> much room for cultivation of taste and skill in
> this department as in any.[110]

A reader of the *Circular* who had practiced the new way
in his own marriage, wrote to share the joy he had un-
covered:

> It introduced an experience entirely new to me
> in this connection, giving a sensation exquisite,
> but chastened.... I felt that I had been led to
> hear one of the great harmonies of the universe;
> and it was the finest chord to which I had ever
> before listened. Common worldly sexual fellow-
> ship is but the faintest type of simple amative-
> ness, in fact, it can hardly be called a type.[111]

This was only one of many letters received from readers
who had followed the advice of Noyes on sexual intercourse. Many wrote to confess that they had never before known the beautiful possibilities of sexual relations until freed by Noyes' theory from the animal,
sensual methods espoused by society. Another writer explained:

> Our sexual fellowship now is as far removed from
> any approach to carnality as it had previously
> been removed from Christ. It is a sacrament to
> us in which we accumulate spiritual vitality in
> contradistinction to physical waste. My experi-
> ence has also been that the theory was utterly
> impractical without the presence of Christ; that
> like the gospels its benefits can only be appreci-
> ated by believers. But no sooner is Christ intro-
> duced into the connexion than the entire nature
> of the transaction becomes so changed that the
> carnal is completely lost in the spiritual.[112]

---

[110] *Male Continence*, p. 16.

[111] *Circular*, 5 February 1866, p. 374.

[112] *Circular*, 5 February 1866, p. 374. Years later,
George Miller, a former Community member, advocated the
beauty of Male Continence in his novel, *The Strike of a
Sex and Zugassent's Discovery or After the Sex Struck*

Critics of Noyes warned their own readers that Male
Continence was unnatural and against the intentions of
the Creator. They insisted that the practice would be
seriously harmful to health. Ellis strengthened this contention by listing the maladies which were sure to af-
flict the woman foolish enough to allow any man to subject her to the selfish practice of Male Continence.
These included acute metritis, chronic metritis, leuchor-
rhoea, menorrhagia, metrorhagia, haematocele, fibrous
tumors, polypi, uterine hyperaesthesia, hysteralgia,
uterine colics, and neuroses, neuralgias, mammary conges-
tion, uterine cancer, diseases of the ovaries and steril-
ity....[113] And similar evils, he warned, should be expected among males who practiced this form of selfish
sexuality, this search for "pleasure without responsibilities."[114] In response to the charge of unnaturalness,
Noyes argued that the long march of mankind toward civil-
ization always involves a war against nature, a resolute
defiance of her primordial edicts. Cooking, wearing
clothes, living in houses, almost everything accomplished
by man, did these not represent departures from natural
ways?[115] In 1870, to silence the attacks of those who

(Chicago, 1905). Referring to Male Continence as "Zugassent's discovery" he puts the following description of
it into the mouth of his protagonist: "...a discovery that
appeared to be the perfection of chivalry, the essence of usefulness,
refinement, civilizing and ennobling man beyond all precedent...."
(p. 88.)

[113]Ellis, p. 201. See also W. F. Robie, *The Art of
Love* (Boston, 1921), pp. 164ff, 201, who argues that the
practice of Male Continence for long periods of time is
very harmful.

[114]Ellis, p. 199.

[115]*Male Continence*, p. 9.

had predicted collapse of health for anyone who engaged
in Male Continence, Noyes commissioned his son, Dr. T.R.
Noyes, who was a member of the Community, to conduct a
detailed study of the medical effects of the practice of
Male Continence on members of the Oneida Community. In
his study, which the editor of the New York *Medical Ga-
zette*[116] described as "a model of careful observation and
discriminative appreciation...(bearing) intrinsic evidence
of entire honesty and impartiality",[117] Dr. Noyes concluded that, on the basis of his medical examinations and
investigations, no deleterious influence on either the
physical or nervous health could be traced to the special
sexual practices of the Oneida Community.[118] Dr. Noyes
admitted that those who abused the practice of Male Continence by approaching too close to orgasm, and then
struggling against the reflex impulse to discharge the
seed, could expect disturbances on the nervous system;
but, then, there was no reason why intercourse for amative purposes should be allowed to approach that point.[119]
Dr. Noyes concluded that Male Continence, carried on with
moderation and without skirting too closely to the point
of orgasm:

> is not injurious to either male or female, while
> it gives rise to all those emotions which are
> refining and ennobling to both men and women, and
> reacts favorably upon the system of the male, by

---

[116]This journal had, earlier in the year, criticized
Male Continence as being likely to prove injurious to
health.

[117]Cited in John H. Noyes, *Essay on Scientific Propagation* (Oneida, New York, 187?), p. 26.

[118]*Essay on Scientific Propagation,* pp. 31f.

[119]*Circular,* 7 November 1870, p. 271; Essay on
Scientific Propagation, p. 31.

> causing an active secretion and absorption of
> the seminal fluid.[120]

Surely, this system eventually results in a loss of
fertility, rejoined the antagonists of Oneida. Again Dr.
Noyes reported no such correlation:

> ...we tested the virile condition of the men by
> microscopical examination of semen, showing that,
> as far as abundant and active zoosperms are evi-
> dence, we have retained our natural powers in
> nearly every case, including those up to 65 or 70
> years of age.[121]

And later, when the Community embarked upon a program of
propagation, statistics of successful impregnation served
to destroy any suggestions that the women had been made
infertile by their experience with Male Continence.[122]

In summary, the Oneida Community supported the practice of Male Continence for the following reasons: (a) it
prevents loss of the male virility through unnecessary
spilling of seed; (b) it protects women from unwanted
pregnancies; (c) it prolongs and enlarges the joy of sexual intercourse; and (d) it raises the passion of love
to the status of a fine art, contributing to the spiritual life of those involved.[123] Noyes was convinced that
with time all men would see the wisdom and beauty of his
proposal. Just as the practice of therapeutic bleeding

---

[120] *Essay on Scientific Propagation,* p. 31. The
people of Oneida believed strongly that the practice of
Male Continence was more healthful for the man than ordinary sexual practices, for it allowed the seminal fluids
to be reabsorbed into the system, which in turn they believed added to a man's magnetic, mental and spiritual
force. See *Male Continence,* p. 18; *Bible Communism,* pp.
45f; Miller, p. 115.

[121] *Essay on Scientific Propagation,* p. 32.

[122] *Essay on Scientific Propagation,* p. 32.

[123] Seymour, *The Oneida Community, a Dialogue,* p. 8.

had been abandoned as a barbarous relic of the unenlightened past, so the day would come when mankind would view
with equal disdain wasteful forms of sexual activity.

As was indicated earlier, the Community sought to
protect their women not only from unwanted pregnancy, but
from slavery to unwanted sexual demands. Within the Oneida Community, no man was to claim a right to the sexual
favors of the women within the Community. The Community
was constant in its insistence that no woman be forced to
receive the attentions of another unwillingly.[124] Each
member was thus prodded to be always on his good behavior,
aware that any boorishness, any selfishness on his part,
would result in a refusal by the women for further "interviews."[125]

Later the Community instituted the third party system, whereby a man, aspiring for the favors of a woman,
was to make his request to her through the offices of an
older woman. This was done, Noyes informed outsiders, to
provide women with the freedom to decline proposals without embarrassment or pressure.[126] However, the Community
admitted that there was a second purpose behind the third
party system, and the observor cannot help wondering
whether it was not, in fact, the primary motivation behind the practice: the third party system brought the
matter of the special intimacies of the members under the

---

[124]*Circular*, 14 January 1867, p. 351. The unpleas-
ant secession of Mr. Mills (see above, p. 140) was occasioned by the refusal of one woman to accept his attentions. The Community apparently did suggest that she
comply, but refused to put any constraint upon her in
this matter, other than advice. Her persistent refusal
led to his withdrawal. (*Circular*, 14 November 1864, p. 274.)

[125]*Oneida Circular*, 2 December 1872, p. 388.

[126]*Circular*, 14 January 1867, p. 351.

inspection of the Community. The third party could bring
to the attention of Noyes and his central committee any
proposed love relation which she thought unfortunate for
one reason or another. The members of the Community
knew that their romances were always subject to the inspection of the elders. But among a people who had been
schooled from youth in the importance of subjecting all
special loves to the spirit of truth and to the good of
the Community, this monitoring need not have caused resentment. The Perfectionists were in agreement that all
fellowships should be open and without secrecy, subject
to the observation and, if necessary, control of the Community.[127] In a report of one children's meeting, we
find the elders stressing the importance of avoiding
secrecy in matters of fellowship. It would appear that
we have here a first lesson in an attitude which was to
be cultivated through life: all fellowships were to be

---

[127]Constance Noyes Robertson, *Oneida Community: the
Breakup, 1876-1881* (Syracuse, 1972), pp. 16f, cites the
following letter written by Dr. Theodore Noyes many years
after the dissolution of the Community: "To get at it, you
must realize that the government of the Community was BY complex
marriage. Much has been said about mutual criticism and in itself
it certainly was a very powerful force in favor of law and order,
but all moral government, no matter how benign, in the end has to
look to penalties for its enforcement. The power of regulating the
sexual relations of the members, inherent in the family at large
and by common consent delegated to Father and his subordinates,
constituted by far the most effectual means of government. Father
possessed in a remarkable degree the faculty of convincing people
that the use of this arbitrary power was exercised for their own
good, and for many years there was very little dissatisfaction and
no envy of his prerogative. Of course I do not pretend to say that
this was the only inducement to good conduct; for the obligations
of religion had a very high place in the Community.... But for the
close relations of complex marriage the power of an arbiter, to
bind and unloose, is an absolute essential, at least in the present
average moral development of human nature." See also *Circular,*
14 January 1867, p. 351; *Handbook 1871,* pp. 51f.

subjected to the spirit of truth, brought to light, and exposed to criticism.[128]

If the Community felt it their obligation to oversee the social relations of the members in general, they were especially vigilant in the case of the young. They were convinced that ill-advised, romantic relations during the younger years would set patterns which would influence every social relation thereafter. Especially were they wary of unenlightened sexual activities during the formative years. This principle gave rise to the practice of having older members of the Community initiate the young into sexual relations, giving them "the means of wholesome and improving sexual experiences as early as they are capable of and liable to perverting and licentious excitements."[129] It was reasoned that if in their first sexual encounters the young experienced sexuality in its most ennobled form, they would be spared the pain and struggle of trying to reform their attitudes in later years. Thus, young men were initiated into the world of sexual intercourse at an early age by women considerably their seniors, and likewise the girls by older men. Chosen for these offices were men and women who had mastered the method of spiritualized and controlled sexual activity.[130]

Oneida always had critics who insisted that the motivation behind the Community's existence was insati-

---

[128]*Free Church Circular,* 20 December 1850, p. 333.

[129]*Circular,* 23 January 1865, p. 355.

[130]This practice had an additional advantage in the case of the young men. By restricting their first sexual experiences to relations with older women, they could master the technique of Male Continence without danger of causing unwanted pregnancy.

able lust.[131] Noyes, in answer, insisted that the members of the Oneida Community did not consider their sexual practices to be even an integral part of their experiment, let alone its ruling motivation. In support of his
position, he pointed to the fact that the Community had
abstained from the practice of their social theory on
several occasions when circumstances warranted it. In
doing so, they had demonstrated their conviction that the
value and success of the Oneida experiment were *not* dependent upon the opportunity to practice sexual freedoms.[132]

---

[131]Consider, for example, the following statements
from Benjamin Warfield's article on the Oneida Experiment
in *Bibliotheca Sacra*: "Noyes himself tells us that he had already adopted this theory of promiscuity in general in May 1834,....
One gets the impression that it held from the first in his mind the
place of an essential principle--we might even say of *the* essential
principle--of his system, while the whole doctrinal elaboration led
up to it and prepared the way for it" (p. 185). In describing
the Bible School at Putney, Warfield comments: "Neither his
purpose nor his interest could any longer be described as theological
or even as religious.... What was really being done was...to supply
his pupils with a religious basis for the practice of sexual promiscuity and to induce them to enter upon the practice of it without
shock, when the time seemed to him to have come to introduce it"
(p. 191).

[132]Noyes pointed out to these critics that he and
his followers had lived every aspect of communal life at
Putney for many years before they entered into the practice of communal love. Likewise, Noyes would cite the
fact that in 1852, as a result of external pressures, the
Community had abstained from the practice of Complex Marriage in order to follow the advice of Paul which requires one to abstain when offense is being caused by
one's liberty. (How long the Community observed this
temporary policy is uncertain. To this author's knowledge, no formal announcement in their journals ever marked
their resumption of Complex Marriage, though references in
articles and notices make it clear to the reader that the Co
munity did so when they felt that danger from external enemi
had diminished.) When the Community established a branch ir
New York City, the members in that house, aware of the objec
tions that their social system would occasion, refrained
from practicing the communal marriage system. Lastly,

The goal of the Community, Noyes would insist to his
critics, was *freedom from the marriage spirit*, freedom
from concepts of possessive and exclusive love.[133] And,
although the practice of Complex Marriage was the social
system most perfectly suited to foster that goal, and
was therefore to be practiced whenever possible, it was
not an absolute necessity. Noyes insisted that the Community would continue to exist whether or not circumstances allowed them to continue the practice of Complex
Marriage. Early in the history of Oneida, Noyes would
point out to these same critics, the Community had promised to relinquish the practice of their social system
if ever they thought that their neighbors' demands warranted it; and, he said, they had never rescinded that
promise.[134] If the people of the Oneida Community believed that their life style was becoming a stumbling
block to their immediate neighbors, or might incite others to work for the disbanding of the Association, then,
without serious regret, Noyes said, they would (as they
had done temporarily in the past) return to marriage arrangements, and continue their search for God and for
holiness in that state. Surely, Noyes concluded, no one
could claim that men and women, who were so willing to
forego their rights in the matter of sexual liberty, had

Noyes pointed to the fact that the Community's business
agents, who were often away from community life, were
quite prepared to abstain from sexual activity during
their absence from home.

    Estlake, p. 41, reports that at certain times in its
history, the Community voted to "fast" from conjugal freedom in order to have a period of spiritual improvement.
These fasts, he says, lasted from a few days to six months.

    [133]*Circular*, 7 March 1852, p. 66.

    [134]*Oneida Circular*, 7 April 1873, p. 118.

formed community solely or even primarily for the purpose
of indulging sexual propensities.

Occasionally, Noyes attempted to refute the charges
of licentiousness aimed at the inhabitants of the Mansion
House by parting the veil of privacy he usually kept
drawn about the intimate life of Oneida. On these occasions, he reported that, if anything, there was less sexual intercourse at Oneida than in the average American
town. Although spectators imagined a state of unbounded
sexual practice within the Community, Noyes reported that
in fact there was a strong tendency on the part of members toward abstinence and reserve.[135] In accounting for
this restraint, the *Circular* observed:

> There are spiritual laws in the case--not outward
> statutes, but the necessities over and in a man's
> own nature, which bind him with adamantine bonds
> to please God and improve in His fellowship in all
> directions, as a condition of liberty in love.[136]

In addition, Noyes pointed to the Community's policy of
extreme scrupulosity in their dealings with visitors and

---

[135]"A just scrutiny of the household habits of the Oneida Community during any period of its history, would show not a licentious
spirit, but the opposite of licentiousness. It would disclose less
careless familiarity of the sexes--less approach to anything like
'bacchanalian' revelry--vastly less unregulated speech and conduct--
than is found in an equal circle of what is called good society in
the world. That we have disclaimed the iron-cast rules...by which
selfishness regulates the relations of the sexes, is true; but with
these conditions we affirm, that there was never in that association,
one-tenth part of the special commerce that exists between an equal
number of married persons in ordinary life." (*Bible Communism*,
p. 20.) "While spectators imagine for themselves a state of unbounded freedom in the Community in accordance with its free love
principles, there has been in fact a strong temptation on the part
of its members at times to feel a restriction far greater than exists in ordinary society." (*Oneida Circular*, 21 September
1874, p. 308.) See also *Circular*, 26 July 1855, p. 106;
Oneida Circular, 17 November 1873, p. 372; Estlake, p.
46.

[136]*Circular*, 26 July 1855, p. 106.

hired labor. Visitors to the Community often mentioned
in subsequent letters of testimony the complete absence
of anything resembling flirtation or innuendoes among the
members of the Community. With regard to their employees,
the Community claimed that it always counseled them to
fidelity in marriage, and censured, even to the point of
dismissal, any kind of licentious talk or action.[137]

It only remains to remark that the members of the
Oneida family often testified that the system of
communal marriage, with all the safeguards which
surrounded it, difficult as it was, introduced them into
a life style which was self-validating. The following
are excerpts from several personal testimonies concerning
the effects of their social practice: "roots out selfishness"..."changed my character"..."brought me very near to
God"..."delivered me from the bondage of an insubordinate
amativeness, which had been the torment of my life"...
"our theory is the greatest safeguard against sensuality"
..."experience proves that it originated in the mind of
God"..."a sense of permanent unity with the Church of God
which I have never felt the like before"..."developed a
love which thinks no evil, envieth not, and seeketh not
its own"..."I have seen great beauty and celestial purity
in it, and I am sure that nothing but omnipotence could
create such blissful, soul-expanding and mind-elevating
realities".[138] To a prospective Community member, the
following advice was given:

> When you come to thirst for the love of a heart
> that can love as no mortal can, and have emptied
> all accessible loves, and tasted that bitterness
> of finding that they have limits while your want

---

[137]*Oneida Circular,* 9 January 1871, p. 11.

[138]*First Report,* pp. 49-53.

has none;...then you will find the door to the
Oneida Community.[139]

PARENTHOOD IN THE ONEIDA COMMUNITY

PHILOPROGENITIVE LOVE

John Noyes regarded amativeness as a passion which,
though good in its simple form, easily degenerates into
a cancerous influence when fused with selfishness. Likewise, he saw the love of adults for children as beautiful
when free of selfishness, but susceptible to distortions,
and capable of undermining the whole spiritual life. If
it was necessary for the Community at Oneida to refashion
the love between the sexes, they believed that it was even
more important to restructure parental love of children,
or, as they called it, philoprogenitive love, separating
the true passion from the dross of selfish exclusivity
and idolatry. In fact, Noyes contended that there is a
direct relation between wrong-headed love of children and
unhealthy sexual love. Both betray the same idolatrous
and selfish spirit. And because this evil spirit estab-
blishes itself first in the stronghold of parental affections, concern to purify the passion of philoprogenitive
love was, for Noyes, a major priority.[140]

----

[139]*Circular,* 15 October 1866, p. 242.

[140]"It is very common for certain persons, and has been for
many, to take possession of babies when they begin to act prettily,
to make idols of them. I observe in the case of C that this tendency is connected with a tendency to special love toward older persons, male and female. Let us study this subject to see whether
the spirit of special love does not establish itself in this stronghold first of all; whether the petters and pets are not soaking in
special love, just as much as though they were lovers in the usual
sense." (*Oneida Circular,* 9 March 1874, p. 85.)

Of the many forms of love open to man, his love for
children is, according to Noyes, the least spiritual and
beneficial (it is, of necessity, a descending fellowship).
Yet, it is the form of love to which men and women are
most attracted. They foolishly abandon themselves to this
descending fellowship, channeling all their love and concern toward children, instead of directing it toward celestial and amative love.[141] As Noyes viewed the situation, most married couples live as though children were
the primary purpose of their love. Noyes protested, to
the contrary, that the primary purpose of love between
man and woman is to create one another:

> It should be observed that the companionship of
> the sexes, pure and simple, is the primary and
> paramount law of society. The interests of pro-
> pagation...are intended to be wholly subordinate
> and secondary to the first combination which is
> that of man and woman. In other words, on the
> natural order, amativeness takes precedence of
> philoprogenitiveness.... Now the tendency of
> society in its apostate condition is to reverse
> the natural order on this point...both (male and
> female) sacrifice the beautiful harmonies of pure
> companionship for an inferior object, which though
> good in its place was intended to be limited
> strictly to the highest interests of the parents
> themselves.[142]

The results of this inversion, the Community insisted,
are seriously damaging to both adult and child. It is
damaging to the adult because constant concern for children can dull his appetite for the ascending fellowship,
thus, in effect, turning him from the source of spiritual
inspiration. Deprived of the strengthening spirit which
the ascending fellowship affords, a man or woman soon

---

[141]*Circular,* 15 February 1869, p. 378.

[142]*Circular,* 16 October 1862, p. 144. See also *Circular,* 26 April 1860, p. 51; *Bible Communism,* p. 43;
Mutual Criticism, p. 61.

loses his taste for spiritual things and becomes the
slave of worldly concern. Lastly, Noyes argued that, despite popular myths, the effect of motherhood is not to
destroy selfishness, but only to enlarge the boundaries
of it, often intensifying it enormously.[143]

Unbridled philoprogenitive love, it was maintained,
has even more unfortunate effects on the child involved,
who, sensing that he controls his parents, learns to ma-
nipulate them in order to obtain his every whim. Instinctively, the child realizes that the hearts of the
parents depend upon him for happiness, and he acts accordingly.[144] Furthermore, parents, out of touch with
God's power, are unable to inspire their children in God's
ways. For all their care and worry about superficial
wants, they deprive the child of what he most needs.[145]
Noyes exhorted his Community to beware of dangers of false
philoprogenitive love, and to search for ways to control
its demands.

The principles developed to purify love between the
sexes are applied to love between parents and children.
First, true philoprogenitive love, though it be intense
and ardent, is free from the feeling that this child is
mine.[146] The members of Oneida were enjoined to obliterate

---

[143]*Oneida Circular*, 5 October 1874, p. 322.

[144]"Let your heart be dependent on your children for happiness
and they will instinctively find it out, and soon act as though you
were made for their pleasure." (*Oneida Circular*, 10 March
1873, p. 83.)

[145]See *Circular*, 13 June 1864, p. 101.

[146]"Parental love is too often a hot-bed warmth, sickly and
dwarfing, but Community love is the sun itself.... We cultivate
philoprogenitiveness true and tender, separate from the feeling of
possession--the little feeling that this child is mine." (*Circular*,
8 August 1864, p. 164.)

any sense of ownership with regard to children, to overcome
every desire to possess a child as their own.[147] The parent, they were taught, who remembers that he does not *own*
his children will never exclude others from showing them affection. Secondly, the members of the Community were exhorted
to expand their love, to be concerned with all children in the
Community, and to show no partiality toward their offspring.
Animals care for their own; the Christian expands his love
beyond the family circle.[148]

Noyes warned his Community that the transformation
of philoprogenitiveness would not come easily--especially
for mothers. The temptation to the contrary spirit would
inevitably be present. Only by daily reflection, examination, and asceticism could they hope to achieve healthy
parent-child relationships, and even then the passion
would be difficult to bridle.[149] Within the Community,
every effort was made to help the members achieve the
proper ordering of philoprogenitive love, and especially
to overcome the feeling of ownership with regard to children.[150] Each person was encouraged to think of all chil-

---

[147] *Free Church Circular*, 20 March 1851, p. 69; *Circular*, 19 July 1855, p. 101.

[148] "What must women do in order to qualify themselves to be
mediums of a good spirit to their children? They must come into
fellowship with the Spirit of Truth and not be narrow minded and
small hearted. The Spirit of Truth is not particularly interested
in my baby or your baby; it loves to see education and every good
thing given to all the babies. We have found the Spirit of Truth
at deadly enmity with idolatrous love between the sexes; and so we
may be sure it is with idolatrous love toward children, and that because idolatrous love takes the place of true love." (*Oneida Circular*, 29 January 1872, p. 34.)

[149] *Oneida Circular*, 29 January 1872, p. 34.

[150] We read in the *Oneida Circular* that the Community
even banned children's dolls from the playroom on this account. They were convinced that playing with dolls, so
popular in the world, only strengthens the innate tendency
toward false philoprogenitive love. (*Oneida Circular*, 14

dren as belonging to the Community. When a new baby was
born at Oneida, its name was given by the Community,[151]
symbolizing the jurisdiction and responsibility of the
Community toward every child within the Community.[152]

Even the aged were warned against the dangers of
philoprogenitive love. Grandparents were advised not to
take charge of their grandchildren, and indeed to avoid
too much interchange with them. One who has had a family
needs to devote the later years of his life to recovering
from the disorders which philoprogenitive love has brought
about, Noyes reasoned. The worst thing would be to continue the cultivation of this sickness by taking on responsibility for a second generation.[153]

October 1872, p. 331; *Oneida Circular,* 19 October 1874,
p. 342.)

[151]Usually this involved an approbation of the parents' choice.

[152]*Circular,* 10 April 1865, pp. 34f. See also *Oneida
Circular,* 11 March 1872, p. 83.

[153]"Another idea which the community broach and maintain is
that grandparents should wisely abstain...from taking charge of
their own grandchildren, and indeed from having much to do with them.
Philoprogenitiveness is so strong a passion, particularly in women,
that one who has had a family of her own needs rather to devote her
after life to recovering herself from the disorders which it has
brought upon her, than to continue the cultivation of it by taking
possession of the second generation. The second growth of this
passion must be in some respects much more perverting than the first.
The position most becoming to aged parents is that which Paul assigns
to widows, when he says: 'She that is a widow indeed and desolate,
trusteth in God and continueth in supplications and prayers night
and day.' In this position a woman who has fulfilled the place of
a mother and blessed her children with her own care may bless her
grandchildren and the whole church by bringing upon them the care
of God. In saving her own soul from the disorders of philoprogenitiveness, she becomes a medium of heavenly spirits to her descendents and to all around her. Such at least is the teaching of experience in Communism." (*Circular,* 2 May 1864, p. 52.) See
also *Circular,* 25 April 1864, p. 52.

THE CHILDREN'S HOUSE

During the first months of life, the child was
placed solely in the care of its mother; but soon after
weaning, it was placed in the Children's House--a section
of the Mansion where all the children were cared for by
specially chosen adults. There, the children were divided into three groups according to age, and graduation
from level to level brought added privileges and responsibilities. Community policy regarding the extent to which
parents retained responsibility for their children varied
over the years, but the trend seems to have been in the
direction of increased Community responsibility. In 1868,
for example, the Central Committee, fearing that the
mothers were smothering their children with too anxious
brooding about clothing, put the responsibility for
clothing the children in the hands of the juvenile department.[154] In 1873, the *Oneida Circular* announced a new experiment whereby children would be placed in the juvenile
department before they had reached the age of one year...
this again because they feared the unfortunate results of
mothers giving too much attention to their children.[155]

The Oneida people regarded the establishment of the
Children's House as a great advancement in educational
practice. It meant that the children grew up under the

---

[154]"We have made more thorough work this spring than ever
before of communizing the children--making them the property of the
whole Community as completely as we have all other possessions.
Heretofore, the mothers have had the care each of her own children's
clothes and kept up more or less special connections.... The
clothes are now put into the hands of those who are in charge of
the juvenile department, the mothers gladly consenting....They are
all better and happier than they were before these new measures
were adopted." (*Circular*, 15 June 1868, p. 100.)

[155]*Oneida Circular*, 23 June 1873, p. 205.

care of adults who by temperament and training were well
suited to educate children. The children there received
the very best health care;[156] they were under the influence of the most spiritual men and women; and they were
protected from the dangers of smothering mother-love. By
comparison to the "hotbed" of mother-love, we are told,
the Children's House was a place of "open air and sunshine."[157] The Community believed that, whereas parents
in the world find it most difficult to refuse their children anything, let alone discipline them, the guardians of
the Children's department could school the young in obedience and responsibility without erratic outbursts of
cruelty.[158] Writing some years later, Pierrepont Noyes
gave the following recollections of his superiors in the
Children's House:

> They were neither indulgent nor were they sadists.
> They seemed anxious about our souls, and felt re-
> sponsible for our health, but they never perse-
> cuted us, nor did they hover over us as doting
> parents do. Within spiritual boundaries and
> rather general limitations of time and space they
> left us to ourselves.[159]

The Community pointed out that the children were not
the only ones to profit from the institution of the Children's House. In addition, it freed the women from many
of the burdens of motherhood. Instead of being confined

---

[156]See *Circular*, 14 September 1868, p. 204; *Circular*,
21 September 1868, p. 212; *Circular*, 28 September 1868, p.
220, for statistics on health in the Children's House.
The figures would seem to support the contention of the
members that the children received better care at the
hands of the superintendents of the House than other
children receive from their own parents.

[157]*Oneida Circular*, 3 July 1871, p. 213.

[158]*Circular*, 4 July 1870, p. 124.

[159]Pierrepont Noyes, *My Father's House,* p. 130.

to the house, slaves to the duties of raising children,
the mothers took their places beside their comrades at
work, at recreation, and at Community meetings. Women,
the Community maintained, are not made for child care
only; their more important duty is to be companions and
lovers for man. The Community claimed that the Children's
Department made it possible for a proper ordering of
loves and priorities to be reinstituted.[160] Yet, the Community did not intend that this new freedom would lessen
the love between mother and child. The Community said
that the system of the Children's House would increase
the love of parents for their children because, by giving
the parties a certain distance from one another, it made
the times together ones of joy rather than burden. Instead of resenting the children who make life something
of a captivity, the young mothers in Oneida would come to
their children refreshed in spirit and mind, eager to
share the love and the inspiration of people fully alive.[161]

It was reported that the adults at Oneida concurred with the ra-
tionale behind the Children's House; they experienced and
rejoiced in the freedom which the system afforded them;
they recognized the fact that their children received
better care and attention in the Children's House than
they themselves could provide.[162] Still, the Community

---

[160]*Oneida Circular*, 23 June 1873, p. 205.

[161]One member wrote: "I now realize as I did not before
that the old way of each mother caring exclusively for her own child
begets selfishness and idolatry, and in many ways tends to degrade
women." (*Oneida Circular*, 23 June 1873, p. 206.) "At
night when I take him he is delighted to see me, but the old claim-
ing, sticky spirit (which made us both miserable) is gone and I have
more enjoyment of him than all the time before of his life." (*Oneida Circular*, 23 June 1873, p. 206.) See also *Oneida Circular*, 20 October 1873, p. 341.

[162]*Circular*, 22 November 1855, p. 175.

knew that heroic self-discipline would be necessary if
the parents, and especially mothers, were to resist their
natural parental instincts in these matters. Should the
parents allow right reason to be overwhelmed by the blind
passion of parental love; should they begin to pamper,
protect or spoil a child; should they regularly interfere
with the policies of the Children's House, then the Community itself was prepared to protect the child and parents from these destructive ways. Noyes said one evening
in this regard:

> I suppose that it is next to impossible for par-
> ents to keep their own affections in subjection
> and rightly manage their children without some
> outside interferences.[163]

While parents were free to visit the Children's House or
to take the children out, Community policy gave the people
responsible for the care of children the right to curtail
this privilege if they thought a child was suffering from
unwise attention.[164] Apparently some of the mothers lived
in fear of the reprisals which were dealt to those who
were judged "sticky" in their attentions to their children.
The children too were warned regularly against the sin of
"stickiness" to parents.[165] A former Community member,
Corinna Noyes, reports that the woman who suffered from a
distorted concern for her offspring was likely to be forbidden to see the child for two weeks.[166] Both she and
her husband, Pierrepont Noyes, describe the agony

---

[163]*Oneida Circular,* 1 April 1872, p. 109.

[164]See *Oneida Circular,* 22 December 1873, p. 412.
See also *Circular,* 17 April 1856, p. 51; *Circular,* 16
June 1859, p. 83.

[165]Pierrepont Noyes, *My Father's House,* p. 64.

[166]Corinna Ackley Noyes, *The Days of My Youth* (Kenwood, New York, 1960), p. 16.

and loneliness which the practice of these rules caused
to mother and child, and the dread which both felt lest
regular visits be curtailed. Pierrepont describes the
constant struggle which his mother underwent to suppress
her "idolatrous" tendencies, a struggle which reflected
itself in a somewhat schizophrenic attitude towards her
son: with sudden transformation she could change "from
the embodiment of tenderness to the severity of a Roman
matron."[167] For example he writes:

> Certain it is that I often wept bitterly when the
> time came to return to the Children's House. I
> remember my mother's terror lest my crying be
> heard. She knew that Father Noyes frowned on any
> excess of parental affection as he did on all
> forms of 'special love,' and she feared that such
> demonstrations might deprive her of some of my
> regular visits.[168]

Yet, we are told that, in spite of this pain, the members
of the Community retained their conviction that the Children's House system was best for the children as well as
for their parents. The *Circular* regularly printed testimonies of parents who wrote of their deep appreciation of
the Children's House and of the "help" given them by the
Community to overcome what elements of philoprogenitive
love remained in their relations with children.[169]

---

[167]Pierrepont Noyes, *My Father's House,* p. 73.

[168]Pierrepont Noyes, *My Father's House,* p. 66. To
what extent, if any, these reports about Community life
reflect the distortions of a child's perceptions is difficult to assess. The same reporter, Pierrepont Noyes,
insists elsewhere that the overall effect of the Oneida
system with children was one of true happiness. He maintains that, despite the trials and pain endured, neither
parents nor children had wanted to return to small family
life again. (Pierrepont Noyes, *A Goodly Heritage* [New
York, 1958], p. 5.) See also Carmer, p. 46.

[169]See footnote 161.

As with the matter of friendship, so here it is easy
for the reader to misjudge the policy at Oneida with regard to the family relation--to assume that the goal was
to annihilate all special love between parent and child.
Yet just as the Oneida Community did not seek to eliminate
all special friendships, but recognized that--when con-
structed according to certain guidelines--they are valuable and important to spiritual growth, so the Community
did not wish to eliminate all special family ties. The
Circular reported that many visitors to Oneida, aware of
the Community's goal to form a single family, were sur-
prised to find that the children there were not all given
the same surname;[170] knew who their parents were;[171] and
were expected to show a special love toward their natural
parents.[172] At the same time that Oneida policy was
critical of families who were guilty of "stickiness", it
encouraged a kind of family closeness which it did not
consider inconsistent with Community principles.[173] Far
from being an enemy of the family, the Oneida Community
saw itself as the preserver of family unity. In the
world, families are broken asunder as first one and then
another of the children leave home to begin new, separate
families. In communal life, the Community pointed out, a
family is never separated, but can look forward to living
together unto death.[174] It was the understanding at Oneida that families, upon entering the Association, ceased to

---

[170]*Oneida Circular,* 21 August 1871, p. 369.

[171]*Circular,* 28 May 1866, p. 84.

[172]*Oneida Circular,* 6 November 1871, p. 354.

[173]*Circular,* 25 July 1864, p. 146.

[174]*Circular,* 7 August 1865, p. 167.

be families in the selfish and exclusive sense. Both
children and parents were imbued with the idea that the
Community was to be their primary family, and that it
was to be the prime focus of their existence. But the
special relation of parents and children, brothers and
sisters, was not to be despised. It was rather to be
subordinated to the communal relation.[175] By loving the
larger society more, a man or woman was not expected to
love his family less.[176] A mother wrote:

> Do I love my child and all children any less?
> No indeed! I love them more, and with a love
> that is far more ennobling than any I ever
> experienced in my state of weakness.[177]

And another writer observed:

> It's ridiculous to say it, but the natural re-
> lation is anything but extinguished. The
> babies do not love their parents less, but
> they love some of the rest of us just as well.[178]

The Community taught that once the selfish element of
family life had been removed from the relationship, then
the preservation of family, that is, the togetherness of,
and special bonds between, brothers and sisters, parents
and children was to be regarded as a good thing.[179] The

---

[175]"Their special relation to their own children, though it is
not extirpated or despised, is reduced to subordination to the general family relation." (*Bible Communism*, p. 13.)

[176]*Circular*, 7 August 1865, p. 167.

[177]*Circular*, 28 March 1870, p. 10.

[178]*Oneida Circular*, 3 July 1871, p. 213.

[179]"Communism is based on a surrender of private claims and
presupposes that each member adopts the interest of the whole, in
place of that of his family or any less organization. Families may
enter the Community in a body, but they thereby cease to be families
in the selfish and exclusive sense.... Now when the selfish element
is taken from family relationships, and the spirit of Christ's injunction is thereby fulfilled--when practically those that do the
will of God are accepted as our kindred, and none others, then the

Circular of 11 July 1864 maintained that if Oneida were
ever divided into several smaller communities, the policy
would be to assign members in such a way as to keep families together: "Communism...will never break up a family
already established in it."[180]   The *Circular* of 2 February 1860, in reporting a dinner party for the "A" family,
who had been dispersed for some time on different Community businesses, observed:

> This family is an interesting example of a house-
> hold becoming dissolved in the community...
> merging all its interests in the public service,
> and yet being able to resume its individuality
> and present a beautiful picture of domestic unity
> on such an occasion as the present.[181]

STIRPICULTURE

The practice of Male Continence made birth control
feasible, and for the first twenty years the Community's
policy was to discourage conceptions among the members.
Because new members brought with them children borne under the rubrics of marriage, there were always young
people about the Oneida household, and there was no need
to conceive children among members. Actually there were
two or three births a year at Oneida. A few of these
were accidental conceptions; the others were from women
who for personal reasons had obtained permission to conceive a child.[182]   But these were exceptions.   The basic

---

preservation of family materials, i.e. the presence of brothers and
sisters and parents and children together in the same community...
is undeniably a good thing...." (*Circular*, 25 July 1864, p. 146.)

[180]*Circular*, 11 July 1864, p. 130.

[181]*Circular*, 2 February 1860, p. 3.

[182]*Circular*, 5 October 1868, p. 228; Anita Newcomb
McGee, "An Experiment in Human Stirpiculture", *American
Anthropologist*, o.s. IV (1891), p. 321.

policy was to abstain from propagation until the Community was "ready".

Noyes explained the delay in this way: he did not want to begin a program of child-bearing until the Community had achieved that level of stability, of unity, of spiritual maturity which would provide the proper atmosphere for nourishing a growing child. Noyes believed that until conflicts from both within and without the Community had been overcome, it was best not to encourage the members to conceive children.[183] In 1868, however, he announced that, because the major obstacles to communal life had been met and overcome, the Community was ready, after years of waiting, to pursue a program of child-bearing.

> The Community has so far perfected the discipline
> of its affections, that it is ready, with one
> heart, for a faithful trial of the experiment of
> rational breeding....[184]

The experiment to which Noyes referred was one of eugenics; he called it stirpiculture.[185] Stirpiculture was a program which aimed at improving the human race by restricting parenthood to those people whose characteristics fit them to bring offspring into the world. Noyes argued that the human race would never make real progress as long as propagation continued to be haphazard and non-

---

[183] "We have had all we could well attend to in maintaining ourselves spiritually and temporally against enemies within and without. Amativeness goes before philoprogenitiveness and we have had to work and watch these twenty years, like frontier settlers, in subduing and civilizing amativeness; hence the demands of philoprogenitiveness have had to be postponed." (*Circular*, 5 October 1868, p. 228.)

[184] *Circular*, 5 October 1868, p. 228.

[185] Stirpiculture: from the Latin "stirpes", meaning race.

selective, as it is in a world which (a) encourages *every*
pair of lovers to marry and bear children, and (b) attempts to restrict propagation to those within the married state. Because it restricts propagation to those
pairs who have married, this system makes it impossible
for the superior man, capable of impregnating many women
and thus giving rise to a superior generation, to do so.
This system limits his value to the production of the
single woman to whom he is married. Thus, Noyes concluded, the world does not fully benefit from the power
of its truly great men. In fact, Noyes would add, this
policy discriminates *against* nobility, for is it not the
immoral man who most often distributes his seed beyond
the bonds of marriage?[186]

The Oneida Community believed that their stirpiculture experiment would be the means of parenting a new,
holier race--a generation of children outstanding in
every way, and especially in their spiritual strengths.
The Oneida people believed that spiritual strengths could
be passed from generation to generation, much as physical
attributes are. In refraining from child-bearing until
they had attained a high degree of spiritual maturity,
the Community believed that they had fitted themselves
to parent children who would *begin* life in a state of
spiritual strength. This new generation, it was expected,

---

[186] "As we have already intimated, marriage ignores the great
difference between the reproductive powers of the sexes, and restricts each man, whatever may be his potency and his value, to
the amount of production of which one woman, chosen blindly, may
be capable. And while this unnatural and unscientific restriction
is theoretically equal for all, practically it discriminates against
the best and in favor of the worst; for while the good man will be
limited by his conscience to what the law allows, the bad man, free
from moral check, will distribute his seed beyond the legal limits
as widely as he dares." (*Essay on Scientific Propagation*,
p. 18.)

would not need to suffer the long and difficult struggle
which their parents had undergone in their search for
holiness and selflessness.[187] They believed that the day
was not far off when their scientific principles would be
applied to all generations so fully and successfully that
the Kingdom of God would at last come among men.[188]

The practice of stirpiculture meant that some members in Oneida might be denied the privilege of child-
bearing. Noyes felt that the individual members of the
Community had attained a level of spiritual maturity such
that they would be willing and able to subordinate personal desires to the welfare of the Community. Speaking
of the stirpiculture experiment, Noyes observed:

> Of course it entirely shuts off some people from
> the propagative part of sexual intercourse. There
> can be no scientific selection...unless all are
> willing that the highest wisdom should control
> social combinations, irrespective of personal pre-
> ference.[189]

Noyes encouraged the members to view the whole project as
a vocation to which some are called, and others are not.
He insisted that all remember that the children who were

---

[187] "We believe on the contrary, that the sexual instincts and
passions can be purified so that we may please God by their proper
exercise, and that the children born of parents saved from sin have
better chances of development than those born haphazard." (*Oneida
Circular,* 12 July 1875, p. 218.) "I believe not only that
children can be regenerated...to grow up in the Holy Spirit, but can
be BORN in the Holy Spirit and need not be regenerated at all."
(*Oneida Circular,* 25 August 1873, p. 274.) See also
Oneida Circular, 5 February 1872, p. 43; Abel Easton, *The
Dissolution of the Oneida Community* [n.p., 1886], p. 2.

[188] "We believe that the time will come when involuntary and
random propagation will cease and when scientific combination will
be applied to human generation as fully and successfully as it is to
that of other animals." (*Bible Communism,* p. 52.)

[189]*Oneida Circular,* 2 December 1872, p. 388.

born would be the children of every person in the Community.[190]   He assured the Community that no one would be
forbidden from propagating; rather he called upon each
and every member to willingly and freely give up his
rights in this matter, and to place himself in the service of the experiment.   He wrote:

> The institutions that scientific propagation waits for
> must be founded in self-government.   The liberty already
> won must not be diminished, but increased.   If there is
> to be suppression, it must not be by castration, and
> confinement, as in the case of animals, or even by law
> and public opinion, as men are now controlled, but by
> the free choice of those who love science well enough
> to 'make themselves eunuchs for the kingdom of heaven's
> sake.'   If mating is to be brought about without regard
> to the sentimental specialities that now control it,
> this must be done only for those whose liberty consists
> in obeying rational laws, because they love truth more
> than sentimentalism.[191]

[190]*Circular,* 22 March 1869, p. 6.

[191]*Essay on Scientific Propagation,* p. 23.   Parker
reports that as a result of exhortations like this,
fifty-three young women of the Community signed the following resolutions: "(a) we do not belong to ourselves in any
respect, but that we do belong first to GOD, and second to Mr. Noyes
as God's true representative.   (b) that we have no rights or personal feelings in regard to child bearing which shall in the least degree oppose or embarrass him in his choice of scientific combinations.
(c) that we will put aside all envy, childishness and self-seeking,
and rejoice with those who are chosen candidates; that we will, if
necessary, become martyrs to science and cheerfully resign all desire to become mothers, if for any reason Mr. Noyes deems us unfit
material for propagation.   Above all, we offer ourselves as 'living
sacrifices' to God and true communism."   (Cited in Parker, p.
257.)   Again Parker cites a corresponding statement,
signed by thirty-eight young men of the Community, and
addressed to Father Noyes: "The undersigned desire you may
feel that we most heartily sympathize with your purpose in regard to
scientific propagation and offer ourselves to be used in forming any
combinations that may seem to you desirable.   We claim no rights.
We ask no privileges.   We desire to be servants of the truth.   With
a prayer that the grace of God will help us in this resolution, we
are your true soldiers."   (Cited by Parker, p. 257.)
    Such were the ideals which Noyes elicited from his
followers.   In actual practice, it would seem that a
policy of compromise was put into action.   Couples wishing

John H. Noyes himself fathered a good number of children
in the Community by different mothers, which is not surprising when one remembers that he was considered the holiest
of men by the Perfectionists at Oneida. Since holiness
was viewed as the prime requisite for being chosen as
father, it seemed obvious to the Community that the founder should bequeath his spiritual strengths to many children.[192]

---

to parent a child applied to the central members, or to
a special committee, who had the power to veto the request. Occasionally, the central members themselves took
the initiative in bringing about combinations which they
thought specially desirable. Parker cites statistics
which state that, of fifty-one applications of prospective parents to the central committee, only nine were
vetoed; and in these cases efforts were made by the de-
ciding body to find other combinations satisfactory to
all concerned which it could approve. (Parker, p. 260.)
T. R. Noyes states that the stirpiculture experiment at
Oneida did little more than make a start in the direction
of eugenics. Its main policy was to veto unions which it
thought obviously unwise. He writes: "It must not be
thought that the community pretends to unusual knowledge upon this
subject (stirpiculture). It has in general attempted little further
than laying a veto upon combinations for parentage which were obviously unfit and even here it has not always succeeded." (T. R.
Noyes, *Report on the Health of Children in the Oneida
Community* [Oneida, New York, 1878), p. 2.) And Pierrepont Noyes observed that, to the best of his memory, almost every male at Oneida fathered one child. Selection
was accomplished by encouraging preferred males to father more than one child. (*My Father's House,* p. 10.)

[192]One wonders to what extent the children born of
the stirpiculture experiment met the expectations of
their parents. The difficulty one would have in answering this question is complicated by the fact that it
would be necessary to separate out the influences of improved eugenics from the influences of conditions at
Oneida: the excellent facilities with regard to health,
education and moral development. For example, the low
incidence of death and sickness among the children born
at Oneida was apparently most remarkable for that period.
According to Parker, p. 261, of fifty-eight live births
during the stirpiculture period, only six deaths had

occurred by 1921, when the stirpicults ranged in ages
from forty-two to fifty-two years of age. He states that
according to actuarial computations based on Elliot's
tables for 1870, the deaths of forty-five out of these
fifty-eight would have been nearer to normal. Dr. T. R.
Noyes, in his report on the health of the children at
Oneida, p. 8, also pointed out that these figures were
unusual, but while not denying that this should be
partially attributed to the stirpiculture experiment, he
reminded readers that the special care given in the
Children's House must also be given some or most of the
credit for this healthiness. (Interestingly, Dr. Noyes
made this observation regarding the effects of better
child care as a reason for introducing the stirpiculture
program throughout society. He maintained that with improved health conditions throughout the nation, the process of natural selection would become less effective,
and in time there would be only a race of sickly adults,
unless steps were taken to prevent the births of unhealthy
children. Such a step he saw represented in the "artifi-
cial selection" process of stirpiculture.) As was indicated above, the Community were hopeful that the children
born within the Community would inherit their parents'
desire for holiness. But Pierrepont Noyes recalls that
children of Oneida were much like any other children of
the same age: selfish. (*My Father's House,* p. 23.)
And Dr. T. R. Noyes, in his article on the children of
Oneida, p. 2, wrote quite simply that the stirpicults
were not very remarkable.

CHAPTER FOUR

THE PRACTICE OF COMPLEX MARRIAGE

IDEAL AND REALIZATION

The question which repeatedly suggests itself when
one studies the Oneida experiment is: to what extent did
the people at Oneida live the goals they advocated in
their writings? Were the principles of non-exclusivity,
non-possessiveness, singleness of heart merely idealistic
dreams which Noyes and a few others regularly articulated,
but which bore little relation to life as it was actually
carried on at Oneida? As has been indicated several
times, it has not been the intention of this study to attempt an answer to that question. However, by way of
conclusion it might be valuable to sketch a response to
be deduced from information found scattered through the
Community journals. Quite obviously, whatever conclu-
sions are derived from this information must be regarded
as extremely tentative because of the nature of the
source material.[1] Nevertheless, this sketch provides an
important starting point for those interested in pursuing
the question. In this last section, therefore, we will
consider the answer which a careful reading of the Community journals gives to those who pose the question: "To
what extent did the Oneida people really practice what
they preached?"

First, the reader of the Community journals finds

---

[1]See above, pp. 124f.

many statements which indicate that the Community sincerely attempted to live out the principles they advocated,
and that progress was made toward achieving the goals
they set for themselves. In 1856, the *Circular* stated
that the Community was gaining an appreciation of the ascending fellowship which would stand any test that could
be put to it.[2] In March of 1857, the Community reported
their conviction that real progress toward the realization of their social goals had occurred.[3] In a reported
Community discussion eight years later, the Community
agreed that there were definite signs of improvement in
the health of the members precisely because they had
learned to grow out of special love; the struggle against
the enemies of true love, they said, was beginning to
bear fruit.[4] In 1865, the readers of the *Circular* were
advised that the higher law of love had won the hearts of
the Community: "...we are now convinced beyond the shadow of a doubt that with us at least the love of the novels has had its day."[5] An 1867 article on the social organization of the Community states that the Community had
little problem in observing, and governing themselves by,

---

[2]*Circular,* 4 September 1856, p. 131.

[3]*Circular,* 19 March 1857, p. 35.

[4]*Circular,* 19 June 1865, p. 108.

[5]"For years all have been free to taste of special love, but
the higher law being in our midst, it has been forced to hide its
diminished head, and we are now convinced beyond the shadow of a
doubt that with us at least the love of the novels has had its day.
It is a new starting point with us and there is no telling the impetus our spirits will acquire under the new regime." (*Circular,*
23 October 1865, p. 252.) "Truly this is not with us a merely
negative matter. We are beginning to reap very sensibly the fruits
of the new graft...oh, the vastness of this universal brotherhood!
You are afloat on a boundless ocean buoyant with the very elixir of
life." (*Circular,* 23 October 1865, p. 252.)

the principles of love that they had advocated.[6] An outsider, who apparently taught at the Oneida Community for
a while, wrote in 1872 that the members of the Community
lived up to their theory in practice; and were the Community dissolved on the following day, it would have
served an important role to mankind by its example.[7]

The Community assured readers that they were as
amazed as the outsider by the degree to which they had
been able to combat false love. One member wrote:

> With a strong natural tendency to idolatrous
> love, the change which has taken place in my
> own heart and in the hearts of my companions
> seems miraculous. I used to ask myself: 'Is
> it possible for me to ever realize a condi-
> tion in which I can love all my brothers and
> sisters and not love some ONE idolatrously...?'[8]

Another correspondent, commenting on the fact that not
one person had eloped from the Oneida family (this was
in 1869) concluded:

> Knowing as we do the great proportion of young
> folk we have always numbered, and knowing that
> the discipline of the passions is more radical
> here than even with the Shakers,...we wonder at
> the fact; and still it is true. A hundred young
> folks have passed the age of temptation at the
> O.C. and yet there has never been an elopement.[9]

The explanation for their success was, of course, the
power of Christ. Christ's answer to the Sadducees in respect to marriage in the resurrection applied to Bible
Communism as well: "Ye do err in your hearts not knowing

---

[6] *Circular,* 14 January 1867, p. 351.

[7] *Oneida Circular,* 16 December 1872, p. 403.

[8] *Oneida Circular,* 3 June 1872, p. 179.

[9] *Circular,* 22 February 1869, p. 390.

The power of God."[10]   What was impossible for man alone
was possible for man under the power of Christ:

> That men can live in close communism...without jeal-
> ousy and dissension is a wonder to the world; it is no
> less a wonder to ourselves. There is a mysterious
> power which comes upon us that we cannot explain....[11]

All of these references would indicate that to a large extent
the Community not only spoke about ideals, but actually did
succeed in enfleshing them in their lives.

On the other hand, in the Community's publications, one
finds reports and statements which balance this picture of
success. In a home talk in 1849, Noyes told the Community
that, because the spirit of false love or selfish amativeness
is a disease which is so difficult to avoid, he had found it
in the past difficult to chastize those guilty of it. However, he wished to challenge the Community to take up the
question of special friendship and to give it a more thorough examination.[12] Apparently, even after many years, there
remained many symptoms of false and unpurified love within
the Oneida Community. In 1856, Noyes commented that too
much of the social activity within the Community was done
in twos, and that there was as yet little appreciation for
the values of group activities.[13]   A discussion reported
in 1858 included the comment that the experience of the Community with regard to the social system had been imperfect.[14]

---

[10]"Christ's answer to the Sadducees in respect to marriage in the
resurrection, brings to view the most important topic we have to do
with in understanding the workings of our social theory. He says to
them, 'Ye do err in your hearts, not knowing the Scriptures nor the
power of God.' The power of God. And that is what we must know if we
mean to understand Bible Communism or the social state of heaven."
(*Circular*, 17 May 1869, p. 65.)

[11]*Oneida Circular*, 11 November 1872, p. 367.

[12]This 1849 home talk was reprinted in *Circular*, 15
March 1869, p. 409.

[13]*Circular*, 23 August 1856, p. 127.

[14]*Circular*, 13 November 1858, p. 170.

In an article written in 1861, Noyes mentioned with some
disappointment that the ideal of the young loving the
old, the handsome the less so, the educated the less
educated had not gained the popularity he had envisioned.[15]
The fact that many spiritual and deserving persons were
not attracting lovers suggested to Noyes that the people
at Oneida had not yet fully digested the true principles
of attraction based on inner beauty. In 1867, Noyes
spoke to the Community of the false love which was being
tolerated at Oneida.[16] In 1868, Noyes insisted on the
need for a new beginning with regard to social policy.
He told the Community that till then his policy had been
to tolerate false relations among the Community members.
When two persons found themselves under ungovernable im-
pulses, so that they had to come together in a special
relation of love, he said that he had allowed them the
freedom to do so, though warning them that they would be
happier without it.[17] But now he felt constrained to
urge the Community to greater discipline and scrupulosity
in matters of the heart:

> But after all the question that is beginning to
> press itself on me is whether it is not compro-
> mising after the time of compromising has gone
> by. Have we not advanced into a position...
> where the absolute principle that he (Paul) fore-
> saw was to come into force in a short time has
> come into force with us? It seems to me that we
> ought to come square up to the principle, and
> public opinion in the Community ought to plant
> itself on the principle that that compromise of
> Paul's is past and gone; and that the only

---

[15]*Circular,* 12 September 1861, pp. 127f; see also
Circular, 28 February 1861, p. 15.

[16]See home-talk delivered on October 15, 1867 and
printed in the *Circular* of 23 November 1868, pp. 281f.

[17]*Circular,* 12 October 1868, p. 233.

rational ground and position for us after having
abandoned marriage for the very purpose of ridding ourselves of its snares and distractions,
is, that we will attend upon the Lord without
distraction. We will not have any interference
of these attractions between the sexes come in to
disturb our relations with the Lord.[18]

We have not quite believed heretofore that the end
of slavery has come. We have thought that things
were partly as they were in Paul's time, and we
must submit to things as they stand. I think this
is a little below our privilege; that it is time
for us to consider that slavery has come to an
end.[19]

In 1869, Noyes stated that the most serious trials with
which the Community had to contend were those involving
false fellowships.[20]

But if the Community at Oneida never perfectly arrived at the goals they proposed, the impression one receives from their journals is that they struggled in that
direction. We read that, repeatedly, Oneida embarked
upon "new starts", "revivals", more intense heart search-
ings with regard to social theory. In March of 1858, reference was made to "what might be called a social revival" at Oneida. "There has been a convicting power at
work, leading to repentance of idolatrous affection."[21]
At a meeting of Community young men early in 1868, those
gathered announced their determination to rid themselves
of every vestige of false love, and to substitute in its
place true brotherly love.[22] Again, in 1874, mention is

---

[18]*Circular,* 12 October 1868, p. 233.

[19]*Circular,* 12 October 1868, p. 234.

[20]*Circular,* 9 August 1869, p. 162.

[21]*Circular,* 27 March 1856, p. 39.

[22]*The Oneida Community Daily,* 13 January 1868, p. 42.

made of a winter renewal, with pledges made to observe a
new fidelity toward the interior social principles and
unselfish love.[23] Speaking of this renewal, the *Oneida
Circular* observed:

> Suffice it to say that the agitation of these
> subjects had strict conviction wherever there
> was any secret unfaithfulness, drawing out
> agonizing confessions...and has gathered all
> hearts together in new devotion to our social
> principles.[24]

The desire of the Community to defeat the enemy of false
love gave rise to a recurring decision to dedicate a
series of Wednesday night conferences to the discussion
and exploration of proper social relations.[25] All these
reported efforts, then, suggest that the Community members in
general were sincere in their desires to live out the
principles advocated by Noyes, though their success was
limited and won at the cost of pain and struggle. This
impression is corroborated by reported examples of individual struggle:[26] for example, it is reported that a
woman in the Community, realizing that her attachment to
one of the Community men was, in fact, bondage to the
spirit of false love, determined to separate from him,
even ridding herself of all mementoes which might prevent
the break;[27] a man, involved in a triangle affair and
tormented with jealousy, turned to Christ and found the
strength to rejoice in seeing his competitor love his

---

[23]*Oneida Circular*, 5 January 1874, p. 12.

[24]*Oneida Circular*, 5 January 1874, p. 12.

[25]*Circular*, 7 February 1856, p. 11.

[26]See Ray Strachey, *Group Movements of the Past and
Experiments in Guidance* (London, 1934), p. 114.

[27]*The Oneida Community Daily*, 10 January 1868, p.
35.

beloved;[28] two lovers, very much attached to one another,
accepted willingly the suggestion of the Community that
they both choose other mates for participation in the
stirpiculture experiment.[29] The Community warned those
who came to them thinking to find a haven of rest, sensual tranquillity and security, that they were badly mis-
informed. For Oneida was the scene of a painful and ex-
acting battle, where those called to Christ's army struggled to win for mankind the war against selfish, exclusive
love. The *Oneida Circular* of 28 September, 1874 observed:

> It will be hard for people to imagine the amount
> of milling and refining a person has to undergo
> before he or she is willing to submit the planning
> of their social or sexual affairs to the good
> spirit, even after they see the way to do it.[30]

Referring specifically to a revival of devotion to the
social principles in 1874, the *Oneida Circular* commented:

> This past winter has been one of great spiritual
> labor and suffering in the Oneida Community....
> (which) could only be adequately expressed by
> such language of anguish as Job's when he says
> to the Lord: 'His archers compass me round
> about.'[31]

---

[28]*Oneida Circular*, 29 April 1872, p. 141.

[29]Estlake, p. 75.

[30]*Oneida Circular*, 28 September 1874, p. 316.

[31]*Oneida Circular*, 9 March 1874, p. 84. The Perfectionists insisted that the discipline of Bible Communism
far exceeded in difficulty and pain the discipline of
Shakerism; that to love and yet renounce worship in love
was far more difficult a cross than the pain of total ab-
stention. See *Circular*, 21 October 1858, p. 155; *Oneida
Circular*, 12 July 1875, p. 219; *American Socialist*, 11
July 1878, p. 222. A writer in the *Circular* observed:
"It seems plain that all that is needed is an enlargement of heart
that should embrace all: a process, however contradictory it may
appear, involving great suffering."   (21 September 1853, p.
354.)

Yet despite the pain involved in this struggle, the Community insisted that their overall experience was one of true joy, a joy unknown to the world. It was their attempts toward implementing this theory of love which provided the foundation stone to their whole venture. Corrina Noyes, a former member of Oneida, observed in this regard:

> Since unselfishness, sacrifice, and dedication
> are qualities which almost by definition, entail
> discipline and even suffering, the history of
> the Community is also a tale of hardships, abnegation and steadfastness; even of suffering. But
> I remember that in her old age my mother, who had
> lived half her adult life in this society, said
> that after living in the world, she realized that
> never again could there be happiness such as she
> had known in the Community. This from a wise and
> honest witness is all I need to say.[32]

The picture then which emerges from this information is one of partial success in implementing the principles of true love. One finds repeated efforts to renew, personal and communal struggle, painful acts of discipline by a people who at times concluded that wisdom lay in a healthy compromise with goals meant for the future. In the *First Report* of the Community (1849), the following admission was made by the communists with regard to their social system:

> The principles in question have never been carried into full practical embodiment, either at
> Putney or Oneida, but have been held by the Association as the principles of the ultimate state,
> toward which society among them is advancing,
> slowly and carefully, with all due deference to
> sentiments and relations established by the old
> order of things.[33]

---

[32] This quotation taken from the un-paginated introduction to Corrina Ackley Noyes, *Days of My Youth.*

[33] Pp. 16f.

Noyes' own description in 1861 of social relations at
Oneida seems to corroborate the impression received: the
social situation at Oneida, Noyes said, was something of
a *compromise*. Life within the Community, he said, was
formed by both the social theory that he had advocated,
and by the principles in which the world imbues its chil--
dren:

> The two forces have met in our body and have sent
> it in the direction it has taken, which is evi-
> dently in some respects a *compromise* between the
> strict lines of both.[34]

Noyes gave for example the principle of non-exclusive
love: while the Community members had effectually turned
away from the world's exclusive institutions, there was
still a tendency to a secondary form of the marriage
spirit, manifested in the partialities of too special
friendships.[35] With reference to the ascending fellowship, Noyes stated that the actual social situation within the Community was hardly a perfect reflection of this
principle. Nevertheless, he argued, the life style within Oneida was very much influenced and modified by the
force of that theory.[36] Perhaps Noyes' description of
the social relations at Oneida in 1861 summarizes fairly
the situation there throughout its history:

> While it is not proper therefore to think of our
> social system as exhibiting the ripe, unimpeded
> fruits of Communism, neither is it just to say
> that our social theory has had no effect--it has
> had effect and it is imperfect only so far as it
> has been embarrassed by the operation of counter-
> acting forces.[37]

---

[34] *Circular,* 25 April 1861, p. 47.   Emphasis added.

[35] *Circular,* 25 April 1861, p. 47.

[36] *Circular,* 25 April 1861, p. 47.

[37] *Circular,* 25 April 1861, p. 47.

THE FINAL DAYS

In August of 1879, Noyes recommended that the Community abandon the practice of Complex Marriage--this without forsaking belief in the principles of the system or in the eventual realization of its program. He recommended this change in policy, he said, under the rubric of prudence, in response to the efforts of a convention of concerned clergymen meeting in Syracuse for the purpose of introducing legislation which would force the Community to abandon its social system.[38] He urged the Community to adopt "Paul's platform" in the meantime: marriage permitted, but celibacy preferred. This proposal, sent by Noyes on the 20th of August, was ratified by the Community on the 26th and published on the 28th of the same month. Thus came to an end the experiment in Complex Marriage.[39] This new venture in Community living was short lived. One year later, on September 1, 1880, the Community signed an agreement to disband, and to reorganize their industries on a new basis. On January 1, 1881, the Oneida Community Ltd., a business company (eventually to become quite successful) in which each member of the Community became a shareholder, was formed. And with this, communism of property at Oneida ceased.[40]

---

[38]*American Socialist,* 20 February 1879, pp. 57ff; *American Socialist,* 4 September 1879, p. 282.

[39]Years later, Pierrepont Noyes reported that the members faithfully ceased all social relations other than those between married couples. This faithful observance of traditional morality, he believed, after years of sharing one another's social company, stood as an eloquent testimony to the integrity of the men and women who had lived the Oneida experiment. (*My Father's House,* p. 164.)

[40]Every man and woman received shares in proportion to (a) the number of years of membership in the Community,

The question which immediately suggests itself is:
why the collapse? Why, after having weathered so many
years of economic and spiritual struggle, just when the
Community should have begun to enjoy the fruits of their
labors, did the Community collapse? Although it is beyond the scope of this book to answer this question, a
few comments of a tentative nature may be in order, especially since there is reason to suspect that problems
concerning the social practices of the Community played a
critical role in the breakup.[41]

---

and (b) the amount of property contributed by the member
to the common fund upon entering. (See Pierrepont Noyes,
My Father's House, pp. 176-181.) Apparently, these financial arrangements were decided upon, and agreed to,
with relatively little contention. William Hinds, a
former member, observed years later that it could have
been otherwise: the talented could have insisted upon
shares commensurate with their special contributions;
those who had brought with them large sums of money at
the outset could have insisted upon *full* recompense for
these donations. (They were given credit for only one
half of the value of the property contributed.) As it
was, the weak and the formerly poor members received
shares beyond what they could have demanded in justice.
Hinds maintained that the smoothness with which these arrangements were made reflected the admirable spirit of
community which had been fostered within Oneida. (*American Communities and Co-operative Colonies*, 2nd rev. ed.
[Chicago, 1908], pp. 216f.) Maren Lockwood Carden gives
a fine account of the evolution of Oneida from an inten-
tional community into a corporation, in her recent study,
Oneida, Utopian Community to Modern Corporation (Baltimore,
1969).

[41]The task of investigating the dissolution of the
Oneida experiment is greatly facilitated by a study of
the breakup of the Community published by Constance Noyes
Robertson: *Oneida Community: the Breakup, 1876-1881* (Syracuse, 1972). A granddaughter of John Humphrey Noyes, Mrs.
Robertson brings to her study a familiarity with unpublished documentation concerning the last years of the
Community's history, which she uses to construct an en-
grossing and convincing account of the last days.

The decision in 1878 to abandon Complex Marriage
was not *intended* as a step toward the final breakup of
the Community; at that time Noyes expressed confidence
that the decision would in no way hinder the continuation
of the Oneida Community. Nevertheless, the agreement to
disband followed one year later, suggesting that the two
events were related in some way. Therefore, we must begin by inquiring into the circumstances surrounding that
first decision.

According to its public statement, the Community
abandoned Complex Marriage because it feared that the efforts of the convention meeting in Syracuse, which had
determined to legally force the Oneida Community to abandon their social practices, would prove successful. In a
reported interview, Mr. William Hinds, speaking on behalf
of the Community, stated with regard to their new policy:

> You may say, sir, and I speak for Mr. Noyes as
> well as the rest of the Community, that this
> movement is a bona-fide one, and we enter upon
> it in the utmost sincerity. The Community has
> always held itself ready to recede from the
> practical expression of its peculiar social
> principles as a matter of expediency and in def-
> erence to public opinion.

He added:

> Our movement is simply a measure of prudence on
> our part, adopted in the spirit of St. Paul which
> says: 'If meat make my brother to offend, I will
> eat no flesh while the world standeth.'

When asked if the Community had been forced into this action, Hinds replied:

> No present pressure is being brought to bear by
> the people in this neighborhood or anywhere else
> to compel this action. We have, of course, been
> cognizant of a general movement on the part of the
> public that was likely, sooner or later, to demand
> some such action on our part, and Mr. Noyes and
> others deemed it best to anticipate it.[42]

---

[42] Cited by Robertson, *Oneida Community, the Breakup,*

Ostensibly, then, the decision in 1879 should be attributed to the successful campaign of these concerned moral-
ists in Syracuse, and not to any dissatisfaction within
the Community over the practice of Complex Marriage. The
fact that the total dissolution of the Community followed
up this decision so closely can be explained without assuming that internal problems were responsible for both
the decision of 1878 and that of 1880. It can be argued
that it was the return to individual marriage which
caused the eventual downfall of the Community; that the
additional problems which were encountered once the Community was composed of individual family units generated
new internal tensions which could not be controlled. As
a matter of fact, Noyes himself had maintained in earlier
years that marriage and community life are incompatible.
In his study of American Communities, Noyes had maintained
that the man with a family inevitably devotes the major
part of his time and interest to that family, placing a
correspondingly smaller part of his energies at the service of the large community. Securing the best possible
circumstances for his dependents becomes an overriding
and excluding passion.[43] Several other members of the
Community had opposed the return to individual marriage
on the same basis: that it would eventually result in
the dissolution of the whole experiment. William Hinds
had argued:

> I will say this much, however, that as communism
> and marriage are based upon fundamentally differ-
> ent principles, it seems to me that the introduc-

---

pp. 163f. See also *American Socialist*, 28 August 1878,
p. 276; *American Socialist*, 4 September 1879, p. 282.

[43]See *History of American Socialisms*, pp. 519ff,
where Noyes cites with approval Charles Lane's analysis
of the conflict between marriage and community life.

> tion of marriage into the Community is a peril-
> ous undertaking that may endanger, sooner or
> later, the most important features of our Com-
> munity life.[44]

And another member, James Turner, who shared the same
position, observed:

> I confess I am not without serious misgivings
> ...as to how the adoption of the modification of
> our social life shall affect the future of the
> Community.... I do not believe that marriage
> and communism can exist together. The only ques-
> tion with me is whether or not this proposed
> change will prove to be an inlet of the spirit
> of marriage which will overcome that of commun-
> ism and at no late day disintegrate the Communi-
> ty. Whether this shall prove to be so or not
> will depend upon ourselves and upon the spirit
> we shall allow to come in upon us. I must claim
> the right of prophecy and if I have the spirit
> of prophecy, I think the Community is to some
> extent in a state of reaction and if, in the
> violence of that reaction, the marriage spirit
> shall take possession of it, it is doomed to dis-
> solution.[45]

The *American Socialist* ceased publication in December of
1879 with the explanation that all the efforts of the
Community would be needed in the difficult task of integrating monogamous marriage in community life. This, the
paper maintained, would be a far more demanding task than
that of creating a community based on Complex Marriage.[46]
But Turner's prophecy came true. In 1880 the Community
agreed that they could no longer live in harmony, and
that dissolution was the solution. Years later, Pierrepont Noyes observed:

---

[44]Cited by Robertson, *Oneida Community, the Breakup*,
p. 157.

[45]Cited by Robertson, *Oneida Community, the Breakup*,
p. 159.

[46]*American Socialist*, 4 December 1879, p. 388.

> They had discovered that family interests in-
> sidiously undermine attachments to group inter-
> ests, and that family selfishness gres apace
> until it destroyed the spirit of self-abnega-
> tion so essential for communal living.[47]

There is, however, another explanation of the facts.
This explanation suggests that the decision of 1878 was
in fact made by Noyes in an attempt to molify a growing
dissatisfaction within the Community by removing what
appeared to be the major cause of that dissatisfaction:
the social system. Subsequent events showed that the
causes of discord were deeper than suspected, and would
not be brooked. According to this hypothesis, then, the
causes of the dissolution of the Community were multiple,
dissatisfaction with the social system being the one
which appeared to be most critical.[48]

---

[47]*My Father's House,* p. 171. See also Warfield
Bibliotheca Sacra, Vol. 78, p. 193; Warfield, *Perfectionism,* Vol. 2, pp. 306f.

[48]This second hypothesis is supported by the study
of Mrs. Robertson, *Oneida Community, the Breakup.* Addressing herself to the question of the causes responsible for the Community's dissolution, she observes: "The
answer to this riddle must be a multiple cause, a weaving together of
a number of strands, each one originally separate and in itself power-
less to bring about the final disaster, but together of irresistable
effect."   (p. 14). Among the strands she lists and studies
in her analysis are: political problems centering upon
loyalty and disloyalty to Noyes in his later years; the
repeatedly unsuccessful, and probably foolish, efforts of
Noyes to make his son, Theodore, his successor (despite
the latter's professed agnosticism); the gradual deterioration in the faith of Perfectionism coupled with growing
interest on the part of some members in Spiritualism and
Revivalism (both of which encouraged an independence of
thought and action which were inconducive to ordered Community life); and the growing dissatisfaction among some
members with the practice of Complex Marriage and stirp-
culture within the Community (pp. 15-21). Robertson
maintains that Complex Marriage, having successfully pro-
moted harmonious unity for over twenty-five years, "became in the end one of the most serious disputes between

This second hypothesis is supported by a passage from the journal of a prominent member in the Community, dated February 5, 1879:

> Everything appears to be going harmoniously. There are no upheavals in the Community at large, at least none which come to the surface so as to be publicly known.... Yet under the surface there is what seems to me a very important and dangerous state of things. The young people as a class, and some of the older ones, are free to speak of their preference for a more limited sexual fellowship than Mr. Noyes has always advocated. The more bold and ultra of them coolly declare in favor of a monogamic relation. They say one man is enough for one woman, one woman for one man.... Perhaps, after all, I ought not to call it a *public* sentiment for it is by no means expressed publicly. I mean that it is a spreading feeling already embracing quite a class.[49]

And the same writer, in a letter to John Noyes five months later (July 19, 1879), having advised Noyes that unless he took immediate action the social system of the Community would collapse, observed:

> But aside from any logical reasoning, I am supported by evidence in asserting as a fact that our system is pretty well broken up already. A number of the young women of Lily Hobart's class do not hesitate to say that they will have no children except by a husband to whom they have been legally married. The next class younger is still more set in this feeling. I have questioned Emily Easton on the point. She tells me that quite a number have decided not to have anything more to do with our sexual system. This feeling has taken such a hold that some of us find ourselves practically monogamist, or nearly, perforce.[50]

---

the dissident parties" and "the subject of a bitter struggle for control between the old regime and the new party which wanted new freedom and new rules." (p. 15).

[49]From the journal of Frank Wayland-Smith, cited by Robertson, *Oneida Community, the Breakup,* p. 91.

[50]Cited by Robertson, *Oneida Community, the Breakup,* p. 130.

The actual course of events in 1879 suggests as well that
dissatisfaction with the social system was an important
factor behind the Community's decision to abandon Communal Marriage, and that fear of the measures to be taken by
the conference in Syracuse was at best a precipitating
cause. First, if the reason behind abandoning Complex
Marriage had been primarily fear of external persecution,
as claimed, then one would expect that the Community
would simply have adopted a policy of *celibacy* as they
had in the past whenever threatened by external attacks.[51]
Instead, they announced that they would return to the
practice of monogamous marriage. Second: Theodore Noyes
assured reporters in 1879, following the decision to dis-
continue the system of Complex Marriage, that there would
be no rush of Community members into matrimony, but that
rather, in accordance with Paul's platform, the disposition would be toward celibacy. The public must not expect to hear of any marriages within the Community for a
considerable time, he concluded.[52] However, his prog-
nosis was proven somewhat inaccurate. Writing in September of 1879 Noyes' sister, Harriet, observed:

> I don't know but you foresaw it all, but MARRIAGE
> fills the eye now of most of the young folks; that
> is, from folks as old as Alfred down: and I should
> think there was very little reference to any counsel
> but personal wishes.... Just now there seems to be
> very little motive working but what impels to mar-
> riage in the world, and it looks as if marriage
> would eat up Communism: but I believe Christ is
> deep in the hearts of many of them, and will make

---

[51] In 1852, in the face of threats from irate moral-
ists, the Community had temporarily ceased the practice
of Communal Marriage. Likewise, the small Community
which was established in New York City maintained the
practice of celibacy during the years of its existence
rather than incite the anger of their "neighbors".

[52] *American Socialist,* 3 September 1879, p. 283.

> their experience turn them back to communism by
> and by.[53]

And a firm supporter of John Noyes wrote in that same
month:

> The rush of attention toward marriage indicated
> a great misapprehension of the recent change of
> social platform, or rather an almost entire failure
> to apprehend it at all. Less than a month has
> passed since the change. We hear very little as
> yet about the turning of the hearts, old and young,
> to the study of the REAL social platform onto which
> the Communist has moved, but instead there is an
> immense amount of talk and excitement and wringing
> of hearts about the marriage of this one and that
> one, just as though the Community had given up Com-
> munism and had started on the broad road to private
> familyism and a general breakup.[54]

And, within four months, twenty new marriages had taken
place within the Community.[55] In summary, then, there
appears to be good indication that the decision in 1879
to abandon Complex Marriage was occasioned in part by a
dissatisfaction, especially among the young, with the
social systems of the Community and that the efforts of
the Syracuse convention were but a contributing factor in
the determinations.[56]

---

[53]Cited by Robertson, *Oneida Community, the Breakup,*
p. 170.

[54]Cited by Robertson, *Oneida Community, the Breakup,*
p. 180.

[55]These marriages, together with marriages formed before entering the Community, meant that there were 90 married persons at Oneida by December, 1879. Still 126 persons, old enough to marry remained unmarried as of that
date. (*American Socialist,* 25 December 1879, p. 413.)
By 1908, when the second revision of Hinds' *American Communities* was published, only a half dozen former members
had followed the advice of Noyes that celibacy was to be
preferred to marriage (p. 212).

[56]See Carmer, p. 46; Jacoby, p. 97; Parker, p. 263;
McGee, pp. 323-325 who mention the dissatisfaction of

If this hypothesis is true, one wonders why the Community, after so many years of successfully following the ways of communal marriage, was unable to keep to this practice in the last years. A tentative answer immediately suggests itself. John Noyes had never tired of insisting that only those who were convinced of his religious principles would be willing or able to undergo the pain and discipline which the practice of Complex Marriage entailed. Many sources suggest that enthusiasm for this religion had waned by the final years of the Community's history. A former member, Allan Estlake, reported that by the 1870s many of the younger members of the Community no longer shared their parents' sense of urgency about the Perfectionist faith. Men, like T.R. Noyes, were avowed agnostics, and others, who had never experienced the conversion of the early founders, held only a nominal relation to the teachings of Noyes. In addition, Estlake reported, many of the more conservative members had allowed their faith to ossify into a religion of doctrine and ritual, equally devoid of real spiritual enthusiasm. [57]

some members in the Community due to (a) the unwillingness of younger generations to submit to the control of their social lives by the elders; (b) the resentment of the younger generations to the advantages of the older men under the stirpiculture experiment, and (c) the unquenchable spirit of monogamy which demanded the return to exclusive relationships. Estlake insists that neither dissatisfaction with Complex Marriage or difficulties with the system of stirpiculture were in any way responsible for the Community's dissolution (p. 74). With regard to the effects of the Convention in Syracuse, Mrs. Robertson concludes that the efforts of that body would not have been able to command the influence necessary to force action against the Community--that they were "largely sound and fury, signifying nothing." (*Oneida Community, the Breakup,* p. 20.) See also *American Socialist,* 20 February 1879, pp. 65f; *American Socialist,* 4 September, 1879, p. 281.

[57]Estlake, pp. 7-16.

Pierrepont Noyes, who was a young boy at the time of the
Community's dissolution, observed years later:

> The majority of these young people had none
> of the religious devotion which the original mem-
> bers brought to Oneida in 1848; hence for them my
> father's heresies lacked effective religious
> sanctions. Among the younger men, too, that
> scientific enthusiasm which, during the latter
> part of the nineteenth century, was challenging
> old beliefs, undermined respect for his spirit-
> ual not to say mystical leadership.[58]

If many of the members had lost their faith, either by rejecting it, or by allowing it to ossify, it would not be
surprising if a loss of dedication to, and enthusiasm for,
the social theory followed soon after. And then, when external attacks were directed at the Community, and more
particularly at its social policies, these "faith-less"
members discovered that they could no longer find either
the reasons or the strength to continue the system.

During these times of change and dissolution, John
Noyes guided his Community from afar. He had departed
Oneida in June of 1879, when he had become aware of the
dissension arising over his leadership. Eventually he
took up residence in a house on the Canadian side of
Niagara Falls, where he was joined by some devoted disciples following the breakup of the Community, and where
he spent his remaining days. With time, several of his
friends bought houses on either side of the Falls, and
regularly gathered around the old man for spiritual guidance. Indomitable, Noyes began making plans to establish
a school for these families, and even considered forming
a new Community. But in 1886, Noyes died.

From what can be discerned, Noyes had reacted to the

---

[58] *My Father's House*, p. 160. See also Carden, "Oneida Community; a study of Organizational Change", p. 89;
Warfield, *Perfectionism*, Vol. 2, pp. 296ff.

collapse of Oneida with calm acceptance, serenity and
detachment. No doubt his followers received their finest
lesson in the meaning of non-attachment, of seeking God
above and in all things, in the demeanor of their founder
in the face of Oneida's failure. Noyes had maintained
from the first days that community life was only a means
and not an end.[59] He did not read failure in the history
of Oneida. It had succeeded in transforming the lives of
many, and it had demonstrated to the world a new *vision*.
His analysis of the situation was optimistic:

> We made a raid into an unknown country, chartered
> it, and returned without the loss of a man, woman,
> or child.[60]

This man who had known how, as few others, to plan, to
work, and to enforce his will thus demonstrated that
fused into his Pelagian character was a wisdom that knew
acceptance and resignation.

ONEIDA'S CONTRIBUTION

     Noyes considered the collapse of Complex Marriage
at Oneida to be only a temporary setback in the war of
Christianity against false and destructive love. He felt
that the Community had made the first difficult essay into the wilderness, and that the record of that attempt
would serve as a guide to those willing to undertake
future forays. Whether others will be willing to take
up Noyes' fallen torch, to adopt his vision, and repeat
his "raid" into the unknown country of un-romantic love
remains to be seen.

---

[59]*Circular*, 23 February 1853, p. 115.

[60]Cited in Pierrepont Noyes, *My Father's House*,
p. 176.

It would seem doubtful that Noyes will ever find a
large audience able to accept his peculiar theological
doctrines. His analysis of Scripture is unsophisticated;
his insistence on the occurrence of the Parousia and the
translation of the Primitive Church to Heaven at that time
remains a stumbling block despite his efforts to prove
the point. Theologically, many of his concepts are anthro-
pomorphic and even offensive. If, then, the value of
Noyes' thinking stands or falls on the validity of his
theology and Scriptural exegesis, one could not expect it
to make any impact.

Of course the study of Oneida provides interesting
insights into the nineteenth-century, and especially into
that idealism which gave rise to communal and social experiments. Especially interesting is the foresight Noyes
evidenced in his stances on the questions of women's
rights, eugenics and the institution of marriage. One
can also find in the chronicle of Oneida the story of a
man to be admired because of his bravery and innovative
insight. One can admire the strength of this man who con-
ducted experiments in human relations despite the opposition of public opinion; one can respect the charism of
this man who was able to form a successful community of
men and women struggling to observe a way of life which
flew in the face of "human nature". But over and above
the chronicle of an interesting experiment or the witness
of a brave innovator, are there values which the study of
Oneida can offer to society?

The present writer believes that Noyes' critique of
romantic love and his suggestions for practicing the art
of true love deserve to be given serious consideration.
The fact that they oppose everything which men consider
obvious about the nature and practice of love does not

destroy the possibility that Noyes' critique is quite
correct and provides a valuable step in the direction of
true, ennobling and rewarding love. Perhaps man should
be encouraged to seek the ability to love in a non-possessive, non-exclusive way. Perhaps it is precisely
man's efforts to possess, to control, to isolate the
loved one--no matter how "natural" these efforts may
seem--which destroys his pleasure and alchemizes the gold
of true love into a lead poisonous to the touch. Noyes'
suggestion that love is only beautiful and satisfying
when it introduces one into an experience beyond the individual; his suggestion that man must learn that all
loves are essentially the same and that one need not
cling to any particular love; his suggestion that one
love never excludes others, but rather calls them into
existence--all these suggestions deserve serious consideration by those interested in aiding man to transcend
whatever prohibits his growth. Noyes' ideas should be of
especial value to those who are attempting one form or
another of communal life, and who are therefore, of necessity, faced with the tension between love for an individual or individuals and love for the larger community.
And, though particularly important to those living within
community, his suggestions with regard to differentiating
and integrating particular friendships and brotherly love
could be applied by every man and woman eager to fulfill
the Christian command to love all men as brothers.

But before Noyes' arguments can make any impression
on other generations, they will need to be translated into language and concepts meaningful to the audience toward whom they are directed. This translation will be
particularly necessary with regard to the theological aspects of those arguments. But these theological aspects

must be *translated*--not *ignored*. The theological dimen-
sion must be retained, not only in order to be faithful
to the author, but, more importantly, because if anyone
is to follow the road which Noyes scouted, he must share
Noyes' hunger for that which man knows by many names,
and which Noyes called the Divine.

Edmonds, Walter D. *The First Hundred Years: 1848-1948.*
    Oneida, New York: Oneida Ltd., 1948.

Ellis, John B. *Free Love and its Votaries.* New York:
    United States Publishing Co., 1870.

Estlake, Allan. *The Oneida Community: A Record of an
    Attempt to Carry out the Principles of Christian
    Unselfishness and Scientific Race-Improvement.*
    London: George Redway, 1900.

Gordon, G. A. *The Void which Oneida Perfectionism Alone
    can Fill.* N.p., n.d.

*Handbook of the Oneida Community: Containing a Brief
    Sketch of its Present Condition, Internal Economy
    and Leading Principles.* No. 2. Oneida, New York:
    Oneida Community, 1871.

Handbook of the Oneida Community, 1875. Oneida, New York:
    Office of the *Oneida Circular,* [1875].

*Handbook of the Oneida Community, with a Sketch of its
    Founder and an Outline of its Constitution and
    Doctrines.* Wallingford, Connecticut: Office of
    the *Circular,* 1867.

Herrick, James B. "A Reminiscence of John H. Noyes", A
    Reprint from the *Quadrangle* (Kenwood, 1908). N.p.,
    n.d.

Hinds, William Alfred. *American Communities and Co-oper-
    ative Colonies.* 2nd rev. ed. Chicago: Charles
    Kerr & Co., 1908.

Holloway, Mark. *Heavens on Earth; Utopian Communities
    in America, 1680-1880.* New York: Dover, 1966.

Jacoby, John E. *Two Mystic Communities in America.*
    Paris: Les Presses Universitaires de France, 1931.

McGee, Anita Newcomb. "An Experiment in Human Stirpi-
    culture", *American Anthropologist,* o.s. IV (1891),
    319-325.

Manuel, Frank E., ed. *Utopias and Utopian Thought.*
    Boston: Beacon Press, 1965.

Miller, George N. *The Strike of a Sex and Zugassent's
    Discovery or After the Sex Struck.* Rev. ed. Chicago:
    Stockham Publishing Co., Inc., 1905.

CONSULTED WORKS

BOOKS, PAMPHLETS AND ARTICLES

Barron, Alfred and George Noyes Miller, eds. *Home-Talks by John Humphrey Noyes.* Vol. I. Oneida, New York: Oneida Community, 1875. Only Volume I was published.

Carden, Maren Lockwood. *Oneida: Utopian Community to Modern Corporation.* Baltimore: Johns Hopkins Press, 1969.

[Carden], Maren Lockwood. "Oneida Community: a Study of Organizational Change". Unpublished Ph.D. thesis, Harvard University, 1962.

Carmer, Carl. "A Reporter at Large. Children of the Kingdom", *The New Yorker,* 12 (March 21, 1936), 26-36; (March 28, 1936), 43-49.

Cragin, George, ed. *Faith-Facts; or a Confession of the Kingdom of God and the Age of Miracles.* Oneida Reserve, New York: Leonard & Co., Printers, 1850.

Dixon, William Hepworth. *New America.* 3rd ed. Philadelphia: J. B. Lippincott & Co., 1869.

_____. *Spiritual Wives.* London: Hurst & Blackett & Co., 1868.

Eastman, Hubbard. *Noyesism Unveiled: A History of the Sect Self-Styled Perfectionists; with a Summary View of Their Leading Doctrines.* Brattleboro, Vermont: By the author, 1849.

Easton, Abel. *The Dissolution of the Oneida Community.* N.p., 1886.

_____. *From the Roman Church to Christian Communism.* N.p., n.d.

_____. *Synopsis of a New Work on the Oneida Community.* N.p., n.d.

Nordhoff, Charles. *The Communistic Societies of the United States*. New York: Dover, 1966.

Noyes, Corinna Ackley. *The Days of My Youth*. Kenwood, New York: By the author, 1960.

Noyes, George Wallingford, ed. *John Humphrey Noyes: The Putney Community*. Oneda, New York: By the author, 1931.

Noyes, George W[allingford]. *The Oneida Community; Its Relation to Orthodoxy: Being an Outline of the Religious and Theological Applications of the Most Advanced Experiment (in Applied Ethics) Ever Made in Any Age or Country*. N.p.: Fielding Star Print, (191?).

Noyes, George Wallingford, ed. *Religious Experience of John Humphrey Noyes, Founder of the Oneida Community*. New York: Macmillan Co., 1923.

Noyes, Hilda Herrick and George Wallingford Noyes. "The Oneida Community Experiment in Stirpiculture", *Eugenics, Genetics and the Family*. Vol. I. Baltimore: Williams & Wilkins Co., 1923, 374-386.

Noyes, John H[umphrey]. *The Berean: A Manual for the Help of Those who Seek the Faith of the Primitive Church*. Putney, Vermont: Office of the *Spiritual Magazine*, 1847.

Noyes, John Humphrey. *Confessions of John H. Noyes, Part I: Confession of Religious Experience: Including a History of Modern Perfectionism*. Oneida Reserve, New York: Leonard & Co., Printers, 1849. Part II was never published.

_____. *Dixon and His Copyists: A Criticism of the Accounts of the Oneida Community in "New America", "Spiritual Wives", and Kindred Publications*. 2nd ed. Wallingford, Connecticut: Wallingford Printing Co., 1874.

_____. *Essay on Scientific Propagation*. Oneida, New York: Oneida Community, (187?).

_____. *History of American Socialisms*. New York: Dover, 1966.

_____. *Male Continence*. Oneida, New York: Office of the *Oneida Circular*, 1872.

_____. *Paul's Prize*. N.p., n.d.

_____. *Salvation from Sin: The End of Christian Faith*. Oneida, New York: Oneida Community, 1876.

_____. *The Doctrine of Salvation from Sin, Explained and Defended*. Putney, Vermont: By the author, 1843.

_____. *"The Way of Holiness." A Series of Papers Formerly Published in the Perfectionist, at New Haven*. Putney, Vermont: J. H. Noyes & Co., 1838.

[Noyes, John Humphrey]. *Slavery and Marriage; A Dialogue*. N.p., 1850.

_____. *The Twofold Nature of the Second Birth*. Putney, Vermont: Office of the *Witness*, 1841.

Noyes, Pierrepont [B.]. *My Father's House: An Oneida Boyhood*. New York: Farrar & Rinehart, Inc., 1937.

Noyes, Pierrepont B. *A Goodly Heritage*. New York: Rinehart & Co., Inc., 1958.

Noyes, T[heodore] R. *Report on the Health of Children in the Oneida Community*. Oneida, New York: (Oneida Community?), 1878.

[Oneida] Association. *Second Annual Report of the Oneida Association: Exhibiting its Progress to February 20, 1850*. Oneida Reserve, New York: Leonard & Co., Printers, 1850.

[Oneida Association]. *Bible Communism: A Compilation from the Annual Reports and Other Publications of the Oneida Association and its Branches; Presenting, in Connection with Their History, a Summary View of Their Religious and Social Theories*. Brooklyn, New York: Office of the *Circular*, 1853.

_____. *First Annual Report of the Oneida Association: Exhibiting its History, Principles, and Transactions to January 1, 1849*. Oneida Reserve, New York: Leonard & Co., Printers, (1849).

_____. *Mutual Criticism*. Oneida, New York: Office of the *American Socialist*, 1876.

_____. *Third Annual Report of the Oneida Association: Exhibiting its Progress to February 20, 1851*. Oneida Reserve, New York: Leonard & Co., Printers, 1851.

[Oneida Community]. "Communism and Separation". A re-
    print of an article from an unnamed Community peri-
    odical. N.p., n.d.

_____. *The Oneida Community: A Familiar Exposition
    of Its Ideas and Practical Life*. Wallingford, Con-
    necticut: Office of the *Circular,* 1865.

*Oneida Community Collection in the Syracuse University
    Library*. Syracuse: N.p., 1961.

Oneida Community, Ltd. *Oneida Community, 1848-1901*.
    N.p., n.d.

Parker, Robert Allerton. *A Yankee Saint: John Humphrey
    Noyes and the Oneida Community*. New York: G. P.
    Putnam's Sons, 1935.

Robertson, Constance Noyes. *Oneida Community. An Auto-
    biography, 1851-1876*. Syracuse: Syracuse Univer-
    sity Press, 1970.

_____. *Oneida Community; The Breakup, 1876-1881*.
    Syracuse: Syracuse University Press, 1972.

Robie, W. F. *The Art of Love*. Boston: Richard G. Badger,
    1921.

Seldes, Gilbert Vivian. *The Stammering Century*. New
    York: John Day Co., 1928.

Seymour, Henry J. "Letter to the 'Outlook'". Reprint of
    a Reply to a letter on "Free Love", dated Feb. 11,
    1903. N.p., n.d.

_____. *The Oneida Community, a Dialogue*. N.p., n.d.

_____. "Oneida Community: Confession of Christ", A
    reprint of a letter, dated Nov. 3, 1897. N.p., n.d.

Shaw, George B. "The Perfectionist Experiment at Oneida
    Creek", *Man and Superman; a Comedy and a Philosophy*.
    Baltimore: Penguin Books, 1965, 227-229.

Strachey, Ray. *Group Movements of the Past and Experi-
    ments in Guidance*. London: Faber and Faber, Ltd.,
    1934.

Warfield, Benjamin Breckinridge. "John Humphrey Noyes
    and his 'Bible Communists'", *Bibliotheca Sacra,*
    Vol. 78, 37-72; 172-200; 319-376.

_____. "John Humphrey Noyes and his 'Bible Commun-
ists'", *Perfectionism*. Vol. II. New York: Oxford
University Press, 1931, 219-333.

Warren, J. P. "Putney Perfectionism", *The New Englander*,
6 (April, 1848), 177-194.

Worden, Harriet M. *Old Mansion House Memories by One
Brought up in it.* Kenwood, New York: By the author,
1950.

PERIODICALS (Listed by year of publication.)

Perfectionist. New Haven, Connecticut. Vols. I, II.
1834-1836.

Witness. Ithaca, New York and Putney, Vermont. Vols. I,
II. 1837-1843.

Spiritual Moralist. Putney, Vermont. Vol. I. 1842.

Perfectionist. Putney, Vermont. Vol. III. 1843-1844.
(Continuation of *Witness* under new title.)

Perfectionist and Theocratic Watchman. Putney, Vermont.
Vols. IV, V. 1844-1846. (Continuation of *Perfectionist* under new title.)

Spiritual Magazine. Putney, Vermont and Oneida Reserve,
New York. Vols. I, II. 1846-1850.

Free Church Circular. Oneida Reserve, New York. Vols.
III, IV. 1850-1851. (Continuation of *Spiritual
Magazine* under new title.)

Circular. Brooklyn, New York and Oneida, New York. Vols.
I-XII. 1851-1853; 1855-1864.

Circular [New Series]. Wallingford, Connecticut and
Oneida, New York. Vols. I-VII. 1864-1870.

Daily Journal of Oneida Community. Oneida, New York.
Vols. I-III. 1866-1867.

Oneida Community Daily. Oneida, New York. Vols. IV, V.
1867-1868. (Continuation of *Daily Journal of Oneida
Community* under new title.)

--

Oneida Circular.   Oneida, New York.   Vols. VIII–XIII.
        1871–1875.   (Continuation of *Circular* [New Series]
        under new title.)

American Socialist.   Oneida, New York.   Vols. I–IV.
        1876–1879.

INDEX